# HOLY WAR

## FOR THE

# PROMISED LAND

# HOLY WAR

## FOR THE

# PROMISED LAND

Israel at the Crossroads

# DAVID DOLAN

BROADMAN
&HOLMAN
PUBLISHERS

NASHVILLE, TENNESSEE

0-8054-2718-X

Published by Broadman & Holman Publishers
Nashville, Tennessee

Dewey Classification Number:956.05
Subject Heading:ISRAEL-ARAB \ MIDDLE EAST

Previously published in 1998 by Fleming H. Revell
a division of Baker Book House Company
P.O. Box 6287, Grand Rapids, MI 49516–6287
First published in 1991 as *Holy War for the Promised Land* by Thomas
Nelson, Inc. Also published in 1992 as *Israel: The Struggle to Survive*
by Hodder and Stoughton

Scripture quotations are from the Holy Bible, New International
Version®. NIV®. Copyright © 1973, 1978, 1984 by International
Bible Society. Used by permission of Zondervan Publishing House. All
rights reserved. Also used, NASB, the New American Standard Bible,
© the Lockman Foundation, 1960, 1962, 1963, 1968, 1971, 1972,
1973, 1975, 1977; used by persmission.

1 2 3 4 5 6 7  08 07 06 05 04 03

# CONTENTS

# ACKNOWLEDGMENTS

I wish to thank the many Jewish and Arab friends who have shared their lives and experiences with me, and so helped me to better understand the raging conflict over the Holy Land.

I am also indebted to my friend, author Lance Lambert, for first alerting me to the large role Islam plays in the Arab-Israeli conflict and for offering the use of his extensive library.

Special thanks to those in many parts of the world who prayed for me when I became ill while writing the original manuscript in the late 1980s.

I would like to express my gratitude to my friends and family in America, and especially my parents, who believed me when I said the turbulent Middle East was where I needed to be.

# INTRODUCTION

The Arab-Israeli struggle is unique among world conflicts. On one side are Israeli Jews—descendants of an ancient people who, according to the Bible, are chosen by God to be his own. The other protagonists, the Arabs, are mostly members of the fastest-growing and most controversial religion on earth: Islam. Closely watching from the sidelines are millions of Christians whose faith stems from history's most famous Jew, Jesus of Nazareth. The world's leading powers are involved in the conflict, as is the United Nations, which oversaw the creation of modern Israel.

One cannot understand the nature of the struggle without an overview of its causes and history, especially since the problems are so complex and deep-rooted. I will begin by taking a look at the persecution the Jews endured from the time of their exile from Jerusalem in A.D. 135 through to the twentieth century. Then I will delve into a short review of Arab history—basically the story of Islam—and then give a broad overview of Israel's modern history.

Most of the books I have read on the Arab-Israeli dispute either play down or ignore the religious struggle at the center of the conflict. Possibly because of my own spiritual convictions, I have spent much time examining the religious beliefs of both Arabs and Jews. It is impossible to comprehend the roots and continuing intensity of the Jewish-Arab struggle without fully appreciating the enormous role ancient beliefs and prejudices play in it. I believe that *Holy War for the Promised Land* will especially make the reader aware of the significant role Islam has played in fueling the conflict.

Almost every chapter, and in many cases even single sentences, have themselves been the subject of entire books. While it is good to examine closely every aspect of the dispute over the Holy Land, I believe it is easy to get caught up in side issues and, therefore, not see the forest for the trees. In my book, we step back and look at the broad picture, especially at the religious canvas on which the conflict has been painted.

Many personal experiences have been woven in throughout this book. Some explain why I came to the controversial land of Israel in 1980. Others were lived out in Israel while covering two Palestinian uprisings, the Gulf War and other major stories, and as a radio broadcaster working in the early 1980s in southern Lebanon. The final chapter is my own personal assessment of the conflict and of the chances for a peaceful resolution.

I do not claim to be a professional historian or theologian; I am simply a journalist who has lived and worked for over two decades with people at the center of the conflict. While doing so, I have come to understand their religious beliefs, political positions, and personal attitudes quite well.

*Holy War for the Promised Land* has been written in such a way that those unfamiliar with the history of the Arab-Israeli conflict can comprehend what has happened and is happening in the Middle East. Yet I believe my book will also be of interest to those better acquainted with the topic, especially to anyone desiring a clearer picture of the fundamental religious elements behind the struggle.

Now, on to the ancient Temple Mount and to the odyssey that brought me to the tiny land of promise.

k ✡ †

# MY ROAD TO ISRAEL

Saddam will avenge us!" shouted someone in the angry crowd, which rapidly dispersed as the shouting continued. Blood flowed thick and fast. Tempers flared on both sides.

"You will *not* take over our sacred mosques!" screamed a woman who held a dying young man close to her bosom.

"Stop shooting, stop shooting! *Allahu akbar!*" cried a male voice from mosque loudspeakers as people ran for cover in two nearby Muslim shrines. Several minutes later Israeli security forces did stop firing at Palestinian rioters on Jerusalem's Temple Mount, but only after killing at least seventeen and injuring scores more, one of whom died several weeks later.

Tension had begun building well before dawn at the site where King Solomon and Zerubbabel had erected the first and second temples to the God of Israel. From 3 A.M. onward, hundreds of Muslims had started to gather on the Temple Mount, which the Muslims call *Haram al-Sharif*, "the Noble Sanctuary," located in the southeastern corner of Jerusalem's ancient, walled "Old City." By 9 A.M. several thousand Palestinian Muslims, most of them men, had assembled on the Mount. They were ready for holy war.

Devout Muslims came to defend the Temple Mount from a group of about thirty-five religious Jews who wanted to march to the site. It wasn't the first time that the small Jewish "Temple Mount Faithful" group had tried to hold ceremonies on the Mount during the Jewish

Feast of Tabernacles. But this year was different. The group—considered eccentric, if not extremist, by a majority of Israelis—had declared their intention to bring with them a three-ton cornerstone of the *third Jewish temple.*

Muslim leaders were officially informed the week before that Israel's supreme court had banned the group from holding the cornerstone dedication ceremony on the Mount. The Israeli justices agreed with police that the proposed ceremony would likely trigger wide-scale disturbances at Islam's third holiest site. The high court's ban had been published in all east Jerusalem Arabic newspapers. Still, thousands of Muslims showed up on October 8, 1990, in answer to calls by Islamic and Palestinian leaders to "defend 'Haram al-Sharif' from Jewish plots to destroy our sacred mosques."

The warm, sunny Monday morning was a special day for religious Jews. It was the fifth day of the annual Feast of Tabernacles, when Jewish men of priestly descent come to the Western Wall of the Temple Mount to say a Levitical benediction over the assembled worshipers. About twenty-five thousand Jews had gathered for the blessing in the large Western Wall plaza, located just below Judaism's most sacred site, where the sons of Levi once ministered in the ancient Jewish temples.

As the priestly ceremony ended, the Temple Mount Faithful came marching into the plaza, singing religious and nationalistic songs and waving Israeli flags. Forbidden to march to the Mount itself, the group quickly made their way out of the Old City's Dung Gate, heading toward the Kidron Valley, where King David had built his capital city. Near the bottom of the valley, just south of the Temple Mount, the group stopped at the Pool of Shiloah to re-enact an ancient Jewish water-purification ceremony.

Just as the marchers were leaving the Old City, Temple Mount loudspeakers started to broadcast sermons from inside Al Aksa Mosque, situated at the southern end of the Mount. The assembled Muslims packed into the sacred Islamic shrine were urged to wage *jihad,* or "holy war," to defend Haram al-Sharif from the Jews planning to march to the sacred site. Palestinian men congregating outside Al Aksa and the nearby Dome of the Rock (also popularly known as the Mosque of Omar) began to gather building blocks, stones, and metal bars from various Temple Mount construction sites. Holy war was about to begin.

Suddenly, all hell broke loose in the City of Peace. "Come, all Muslims, and defend us! The Jews are invading!" cried a Muslim official from a loudspeaker on a mosque in Silwan Village, where the Pool of Shiloah is located.

Muslims on the southern edge of the Temple Mount heard the cry and sounded the alarm. "The Jews are coming!" Several hundred primed and ready Palestinians then rushed to the western edge of the Mount, with rocks and other weapons in hand. An enraged crowd of several thousand Muslims quickly began to move in the same direction. As they did so, a tear gas canister was hurled into the crowd by an Israeli policeman, who apparently tossed the canister at random after it accidentally went off while being thrown to him by a fellow officer.

Taught that a Muslim who dies defending Haram al-Sharif goes immediately to the highest state of paradise, the jihad-frenzied Arabs then attacked a row of forty-four Israeli policemen standing near the edge of the Mount above the Western Wall.

The vastly outnumbered security forces, some wounded from the barrage of stones and other objects, shot tear gas canisters and rubber bullets at the Palestinians. But the crowd kept surging forward, seemingly impervious to injury or death. Within minutes, the overwhelmed Israeli policemen were forced to flee the Temple Mount through two nearby gates.

Angry Muslims took advantage of the police retreat to move up to the edge of the mount. Two policemen standing on a ledge above the Western Wall called to Jews near the wall to quickly evacuate the area. Soon afterward many of the Palestinian rioters began to hurl rocks and stones onto the Western Wall plaza below. A majority of the thousands of assembled Jewish worshipers had already left the plaza, but hundreds were still in the vicinity of the wall. Jerusalem police said that about a dozen Jewish worshipers were injured in the barrage. Some of the wounded were hit by stones, while others fell and were bruised during the rush to get away from the wall. None were hurt seriously.

The pavement in front of the ancient Temple Mount wall was soon carpeted with rocks and stones. Lying amid the debris were a number of Jewish prayer books, knocked off their stands by the deluge of missiles.

As Israeli marksmen began shooting from a police lookout on the mount, Muslim rioters attacked a nearby police outpost. Two Arab guards stationed inside the outpost called over a two-way radio for help. Minutes later the two were allowed to flee the outpost as the rioters entered the building. Beefed-up security forces preparing to reenter the Mount heard the appeal for help over hand-held radios.

■ ■ ■

Soon afterward, the Israeli force broke through, met by a hail of stones and other objects. Their main goal was to get to the police outpost as fast as possible to free the two guards whom they assumed were being held captive. Unaware that the Muslim rioters had freed the two police guards, and suspecting that they had stolen guns and other weapons from the sacked outpost, the entering security forces quickly opened fire. In many cases, they seemed to be shooting to kill.[1]

Many Palestinians in Jerusalem and elsewhere stayed up late on the night of the tragedy, waiting for Iraqi chemical-tipped missiles to wipe out Tel Aviv, Israel's largest Jewish city. But their hoped-for avenger and savior, Saddam Hussein, did not come through, at least not right away.

The Palestinians, echoed by Saddam and other Arab leaders, called the Israeli shootings a calculated massacre. The Israelis, suspecting that the attack on Jewish worshipers at the Western Wall was planned in advance by the PLO, in collusion with Saddam, said their security forces had acted in justified self-defense. The United Nations, supported by the United States, condemned Israel, calling for a special U.N. investigative commission to go to Jerusalem. The Israeli government demurred, saying all of Jerusalem, including the Old City, was sovereign Israeli territory, and therefore, the Israelis would handle the matter themselves.

Several weeks later, a special Israeli government-appointed committee blamed the Palestinians for starting the riot, and for no justifiable reason. But the committee also charged police officials with negligence in being unprepared for major rioting on the day of the clash and said without elaboration that there had been "unsupervised use of live ammunition" by police trying to quell the rioting. The Palestinian uprising leadership, having already issued leaflets ordering revenge knifings and other attacks on Israeli soldiers and civilians, called the report a whitewash.

The riot and shootings took place just one mile north of my Jerusalem apartment. I was home on the morning of the violent clash, leisurely sipping coffee and reading the *Jerusalem Post* newspaper. Since I was not on duty that day for CBS Radio, I didn't react too quickly when the barely audible sounds of distant shooting and police sirens began to filter into my living room. Such sounds are, sad to say, not all that uncommon in the City of Peace. Indeed, identical sounds from the same location ten years later would signal the start of another, far more deadly Palestinian uprising. After the noise continued for more than ten minutes, I thought I'd better find out what was going on.

## FROM IDAHO TO ISRAEL

It was on an earlier October morning during another Jewish holiday that I first noticed the rumbling sounds of the distant Arab Israeli conflict. The autumn sun shone brightly as I settled into my stuffed pillow chair, newspaper and coffee in hand. Local news dominated the headlines on that warm Saturday morning—another fatal road accident, city council intrigues, and ongoing preparations for the Expo '74 World Fair in nearby Spokane, Washington. There were also the usual reports on the deepening Watergate crisis. After a quick glance at these stories, I turned to something a bit more interesting: Charlie Brown and his Peanuts gang.

After taking a serious look at the comics and sports pages, I switched on the radio to catch the latest news. "War has broken out in the Middle East," said a very somber voice. "Egyptian and Syrian forces launched a full-scale military attack against Israel several hours ago. Israeli troops and army reserve forces are being quickly mobilized to counter an Egyptian assault in the Sinai Desert and a Syrian offensive on the Golan Heights. The surprise attack came as most Israelis were observing the holiest day of the Jewish year—Yom Kippur, the Day of Atonement."

When the newscast was finished, I turned off the radio and quietly mulled over this unexpected and obviously serious development. But instead of coherent thoughts, I found myself overwhelmed with emotion. Tears welled up in my eyes from somewhere deep inside of me. Waves of sorrow were rippling through me as the tears began to pour down my cheeks.

Why was I reacting like this? Just out of high school and eighteen years old, I was only marginally interested in the Arab-Israeli conflict, even though my friends considered me a bit of a newshound. I didn't know any Jews or Arabs who might lose loved ones in this latest chapter of the decades-old dispute. True, I had become somewhat sensitized to the horrors of war by watching television reports from Vietnam, as had many Americans, yet I realized that this alone couldn't explain the depth of my sorrow. It was as if some other being—maybe even God himself—were crying deep within me.

■ ■ ■

The Arab oil embargo following the 1973 Yom Kippur War was just beginning to produce major disruptions in America's lifestyle when my childhood faith in Jesus was renewed in January 1974. Increasing international attention was focused on the Middle East as drivers in the United States and parts of Europe suddenly found themselves waiting in long lines to fill up their gas tanks. Against this background, I soon found myself devouring various Christian prophecy books that pointed to the Arab-Israeli dispute as the centerpiece of God's prophetic "end-time plan" for the world. These books usually portrayed Israel in a very positive light. But, I was soon exposed to other, less charitable views of the Jews and Israel.

"It's all part of the Jewish conspiracy to take over the world," said my friend Doug, referring to the crisis that followed the Arab decision to cut off oil supplies to the United States because of its support for Israel.

"How could that be," I responded, "since the embargo is designed to hurt Israel?"

"Oh, the Jews are very clever," Doug assured me. "This is just part of their international deception. They're lulling the world to sleep while preparing for their final moves. We white Americans and Europeans must do everything we can to stop them!"

Doug was echoing the teachings of a group he had just joined, the Church of Jesus Christ Christian, Aryan Nation. Several years earlier, the group's leader had moved from California to Hayden Lake, Idaho, just a few miles north of my hometown, Coeur d'Alene. Many of the neo-Nazi white supremacists that followed him to Idaho were busy recruiting local people to their movement. Doug, of Germanic background, turned out to be easy prey, to everyone's great surprise.

Despite my newfound intense interest in the Arab-Israeli dispute, I didn't think I had ever met any Jews, or Arabs for that matter (although I later discovered that the father of a childhood classmate was Jewish when his Hayden Lake restaurant was painted with swastikas and set on fire by Aryan Nation followers). But now I was meeting Nazis, or their 1970s American equivalent, in my own hometown!

I was increasingly shocked, as were most of my fellow Idahoans, to discover the things that were going on in the Aryan Nation compound just outside of Hayden Lake. Hitler's Nazi flag was prominently displayed. Armed men in Nazi uniforms marched in "training exercises" around the compound. Wooden crosses were burned in the worst tradition of America's white supremacist underground movement, the Ku Klux Klan.

I easily resisted Doug's repeated invitations to attend a "Sunday service" in the fenced compound, but several mutual friends did go.

"Their leader said only white people in white robes would make it into heaven," chuckled one of them. "He also insisted that we white Christians must overthrow what he called ZOG, the Zionist Occupation Government, which he said has long controlled Washington, D.C."

Several years later I experienced Aryan Nation persuasion firsthand. I was working at a Coeur d'Alene radio station after completing a year-long broadcasting course in Spokane. The radio station's news director was preparing a story about an armed attack on the home and car of a local attorney who had represented several Aryan Nation members and others in a lawsuit against a Spokane dental clinic. Doug told me the claimants had been "ripped off" by the previous owner of the clinic, Jewish dentist Dr. David Cowan. It seemed that the new owners of Cowan's dental clinic would not honor his lifetime guarantee on every set of false teeth he had sold. The attorney apparently had been attacked by disgruntled claimants unhappy with his out-of-court compromise settlement, which they complained did not give them sufficient compensation.

The radio station's news director showed up late one evening while I was on the air. "I interviewed that guy the neo-Nazis tried to kill," he told me. "I'll get the story to you for your next newscast."

"Good for you!" I replied. "I'll be waiting for it."

Soon after our brief conversation, the telephone rang. I could see the news director pick up the phone in a nearby editing room. I was pretty sure I knew who was calling. The day before, the owner of Coeur d'Alene's only newspaper, who also owned the radio station, had received a telephone threat: the publisher's family would be much better off if he stopped printing the attorney's allegations that Aryan Nation members were responsible for the attacks against him.

I listened in on the call over a nearby studio monitor. "We understand you did an interview with that man whose house and car were firebombed and shot at," said the unidentified caller. "We will be very glad if you do not run it. Your children and wife will be glad too."

After pausing for a few minutes, the news director walked into the on-air studio and announced that the story would not be available that evening.

"They threatened you," I said, not revealing that I had monitored the conversation. He frowned, but didn't answer. "We mustn't let these people intimidate us," I insisted with rising emotion. "This is how Hitler got started!"

"Then *you* run the interview," he shot back, "but it won't have my voice on it!"

I went ahead and played part of the interview on my 11 P.M. final newscast. Immediately two phone lines lit up. I decided not to answer. Soon afterward, in the spring of 1978, I left Coeur d'Alene for what I hoped would be saner pastures in California.

■ ■ ■

"Down with the oppressive Shah! Down with the satanic puppet!" shouted the Iranian students over loudspeakers as they drove around the University of California campus in Berkeley. It was there, where the 1960s "free speech movement" began, that I first met Arabs and Jews. I didn't, however, meet any dissident Iranian students, although all of us were awakened many mornings by their anti-Shah slogans broadcast over an automobile loudspeaker. Within a year their wishes would come true, as the Shah of Iran was overthrown in early 1979 by a Shiite Muslim leader named Khomeini.

My next-door neighbor didn't think the Iranian Muslim fundamentalists were going to succeed in ousting the pro-Western Shah. Aaron was a Jewish law student at the university. He was interested to hear that I had come to California to work with a Christian anticult group called the Spiritual Counterfeits Project. "Sounds far-out to me," said Aaron. "There are certainly enough religious kooks around the Bay area to investigate!"

Aaron was quite right, as I soon discovered. The folks at Spiritual Counterfeits had conducted an investigation of an unusual San Francisco "church" headed by the Reverend Jim Jones. Four months after I arrived in Berkeley in May 1978, Jones and hundreds of his followers committed suicide in Jonestown, the cult center he set up in Guyana, South America. Some of the survivors of Jones's cult threatened to harm members of those groups, such as the one I was now with, who had conducted investigations of it. Shortly after the horrific mass suicide occurred, the mayor of San Francisco and a city councilman were assassinated.

The cult-induced deaths of so many poor, mostly black San Franciscans in Guyana, followed by the killing of the two most prominent politicians in the city, left most Bay-area residents in a state of shock. Such things were a bit too much for an Idaho boy, even one who had already experienced neo-Nazi close encounters of a weird kind. My thoughts turned increasingly toward the relative sanity of northern Idaho. In December, I returned to the snowy Pacific Northwest. Several months later, I began working as a radio announcer at a station owned by the Moody Broadcasting Network in Spokane.

My sensation-filled time in the San Francisco area taught me that California, while a nice place to live in many ways, is definitely *not* the Promised Land. But it was there that I had my first deep longings to visit the *real* land of promise, Israel.

During my third month in "Berserkeley" (as the city is affectionately called by many), I had been invited to attend a Tuesday night Bible study at the Jews for Jesus headquarters in San Francisco. Almost every week after that, I would pile my car full of Christian friends and cross the Bay Bridge into beautiful, troubled San Francisco. Although we were mostly Gentiles, the "Berkeley crew" always received a warm welcome at the study.

I especially remember one meeting just before Yom Kippur. Tears filled my eyes as I listened to the beautiful songs sung by the musical group known as Liberated Wailing Wall. As the Bible study leader spoke of Yom Kippur, I recalled the first time I ever heard of the holy day—sitting in my pillow chair listening to the news about a new war in the Middle East. *Maybe I'll live in Israel one day,* I mused. But I quickly dismissed the idea as highly unlikely.

■ ■ ■

Yet Israel was indeed in my future. Two years later, in November 1980, I was on my way to live in the Promised Land, but only for a year, I assured my not-too-thrilled parents. I still couldn't believe I was really going, even as I boarded an Israel-bound airliner with a group of twenty young American Christians. We were on our way to live and work for a year on an Israeli *kibbutz*—the world-renowned collective agricultural settlements that played such a vital role in the formation of the state of Israel earlier this century.

Many passengers applauded as our plane touched down at Ben Gurion Airport near Tel Aviv. We were in the Holy Land! After a harrowing taxi ride that should have taken twenty minutes but lasted only ten, we arrived at Baptist Village, a Southern Baptist Christian center near Tel Aviv. There we were joined by another ten young people from Britain, Denmark, Africa, and Australia. The next day we began a six-week orientation program to prepare for our year-long stay in Israel. We had come under the sponsorship of Project Kibbutz (P.K.), a U.S.-based ministry that placed teams of young Christian workers on Israeli kibbutz settlements.

Despite a severe case of jet lag, I enjoyed the P.K. orientation program. Well, maybe I wasn't exactly thrilled about the mandatory 5 A.M. daily jog around the village, but the continuing excitement I felt at being in the Promised Land made any other feelings, including exhaustion, irrelevant. My main goal besides staying awake was to visit the "City of the Great King," Jerusalem, just thirty miles away. We were scheduled to have a three-day tour of Israel's capital city at the end of the program. There was no way I was going to wait that long.

Niels Christiansen from Denmark had the bunk bed just above mine. While the rest of us had flown in from various parts of the globe, Niels had pedaled his bike from Jerusalem, where he had worked as a volunteer with a Danish group helping the elderly for a year. Every day during the first few weeks of the P.K. orientation he would gleefully describe the city to me, knowing my eagerness to get there.

"Oh, Lord," I prayed, "you must have some way to get me to Jerusalem soon. I can't stand being so close to your city, yet having to wait another month to see it." The Lord heard my cry.

"I need someone to go up to Jerusalem to help me pick up the rest of my belongings," said Niels, with a glint in his eye. "You wouldn't be interested, would you?" Several days later we were on a crowded Israeli bus, weaving our way up the tree-lined hills to Jerusalem.

My first experience in the Holy City was nothing less than delightful. After arriving at the almost-empty central bus station in western Jerusalem, Niels suggested we go and visit friends of his in a nearby apartment building. We walked in just as his Israeli friends were about to light the Friday evening Sabbath candles.

It was a special Sabbath, coming in the middle of the week-long Jewish festival of Hanukkah. The holiday marks God's deliverance of Jerusalem in 165 B.C. from Syrian-Greek control, and the miraculous restoration of the ancient Jewish temple, which had been defiled by Greek pagan practices. We were handed Jewish skullcaps, or *yarmulkes,* to put on our heads before the woman of the house lit the candles. *"Baruch Ata Adonai Eloheinu, Melech ha Olam,"* she proclaimed, which is Hebrew for "Bless You, O Lord Our God, King of the Universe." After the prayers were finished, we retired to the kitchen to eat jelly doughnuts, the traditional Hanukkah treat.

"This is not the way the city usually looks," Niels assured me as we walked along almost-empty streets heading for Jerusalem's ancient walled Old City. "This place really shuts down on Friday nights and Saturdays. The Sabbath is the Sabbath in Jerusalem!" To me, the quiet only added to the awesomeness I already felt at being in the city where Jesus died and rose again—the city where, according to the Bible, he will return one day in glory.

My excitement grew as we spotted in the distance the high stone wall surrounding the Old City, beautifully lit up by pink and white floodlights. Soon we were walking through the Damascus Gate, the main northern entrance to the Old City. All was quiet as we made our way along deserted narrow lanes. Finally we reached the Western Wall plaza. Here thousands of religious Jews gather daily to pray for the coming of the Messiah and the rebuilding of the temple. Their heartfelt, sometimes tearful prayers over the years have led many Western visitors to dub it "the Wailing Wall." I was bubbling with excitement and anticipation as we entered the plaza. "We're approaching the heart of Jerusalem—and of the whole world," proclaimed Niels.

I was certain I had died and gone to heaven! Five large, gas-powered candles positioned close to the Western Wall shed a beautiful, other-worldly, reddish orange light all over the empty plaza. The flickering firelight danced on the venerated ancient wall and on all the surrounding buildings. The burning candles were part of the eight Hanukkah lights lit by Jews around the world each year, one day at a time. The candles commemorate a miracle said to have occurred in the ancient temple, which once towered just above where we were standing. When the Jews drove the Syrian-Greeks out of the temple, records the Jewish Talmud, only enough oil remained to fuel the seven-pointed temple lamp for one day. But miraculously, the oil lasted eight full days.

As Niels and I marveled at the sight before us, we spotted one lone Jew praying silently next to the wall. He didn't seem to notice us as we quietly approached the wall and began praying to the God of Israel through his anointed Messiah.

■ ■ ■

Although I was on cloud nine for several days, I didn't fully appreciate until a few weeks later just how special my first visit to Jerusalem actually had been. When I saw the city a second time, it was as most visitors see it: full of the hustle and bustle, the crowds and the noise, of any city on earth. Our Project Kibbutz tour bus hobbled through streets packed with cars and noisy, smelly city buses. Shoppers carrying packages lined the route, darting to and fro between the slow-moving vehicles. Even the Western Wall plaza was not the same. Hundreds of tourists, many in odd-looking blue hats provided by their tour guides, mingled with Jewish worshipers. Arab vendors busily sold breadrolls nearby. This was the Jerusalem that I became quite familiar with over the next two decades. But the memory of my first visit will never leave me.

Nor will the memory of my first tour of Yad vaShem Holocaust Memorial, located near Mount Herzl in southwest Jerusalem. I, like my companions, was familiar with the Nazi holocaust of World War II that wiped out one-third of world Jewry. I was aware that well over a million Jewish children were among the dead. I knew millions of Jews had perished in gas ovens; had been shot near open pits; had been dissected like frogs; had been burned alive, raped, pillaged. Still, I was not fully prepared for what I would see on that cold day in December.

The others in my group went through the horrifying hallways—lined with pictures, documents, maps, and actual remains of history's worst mass slaughter—more quickly than I did. Maybe I took longer to absorb what I was reading and seeing because I knew firsthand that Nazi ideology is not a thing of the past. Maybe it was because of my experiences with the Church of Jesus Christ Christian, Aryan Nation that I was moved to tears by a large photograph prominently displayed at the end of the first hallway.

The picture, the only one without an accompanying text, showed a large outdoor crucifix located in the yard of a German monastery. Just outside the yard, in the direction the head of the crucified, blood-stained Christ was facing, was posted a large sign in German: *Juden Sind Heir Nicht Erwunscht,* "Jews are not welcome here."

*How could such a wholesale slaughter have happened anywhere on earth in the twentieth century?* I asked myself as I neared the exit door. And, even more puzzling, how could it have taken place in Germany, one of the most advanced "Christian" nations in the world? Despite the fact that I knew the others were waiting for me outside, I had to take a few minutes at the end to find a dark corner—and weep.

# CHAPTER 2

## RACHEL WEEPS

"Y ou have two choices," said Art Carlson, the founder and leader of Project Kibbutz. We were at the end of our six-week orientation program, which included full lectures on Israel's history and the Middle East, plus Hebrew language lessons. "You can either go to a kibbutz in the south near the town of Ashkelon, or to one along the Israeli border with Lebanon. But I have to warn you," he continued gravely, "the northern kibbutz is sometimes shelled by PLO forces located just over the border in south Lebanon."

Naturally, as a radio broadcaster, I wanted to spend my year near the action, so I chose the northern kibbutz called Hagoshrim (Hebrew for "the bridge builders"). My Danish friend Niels also anticipated an adventure in the north, as did a dozen other orientation participants. It was undoubtedly for the best that none of us realized just how much action we were about to experience!

I arrived at Hagoshrim on Christmas Day 1980, along with my two team leaders, who were both from Great Britain. The three of us were sent up before the rest of the team to make sure that everything was in order. It was a bright, warm Christmas Day, marred only by what sounded like a distant thunderstorm. But there were no clouds on the horizon.

"I bet you're wondering what that noise is," said Eliyahu, a delightful Turkish-born Jew who was in charge of overseas volunteer workers at Hagoshrim. "That's the PLO's traditional Christmas gift to the Christians of south Lebanon!" My puzzled expression prompted a further explanation.

"The PLO always shoots extra shells at the south Lebanese Christians on their religious holidays," Eliyahu told me. As I began to digest this, he said, "Let's just hope they don't send anything our way." I could have gone all day without hearing that comment!

"Are people being killed?" I asked.

"Maybe some, but not many. The Israeli army provides bomb shelters for them."

*What a sad way to spend Christmas Day,* I thought, *and how different from what I'm used to!*

Not much time passed before we began living in underground bomb shelters ourselves. Tension rose sharply in mid-January after the nearby Israeli town of Kiryat Shmona was shelled. The PLO had used the town as a frequent target of attack ever since setting up a ministate in south Lebanon in the mid-1970s. The Palestinian attack began a new round of tit-for-tat shelling from both sides of the border. It climaxed with several weeks of heavy bombardments in April. One of the main Israeli gun emplacements was just next to Hagoshrim, a fact that was regularly brought to our attention. The shooting calmed down for a couple of months, but intensified again in late June. July was a real blast! We ate and slept in our sweltering shelter for several weeks straight while bombs crashed down around us.

The Jews of Hagoshrim, who had lived through similar bombing blitzes for decades, were certain that some of us would return home. Taking off was the normal, and quite understandable, reaction of most foreign volunteers during periods of heavy shelling. Yet, although we were tempted at times, and despite some parental encouragement to come home, none of us left the kibbutz. We wanted to show our Jewish hosts that we would not run away at the first sign of trouble.

Our determination to stay was noted and appreciated by Hagoshrim's five hundred or so Israeli residents. A few would drop by our bomb shelter to hear us sing songs of praise and worship to the Lord. "The Lord is my life and my salvation. Whom shall I fear, whom shall I fear?" We especially liked to sing "Hiding Place," written in late 1980 by Project Kibbutz member Michael Ledner. He taught the song to me, then together we taught it to several P.K. teams gathered for a spring seminar on the shores of the Dead Sea—the lowest place on earth. "You are my hiding place. / You always fill my heart with songs of deliverance. / Whenever I am afraid, / I will trust in you, / I will trust in you. / Let the weak say, 'I am strong / in the strength of the Lord!'" Comforting words indeed while sitting in an underground bomb shelter, or at the lowest spot on earth.

A late-July cease-fire, engineered by U.S. special envoy Philip Habib, gave us a break from the shelling for the remainder of our stay on Hagoshrim. Finally, we were able to get to know the kibbutz members in a relaxed atmosphere. Many of them immigrated to Israel from Turkey, whose once-great Jewish community consisted mainly of descendants of Jews expelled from Spain in the late 1400s. Some had fled Europe during World War II. One woman had lost more than two hundred relatives in Hitler's gas chambers. A few had come before the war, foreseeing that Hitler meant it when he said that Europe must be rid of its Jews. Several had fled from Iraq and other Arab countries in the early years of the Jewish state. Only a handful were survivors of Hitler's death camps.

I was overwhelmed by the stories I heard—some heroic, some pitiful, most a mixture of the two. As I listened, I realized that I knew so very little about the Jewish *diaspora*, or "dispersion," which had lasted for most of the past two thousand years.

"*Diaspora* is a Greek word," someone on the kibbutz pointed out to me. "The word we use in Israel is *galut*, Hebrew for 'exile.' We weren't simply dispersed. We were cast out, exiled from our land."

I soon realized that knowledge about the many years of Jewish *galut* is essential if one is attempting to comprehend what lies behind the creation of the modern state of Israel and the Arab-Israeli conflict. I knew that the history of "Christian" persecution of the Jews didn't begin with Hitler's Germany. Still, I was shocked to discover in subsequent research that it was only the tip—even if an excessively horrendous one—of a very ugly iceberg.

## MARTYRS AND HEROES

As I begin writing this brief overview of Jewish history from the time of the Jewish dispersion from the Holy Land in the second century A.D.,

Israel is observing its annual Holocaust Martyrs and Heroes Remembrance Day. This morning I stood on my balcony at 10 A.M. as sirens wailed for two minutes across Jerusalem and the rest of the country. Cars and trucks came to a halt as Jews throughout the land stood in silence to commemorate the millions killed by Hitler's Nazi death machine. This special day also reminds many people of the centuries of persecution their ancestors endured in Christian Europe and Russia. Last evening, as the sad day began (all Jewish days begin at sunset), I was in the home of messianic Jewish author Lance Lambert, whose father and other relatives perished in the Auschwitz death camp. I sat quietly as Lance and his sister Teresa lit a candle in their father's memory.

Lance's father was taken to Auschwitz from his home country of Italy, where a thriving Jewish community had lived for many centuries in relatively peaceful conditions. Yet despite the traditional warmth and moderation of the Italian people, the Mediterranean nation of Italy is generally not fondly remembered by Jews. The reason for this is quite simple. The heart of Italy is Rome, and for centuries the heartbeat of Rome has been the Vatican, the seat of the Roman Catholic Church. It was the Vatican that gave an official Christian imprimatur to the persecution suffered by the Jewish people in the early days of Christianity and beyond, an imprimatur that was at least partially carried on by most of the Reformation churches.

The ancient church laid the foundation upon which the holocaust was built. In fact, a thousand years before Hitler took control of Germany, Jews were being slaughtered throughout "Christian" Europe. It must be noted that anyone holding religious views dissimilar to the Church of Rome's was liable to be ostracized, if not actually persecuted, be they Jew or Gentile. But no other sect or nationality suffered such deep and consistent hostility, hatred, and violence as the Jews.

"The vast majority of Christians, even well educated, are all but totally ignorant of what happened to Jews in history, and of the culpable involvement of the Church," writes Edward H. Flannery, a Roman Catholic priest, in the introduction to his excellent, though very sad, book *The Anguish of the Jews: Twenty-three Centuries of Antisemitism.*[2]

The author's lament, which I can verify from my own experience, is followed by the observation that Christians are generally ignorant of the church's historical anti-Semitic record because most Christian history books omit or play down its intensity. Christian anti-Semitic teachings and actions were hardly even mentioned in the Catholic school I attended in the 1960s. Father Flannery then goes on to note that most Jews are *acutely* aware of this historical hatred and persecution, which so often ended in violent death. Having lived many years in Israel, I can confirm that statement as well.

Is the church's record really that bad? some may ask. And didn't the Jews deserve it just a little? The answer to the first part of that question can be found in history, which we will look at briefly in the coming paragraphs. The answer to the second part is a matter of opinion. As someone who has lived with Israeli Jews since 1980, I can testify that they are as human as anyone else. It was, after all, the ancient Jewish prophets who pointed out the sinful and fallen state of the chosen people of God. Many Jews are wonderful people, and others not so nice.

Whatever the case, true Christians have no excuse for hating or persecuting anyone, since they are followers of the Jew who taught us to love all people equally, whether we like them or not. Yet it was the Bible, and especially the New Testament, which was so often quoted to justify Christian attacks against the Jews.

## A LEGACY OF HATRED

Within several centuries after Jesus' death and resurrection, many of the church fathers seemed to have forgotten that their Savior, his mother Mary, his earthly father Joseph, all of the apostles, all but possibly one of the New Testament writers, and most members of the early church, *were Jews*. They began preaching from churches—mostly named after these Jews—that God had forever cursed the physical brethren of Jesus who had totally rejected him as Messiah. They taught that the New Testament church is the new Israel, which has totally supplanted the old.

The church accepted this interpretation as authoritative despite the contextual evidence throughout the New Testament that, although the Gentiles are now partakers of the covenant blessings of God, the term *Israel* still refers, with one possible exception, exclusively to the Jewish people.

These same church leaders apparently overlooked the fact that many thousands of Jews accepted their fellow Jew, Yeshua, as the Messiah *before* Gentiles even had a chance to hear the gospel. We know from the New Testament Book of Acts that in the immediate years after the Lord's ascension, "the word of God spread. The number of disciples in Jerusalem increased rapidly, and a large number of priests became obedient to the faith" (6:7).

Even before this, just after Jesus' crucifixion, many Jews were sympathetic to him, deeply regretting his death. Luke records that following the crucifixion and darkness that fell over the land, "all the people who had gathered to witness this sight . . . beat their breasts and went away" (Luke 23:48). Breast beating is a traditional sign of great mourning. Yet in the writings of many of the early church fathers, the Jewish multitude were pictured as totally evil, gleefully jeering the Lord as he was led to the slaughter.

Flannery points out that church fathers such as Origen, Justin, and Chrysostom seemed to have forgotten that any Jews had ever trusted Jesus as their Savior. Jewish Pharisees and priests were exclusively portrayed as conniving and totally hostile to the gospel. The fathers used selected statements made by the apostle Paul to attack these groups, ignoring Paul's own testimony that he was proud of his Jewish heritage, including his upbringing as a Pharisee. Nicodemus, a leading Pharisee in Paul's day, confessed to Jesus that many of his contemporaries were awestruck by this rabbi from Nazareth: "We know you are a teacher who has come from God. For no one could perform the miraculous signs you are doing if God were not with him" (John 3:2).

Many church fathers seemed to have assumed that none of the people spoken of by Nicodemus, and none of the multitudes who beat their breasts over the Lord's crucifixion, ended up following the one who proclaimed himself the long-awaited Messiah of Israel. Of course, even if none had believed, there was no "Christian" basis for vicious attacks against the Jewish people.

Paul's affection for his kindred and their religion, spelled out in his letter to the Romans, was not emulated by these early Roman church leaders. Instead there was enmity, hostility, and finally outright hatred for the

Jews. Paul taught that God's rejection of that part of the Jewish nation that did not believe led to "riches for the Gentiles" who were then grafted in as "wild olive branches" onto the tree of Israel. (How can the church be grafted onto a tree it has previously supplanted?) Many of Paul's successors seemingly wanted to destroy the Jewish roots of the tree, along with the rejected branches, apparently ignoring the fact that a tree without roots will soon die.

The Roman destruction of the Jewish nation of Judea in A.D. 135 was deserved, wrote Justin to an unidentified rabbi in his *Dialogue with Trypho,* "because you have murdered the Just One."[3] This theme would be echoed frequently down through history by Christians persecuting Jews. The fact that Jesus himself taught that he *had to die* in order to redeem humankind somehow escaped Gentile persecutors, along with the fact that it was *Roman* soldiers who actually killed him.

Origen concluded that the Jews "will never be restored to their former condition. For they have committed a crime of the most unhallowed kind, in conspiring against the Savior of the human race."[4] Apparently overlooked was Paul's teaching that Gentile Christians should not behave arrogantly toward the broken-off Jewish branches, for "God is able to graft them in again" (Rom. 11:23).

Father Flannery cites many other instances of growing hostility toward the Jews by early church fathers. This hostility reached its height in the sermons and writings of John Chrysostom (A.D. 344–407), the most popular preacher of the fourth century. According to Flannery, Chrysostom "stands without peer or parallel in the virulence of his attack."[5] He quotes from eight of Chrysostom's sermons in which he called the Jews "lustful, rapacious, greedy, perfidious bandits, inveterate murderers, destroyers, men possessed by the devil" with the "manners of the pig and the lusty goat." Jews "worship the devil," and their religion is "a disease." They have fallen into such a state because of their "odious assassination of Christ."

Therefore, according to Chrysostom, God hates the Jews, who will always remain without the temple or a sovereign nation. If all of this did not lead to obvious conclusions among his Christian audience, Chrysostom spelled it out even more explicitly for them, calling for a perpetual Christian "holy war" against the Jews: "He who can never love Christ enough will never have done with fighting against those who hate Him."[6]

Such statements as these would be of only marginal historical interest if it were not for the awful, tragic fact that many Christian leaders and laymen used them as a basis for persecuting, and even killing, their Jewish neighbors. It does not matter that Jewish hostility against Christians might have, at times, preceded Christian persecution of Jews, as Justin argued in his *Dialogue with Trypho*. It was, after all, Christians, and not unbelieving Jews, who were supposed to be the bearers of the full revelation of the Messiah. It was Christians who had the high moral and ethical standards of the Jew Jesus to emulate.

There were, of course, individual Christians down through the years who followed the Messiah's teachings and example of love, compassion, and forgiveness in dealing with their Jewish neighbors. But, as in Nazi Germany, such people were always relatively few. And most of them were forced to go against official church teachings and laws in order to fulfill Christ's command to "love your neighbor as yourself."

## ENFORCED DISCRIMINATION

It wasn't long before anti-Jewish sentiments emanating from various pulpits around the Roman Empire were turned into anti-Jewish church legislation. Around A.D. 306, church leaders meeting in Elvira, Spain, issued a decree forbidding close relations of any kind between Christians and Jews. In particular they banned Jewish-Christian marriages, which was understandable in light of Paul's admonition in his second letter to the Corinthians that Christians should not be "yoked together" with unbelievers (6:14).

The Nicaean Council of 325 took another step to insure that Christians would have "nothing in common with this odious people," ruling that the calendar date for Easter should be unlinked to the Jewish Passover Festival. The Council of Antioch in 341 explicitly prohibited Christians from celebrating Passover with their Jewish neighbors (a command I've broken many times!). The long-running Council of Laodicea

(434–481) told Christians they could not keep the Jewish Sabbath, or receive gifts or unleavened bread from Jews observing the Passover.

The Roman emperor Constantine converted to Christianity in 312 and later declared his new faith to be the official state religion. His subsequent moves regarding the Jewish people were not exactly sterling displays of the Golden Rule. Constantine ordered all Jews to leave Rome in 325, signaling hard times ahead for the ancient chosen people of God. British Old Testament scholar H. L. Ellis wrote that Constantine's legalization of Christianity was a turning point for the Jews: "When the church became recognized by Constantine, legal discrimination against Jews increased and they were gradually deprived of all rights."[7]

At least Constantine and his successors frowned on the growing Christian practice of burning down Jewish synagogues (a practice fanned, no doubt, by Chrysostom's sermons in Antioch). There was still some appreciation for the fact that the Jews had been the first to bring knowledge of the one true God of Israel to Rome and its provinces, but it was insufficient to hold back the tidal wave of anti-Semitism that was about to crash on the Mediterranean shores and flood the entire empire.

Conversions to Judaism, which had been a legally protected religion, were outlawed for all Roman citizens, while formulas were drawn up for Jews converting to Christianity, which included renunciations of the "detestable practices" of Judaism. Jewish converts were to break off all ties to any family member or friend still practicing the "nefarious religion." The official slide into anti-Semitism was halted only briefly during the reign of Julian (361–363), who did not claim to be a Christian, but resumed again with his successors, who were professing Christians.

Emperor Theodosius banned all Jews from holding any form of public office in A.D. 438. This law, along with other restrictions enacted around this time, constituted the legal basis on which all later European anti-Semitic legislation was formulated.

With the legal door now closing on Jewish life, persecution began in earnest. The ancient Jewish community in Alexandria became the first victims of wide-scale attack early in the fifth century. Zealous, misguided preachers encouraged the sacking of synagogues all over the empire. Many thousands of Jews perished in these attacks.

The official Roman Catholic Church attitude toward the Jews—which was more benign than the practice of many of its members—was solidified by Pope Gregory, who ruled from 590 to 604. Physical violence was condemned, but other forms of persecution were tolerated and even encouraged. God did not intend for Christians to kill Jews, said Gregory. Instead, the Jews were meant to exist alongside Christians as an "active witness" that God always punished sin. The Jews, in their degradation, provided such a testimony. While their conversion was to be worked for, force should not be used. The Jews could keep their synagogues, but no new ones should be built.

Popes down through the centuries were generally able to enforce these policies in the immediate vicinity of Rome, even as the empire fell apart. But elsewhere, many bishops and secular rulers, believing that the Jews were eternally cursed by God, carried the official church position to its logical conclusion. Forced conversions under penalty of death were ordered in many places (not a few Jews died rather than undergo baptism). The burning and looting of synagogues continued throughout Europe. Jewish children were forcibly taken from their parents and raised as Roman Catholics. Jews were forbidden to work in many professions.

They were, however, encouraged to be moneylenders since the church forbade its members to be involved with usury. (Thus, the anti-Semitic charge, heard to this day, that "Jews control all the money" was to a certain degree true, but only because of the Roman Catholic Church's own laws!)

## JUDENRIND

The first mass expulsion of Jews from their homes was ordered by King Dagobert of Gaul in 626. The decree was rapidly emulated in nearby Burgundy and in the kingdom of Lombardy in northern Italy. These expulsions came as King Sisebut of Spain was outlawing the practice of Judaism in his country. Still, the great Spanish Jewish community continued to flourish for many centuries, despite growing persecution, and some Jews even attained positions of power and influence.

However, Jewish fortunes declined sharply in the ninth century as Christians and Muslims fought over the Iberian Peninsula. Jews were expelled from the kingdom of Granada in 1066. Many were put to death by Muslim conquerors in southern Spain. Muslim victories in Spain only added to the growing cry in Europe for a holy war against the Islamic "infidels" who had conquered the Holy Land four centuries earlier.

The first "Crusade" to retake Zion from Islam was launched by Pope Urban II in 1095. For the next several hundred years, Jews would be viciously slaughtered throughout Europe and the Middle East by European soldiers and civilians who believed they were doing the will of God. Hatred of the Jews exploded into mass violence everywhere. Jews were burned alive in their synagogues, raped, driven from many towns, accused of killing Christian children in order to use their blood in Passover rites, accused of poisoning water wells.

Jews were forced to wear distinctive hats or yellow patches for identification. Their property was seized and plundered, their crops destroyed, their animals stolen or killed. All of this happened, and much more, in the name of the Jewish Messiah.

When the crusaders "captured Jerusalem for Christ" in 1099, they gathered the small Jewish remnant of David's ancient capital city into one of Jerusalem's synagogues and set it on fire, killing everyone inside. In 1189 during the Third Crusade, the Jewish quarter of London was set aflame, leaving many people dead. Jewish centers were then destroyed all over England, as they had been earlier in France and Germany. Anti-Jewish rioting against "the Christ killers" was usually at its worst around Easter. Jews came to dread this Christian holiday more than any other— even though it was a holiday meant to proclaim the Messiah of Israel's victory over sin and death.

As the Crusades came to an inglorious end with Jerusalem back in Muslim hands, a wave of expulsions began in Europe. Jews were ordered out of England and Wales in 1290, from Paris and other parts of France in 1306, from the Rhineland in 1348, from Hungary in 1349, from southern France in 1394, from Spain in 1492, and from Portugal in 1497. The expulsions came in the wake of the Fourth Lateran Council in 1215, which strengthened earlier Roman Catholic legislation aimed at restricting the Jews. Among other things, the council ordered Jews to begin wearing a yellow or crimson badge in order to prevent unwitting sexual intercourse between Christians and Jews—an offense punishable by death in most places.

In the midst of these expulsions, Europe experienced its most deadly plague ever—the Black Death. The scourge, which wiped out a third of the continent's population (including, of course, Jews) between 1347 and 1350, was blamed by the masses on the Jews. They had become the usual scapegoat for anything that went wrong.[8]

The populace believed that the Jews had poisoned Europe's water supplies with a concoction of sacred hosts, human hearts, and various insects and animals. Untold thousands of Jews were massacred in southern France, Spain, Switzerland, Germany, Austria, Poland, and Belgium because of this ridiculous charge. More than two hundred Jewish communities were entirely wiped out. To his credit, Pope Clement VI tried to stop the carnage, but he could not.

The expulsion of the Jews from Spain and Portugal followed what was probably the saddest feature of Roman Catholic Church history: the Inquisition. Pope Sixtus IV issued a papal bull in 1478 to set up the "holy tribunal" in Spain. Its purpose was to seek out and expose all heretics living in the land. The Roman Catholic inquisitors ordered tens of thousands of people burned alive at the stake, most of them either Jews who had been pressured to convert to Christianity or their descendants. Many confessed, often under torture, that they clung to Judaism despite their conversions.

The practice of forcing Jews to live in walled ghettos was already widespread when it was officially legislated by Pope Paul IV in 1555 as part of his fight against the dreaded Protestant Reformation. The idea was to keep Jews, thought to be sympathetic to Martin Luther's reforms, away from their Christian neighbors. The ghettos, usually overcrowded, were ordered sealed off at night and on Christian religious holidays. In Rome, Vienna, Prague, Frankfurt, and other European cities, Jews were forced to live like rats in a hole for no other reason than that they were Jews.

The Reformation was in fact welcomed by many Jews as a possible breath of fresh air in an otherwise stifling Europe. Martin Luther had proclaimed that Christians must be guided in their dealings with the Jews, "not by papal law, but by the law of Christian love." Yet a mere twenty years later, Luther—upset that "Christian love" had not won mass con-versions—declared the Jews "disgusting vermin" who should be deported from Germany. His pamphlet "On the Jews and Their Lies" (1543) called for seven steps to be taken against the Jews, including the burning of their synagogues, the razing of their homes, the banning of their holy books, and the seizure of their assets.

Although conditions gradually improved for European Jews after the Enlightenment took hold in the late seventeenth century, persecution and discrimination still continued in many places, especially in Eastern Europe and Russia. And Luther's suggestions were definitely not forgotten. They were put into effect four hundred years later (along with many other measures that would have horrified even Luther) by a German führer whose ultimate aim was to make Europe, and ultimately the entire world, *judenrind*—without Jews.

CHAPTER 3

k ✡ ✝

# BUSTING OUT OF ARABIA

The windows in my room shook fiercely as artillery and tank shells rained down on the nearby Golan Heights. *This time*, I thought to myself as I quickly became fully awake, *I'm not in Idaho listening to radio reports about a Syrian surprise attack against Israel . . . I'm in the valley right below the battle!*

It was the middle of the night, in September 1981. I was all alone in the Hagoshrim medical clinic, recovering from a bad case of hepatitis. The kibbutz resident doctor said I probably caught the disease by drinking un treated water from the Jordan River. "They'll have to carry me down to the bomb shelter," I reasoned out loud while listening to the heavy bombardment on the heights above.

But several hours passed, and no one came to rescue me. My imagination rapidly slipped into overdrive. Pictures of Syrian soldiers carting me off from the clinic flashed through my mind. As my sense of panic grew, I prayed fervently that God would send someone from my Project Kibbutz team to retrieve me before the Syrians began bombing Hagoshrim.

By morning, the noise of battle had died down. "Would you please tell me what's going on?" I demanded of my teammate Pat as he prepared to pass me breakfast through an open window near my bed.

"Oh, you mean the stuff during the night. Did it bother you?" he asked with a rather obvious sparkle in his eye. Before I could protest, Pat went on to explain that the sounds of war had come from an all-night

Israeli army exercise. "We were all a bit excited. Sorry I didn't come to clue you in on what was happening. Eliyahu came and told us what it was. Boy, was he mad, and so were the other kibbutzniks!"

"Why is that?" I asked, more than a little relieved to find we were not at war.

"Well, it seems the army didn't inform them about the exercise in advance," answered Pat. "The kids were all sent down into the shelters, and the men were grabbing their uniforms and guns to go off and fight the Syrians before word came that it was only an exercise!"

Although the "battle" on that September night in 1981 proved to be one-sided, Israel and Syria would indeed clash in war before another summer passed.

One month later, I had recovered enough to begin the long journey back to North America. Yet somehow I didn't feel right as Niels and another teammate carried my bags to Hagoshrim's bus stop. Maybe I felt guilty because we had only a couple of months left of our year-long commitment to the kibbutz. Here I was, the one who had encouraged everyone else to stay during the heavy shelling earlier in the year, flying home because of a little illness! But Niels and the others, seeing my poor health, urged me to go and rest for a few months.

"I'm certain that I'll end up on another kibbutz after this one," he assured me, "a quieter one, I hope! So you can come back and finish your year with me in 1982!" Tears filled my eyes as I waved good-bye to my friends. With a heavy heart, I took one last look at the Golan Heights, Mount Hermon, and the brown hills of Lebanon as the bus moved south toward Jerusalem.

By the time I spotted the Dome of the Rock Muslim shrine on the ancient Temple Mount four hours later, I was certain that, like Jonah, I was heading in the wrong direction. Still, I proceeded with my plan. My next stop was the Garden Tomb near the Old City—the place revered by many Protestants as the possible site where Jesus was buried and rose from the dead.

Good friends from Hayden Lake, Idaho—Claude and Jerry Carey—were serving as volunteer administrators at the Garden Tomb. The Careys met me with their usual warm hugs. However, my surrogate parents for the year were not pleased to hear that I was suddenly thinking of staying in Israel.

"You need to go home to your parents' place and really recover," said Jerry as Claude nodded in agreement. As longtime missionaries, they knew something about hepatitis.

"But I feel like I'm running away from God," I responded.

"Well, why don't you go out to the garden and pray about it for a while, then come in and we'll have a good meal," said Claude, seemingly certain that God would show me the way back . . . to Idaho!

As I sat down to pray in a quiet corner of the garden, one thing especially weighed heavily on my mind. I strongly believed that the Lord had shown me, while sick in bed, that I would be serving him in Lebanon the following year. I had even shared this belief with some of my Project Kibbutz teammates. Yet here I was journeying back to America, with little prospect that I would return halfway around the world to the Middle East in 1982. "Please, Lord," I prayed, "show me what you want me to do!"

His answer came quite quickly. I felt the Holy Spirit gently prompting me to walk over to another part of the beautiful, well-kept garden. There, I came upon a gathering of about fifty people just beginning a communion service. As I joined in singing the familiar Christian hymns, I noticed the light blue windbreakers worn by everyone in the group. "The Voice of Hope" was printed in large letters across the back of the jackets. The name belonged to a Christian radio station that I had often listened to at Kibbutz Hagoshrim. The Voice of Hope broadcasts came from southern Lebanon.

After the service ended, I announced to the Careys that God had clearly shown me that I was to return to the kibbutz. I didn't quite have the nerve to add that the Lord also confirmed that he was about to open a door of service for me in war-torn southern Lebanon.

In early 1982 there were really only two possible ways of entering the Land of the Cedars from Israel. You had to be an Israeli or United Nations soldier beginning a tour of duty in or near the south Lebanese security zone, a border enclave set up by Israel in the late 1970s to stop terrorists from infiltrating into northern Israel. Or you had to be an employee or guest of the American-owned Voice of Hope radio station.

I certainly wasn't about to join the Israeli army in order to get into Lebanon. But I was not overly eager to work at the Voice of Hope either. I knew that the station was a frequent target of PLO shelling from Beaufort Castle, a nearby crusader fortress used as a forward military base by Yasser Arafat's fighters. On top of that obvious drawback, I had already decided to leave the field of broadcasting before I ever left the United States. I did not respond enthusiastically when station manager Chuck Pollack suggested during the summer of 1981 that I consider working with his crew in southern Lebanon after completing my year at Hagoshrim.

"If you have any life insurance, don't count on anyone collecting on it for anything that happens here," said Chuck as we crossed the border into Lebanon, adding that "your insurer will say that anyone crazy enough to come here deserves to die."

I had met the Voice of Hope director again at a wedding soon after I returned from my "Jonah journey" to Jerusalem. He renewed his offer to me to come work with him. Chuck said he was beefing up his staff, especially the news department, in anticipation of a large-scale Israeli army operation sometime in 1982.

After touring the station, and after much thought and prayer, I finally decided to join the Voice of Hope's English-language staff. My first day on the air was in mid-April. Less than two months later, thousands of Israeli soldiers poured across the border to push the PLO out of southern Lebanon.

The first Israeli citizens I met after arriving at Ben Gurion Airport in 1980 were Arabs. They were Christian Arabs from Nazareth who worked at Baptist Village. But from the time I moved to Hagoshrim, I was, naturally enough, surrounded by Hebrew-speaking Jews. It was quite a change to suddenly find myself at a Christian radio station in the Arab country of Lebanon, even if I was not far from the Israel-Lebanon border and only a few miles north of the kibbutz.

Several English-speaking Voice of Hope staff members, including myself, took turns broadcasting in the mornings. Several Lebanese Christians rotated as hosts of the afternoon Arabic show. I quickly became friends with my Lebanese coworkers, who all spoke passable English, and began picking up a few phrases in Arabic. I often practiced my newly acquired "pigeon Arabic" over a cup of thick, black Turkish coffee with several of the Christian and Muslim guards who protected the station from armed attack.

One of the conditions for working at the Voice of Hope was that I purchase my own vehicle—essential since we Westerners were not allowed to live in Lebanon and had to cross the border daily from our homes in northern Israel. A friend told me about a good, used Volkswagen station wagon that an Arab Christian pastor needed to sell in Haifa. Although the car was already ten years old, it seemed like just the right vehicle for the potholed roads of Lebanon.

After signing a purchase agreement with Samir, we discussed the Middle Eastern situation. It wasn't long before I discovered that he had a very different perception of the fighting in Lebanon than did my Jewish or Lebanese Christian friends. I also learned that Samir termed himself a "Palestinian Israeli," not an "Israeli Arab" as Israeli Jews generally called him. Our discussions about the Arab-Israeli conflict continued whenever I took the car for a checkup to Samir, who was also a good mechanic.

My growing contacts with Arabs from both Israel and Lebanon showed me just how little I knew of Arab history, even as my time on Kibbutz Hagoshrim had pointed out the large gaps in my knowledge of Jewish history. As I studied Arab history in depth, I quickly realized that it is largely a story springing from one man—a desert-dweller named Muhammad.


## WHAT'S IN A NAME?

It is difficult to know exactly what we are talking about when we say "Arab history," because it is difficult to precisely define who an "Arab" is.

Historians say the original Arabs were a seminomadic, Semitic-speaking tribal people who dwelled in the northern section of the Arabian Peninsula, southeast of the Holy Land. The Bible records that the peoples who roamed the northern Arabian Desert area were largely the descendants of Abraham's firstborn son, Ishmael, and Isaac's son Esau, also known as Edom. God promised Abraham that he would make Ishmael a great nation, although he made clear that he would establish his covenant with Isaac (Gen. 17:20–21). The God of Israel also foretold that there would be enmity between the descendants of Isaac's twin sons, Jacob and Esau (Gen. 25:23). Esau's children began to fulfill that prophecy when they refused passage to the children of Israel, who were on their way from Egypt to the Promised Land.

The Bible first uses the term *Arabs* in 2 Chronicles 17:11, where we are told the Arabs gave tribute, along with the Philistines and others, to the highly honored Jewish king Jehoshaphat, who ruled in the ninth century B.C. Later on we find the Arabs joining the Philistines in an attack against Jehoshaphat's son Jehoram (2 Chron. 21:16–17). With God's help, the youthful King Uzziah defeated the Arabs and the Philistines in the eighth century B.C. (2 Chron. 26:7). By the time of Christ, all of the desert peoples who lived east and southeast of the Promised Land were known as Arabs.

Arab-Jewish enmity was evident when the Jews returned to their homeland from the Babylonian exile in the sixth and fifth centuries B.C. Arabs were apparently among the peoples who settled in the land during the exile, since they are listed as among those who were angry that returning Jews were rebuilding the destroyed walls of Jerusalem (Neh. 4:7). Earlier, Nehemiah had told his opponents, including "Geshem the Arab," that God was behind the rebuilding project, adding that these Gentiles had "no share in Jerusalem or any claim or historic right to it" (Neh. 2:20).

In modern terminology, an Arab is generally thought of as anyone whose native tongue is Arabic. This is basically how I have chosen to use the term in this book. However, the peoples who lived in the vast North African region from the Sinai Peninsula to the Atlantic Ocean only began to seriously mix with the warrior-tribesmen of Arabia in the seventh century A.D. Likewise, many of the inhabitants of Syria, Persia, Mesopotamia, Lebanon, and the Holy Land probably had very little Arabian blood in them before the Islamic conquests of that century.

Today most Arabic-speaking people have at least some genuine Arab ancestry. This is probably less true of those indigenous peoples who did not convert to Islam in the centuries following the Arab conquest—such as the Maronite Catholics of Lebanon, the Copts of Egypt, and the Greek Orthodox and Syrian Orthodox Catholics of the Middle East.

Except in Lebanon and Egypt, present-day Middle East Christian communities are tiny minorities in the countries where they reside. This is true despite the fact that Christianity became the dominant regional religion by the fifth century. The Lebanese Christians, who belong mainly to the Rome-affiliated Maronite Church founded in the fifth century by a Syrian monk, consider themselves descendants of the Phoenicians who plied the ancient seas from Lebanon's shores.

In fact, they are probably a mixture of various peoples, as is common in the region. The Egyptian Copts, whose church was said to have been founded by the Gospel writer Mark, say they are the true descendants of the ancient Egyptians who once ruled half the known world. This claim is also undoubtedly only partially true.

Mideast church historians believe that at least some of the ancient ancestors of the indigenous Christians of modern-day Israel, Jordan, Judea, and Samaria were the original converts to the faith in the first century of church expansion. In other words, many such Christians actually have Jewish ancestry, since the early church was almost entirely Jewish. Their ancestors' Jewish memory faded as the church grew in strength and as rejection of anything Jewish became a part of mainstream Christian theology.

The Arabic-speaking Arabian tribesmen who conquered the Middle East, the Horn and North Africa, and the Persian Empire for Allah turned the world upside down in just a few short decades. The Arab-Islamic expansion into these areas was swift and complete. Some Christians and Jews fled the rapidly advancing Muslim warriors, while many others were killed. Others converted—often at the point of a sword.

The common thread, then, that ties the histories of the Arabs of Northern Africa and the Middle East together is a religion—Islam. But Islam is much more than a religion. It is an all-encompassing code of life that does not separate Caesar from God. The Islamic conception of the absolute unity of religion and government is very much a part of the Middle East drama unfolding in our day.

## ALLAH'S ANOINTED

Arab history was mostly uninteresting until around A.D. 570. In August of that year (the date established by Muslim tradition), a baby boy named Muhammad was born in the Arabian trading town of Mecca. A member of the Quraish tribe that had seized Mecca more than a century earlier, the somewhat mystical, moody orphan had been brought up by one of his uncles following the death of his parents and beloved grandfather, who was one of the leading men in Mecca.

As an adult, Muhammad would often go out to meditate in the hills surrounding Mecca. It was there, during the month of Ramadan in A.D. 610, that the "Angel Jibril" (Gabriel) appeared to the thoughtful mystic. The "angel" instructed Muhammad to declare to the world what he would reveal to him.

Three years later, the forty-three-year-old Arabian stood in Mecca and proclaimed the revelations given to him. He spoke out against the pantheistic idol worship then prevalent in Mecca, and in favor of the one God associated with Gabriel: the God of Abraham, whom he called Allah. But it soon became apparent to Arabia's Christians and Jews—the first targets for conversion by Muhammad and his followers—that Islam's founder was definitely not speaking about the God they worshiped.

When he was twenty-five, Muhammad led a trade caravan to Syria on behalf of a local wealthy widow, Khadija, who later became his first wife (he had about fifteen altogether). Scholars believe he may have absorbed much of his knowledge of Christianity while visiting the Byzantine-controlled city of Damascus. However, Muhammad apparently did not correctly comprehend several theological fine points. For one thing, the prominent position that the Eastern Orthodox Church allotted to Mary led him to assume erroneously that she was the third person of the Christian Trinity (an assumption still held by the average Muslim today).

The Christianity with which Muhammad came into contact was largely corrupt and riddled with internal, often violent, disputes over theological and political questions. It is, therefore, perfectly understandable that an outsider would have difficulty determining exactly what the church's doctrinal positions really were.

Many Christian experts on Islam maintain that Muhammad's often-confused accounts of the life and mission of Jesus—recorded in the Muslim holy book, the Koran—may have been influenced by contacts with the heretical Christian Nestorian sect, which believed that separate divine and human natures and persons were manifested in Jesus Christ.

Whether Muhammad's ideas about Jesus came from himself, from Nestorian members, from the "Angel Jibril," or some combination of the three seems impossible to say for sure. However, one thing is quite clear: the Islamic Jesus is not the divine being portrayed in the New Testament or worshiped throughout church history.

According to the Koran, Jesus is not the Son of God, but "the son of Mary," since God could not have a son. Those who declare that Jesus is God are "unbelievers" who will be "forbidden entrance into paradise, and will be cast into the fire of hell," for "the Messiah, the son of Mary, was no more than an apostle" (Sura 5:73–75).[9] The Galilean was a great prophet, but not the Savior of the world. He did not die on the cross, but only appeared to do so. He was actually taken up alive to heaven before an embodied spirit resembling him appeared to undergo crucifixion.

Since Jesus did not die, according to Muslim teaching, he was not raised from the dead. His unshed blood did not atone for the sins of mankind. He will come again to earth just before the day of judgment, proclaim that Muhammad was God's final and most sublime prophet, and lead all of mankind into Islam. Then "the son of Mary" will die like any other mortal man and be raised to life along with everyone else on the last day.

The Koran's version of the birth of Jesus is very different from the Gospel accounts. In Sura Mary (*Sura* means "revelation"), the Holy Spirit is sent to Mary in the form of a full-grown man who tells the frightened Jewish maiden that he has "come to give you a holy son" (15–20). The koranic account then reveals that Jesus came into the world while Mary rested under a palm tree somewhere in "the east." Suddenly a voice comes "from below" her, apparently the newborn baby Jesus, who tells Mary to shake the tree and eat of its fruit (24–27). Later the infant surprises Mary's relatives by speaking from his cradle, saying, "I am the servant of Allah." He then goes on to describe his mission on earth.

The Koran then reveals that "this is the whole truth, which they [apparently Christians] are unwilling to accept," adding that "Allah forbid that He Himself should beget a son!" (29–36).[10]

Islam has as many distortions in its portrayal of the Hebrew Bible, upon which Judaism is founded, as it does of the New Testament. For instance, the Koran says that Abraham had two sons, not eight as recorded in Genesis. The patriarch is said to have raised his family in Mecca, not in Hebron as the Bible says. Allah's covenant blessings were passed down through Ishmael, not through Isaac. The Islamic holy book states that Moses was adopted by Pharaoh's wife, not his daughter as recorded in Exodus 2:5–10.

Haman, the evil Persian court official who opposed the Jews in the fifth century B.C., is said to have been a minister in Pharaoh's court. The Bible records that Aaron molded the golden calf in the wilderness; the Koran says it was a Samaritan, despite the fact that the Samaritans did not appear in the Holy Land until the time of the Babylonian exile.

The Koran, which calls itself a holy book sent by God from heaven to Muhammad (3:1–2), contains many denunciations of the Jews and their religion, especially in chapters 2 through 5. After the sins of the children of Israel in the wilderness are recounted, Allah castigates the Muslims for thinking that the Jews, who "knowingly perverted" his word, would trust the Muslims (2:75). Allah has forever cursed the Jews for their unbelief, and especially for deliberately rejecting his final revelation, the Koran, which they know to be a holy book (2:88–90). The Jews are evildoers who "love this life more than the pagans do" and are enemies of Allah and of his angels, his messengers Gabriel and Michael (2:95–99). Jews worship their rabbis (9:31), who cast off the Islamic holy book, are influenced by devils, and teach spells and witchcraft to their followers (2:101–102).

The Jews have deliberately "perverted the words of the Scriptures," and, therefore, "Allah has cursed them," except for a few who have faith (5:13; 4:46). Although "a portion of the Scriptures, was given" to the Jews, they are enemies of the Muslims and want to see them "led astray" (4:44). Any Jew who does not repent and turn to Allah—along with all other unbelievers—will roast in hell, constantly receiving new skins to be burned in order to receive a thorough taste of Allah's "scourge" (4:55).

Muhammad was probably familiar with the basic tenets of Judaism since many Jewish tribes lived in Arabia, especially around the town of Medina. This is the town where he fled after being rejected as a prophet in Mecca. Scholars say his negative attitude toward the Jews, partially founded on denunciations of them in the Bible, probably congealed after local Jewish tribes resisted conversion to his fast-growing faith in the early years of Islamic expansion.

Islam's founder is also thought to have learned something about Judaism and Christianity from visiting preachers who occasionally stopped off at Mecca's main tourist attraction—the Kaaba Shrine—to try to convert the crowds gathered at the cultic site. The Arabian Peninsula's most popular pagan shrine housed a black stone said to have fallen out of the sky in ancient times. Before Muhammad's reformist religion took hold, the Kaaba Stone was the centerpiece of Arabian polytheistic idol worship. Muhammad ordered the idols destroyed and declared the site to be an Islamic shrine. Muslim tradition later held that either Allah or Gabriel had given the black Kaaba Stone to Adam when he was cast out of the Garden of Eden. For more than twelve centuries, Muhammad's followers all over the world have turned to face the stone shrine while reciting their daily prayers.

Another tradition connected to the Kaaba Shrine illustrates how Islam reinterprets certain parts of the Hebrew Bible, along with New Testament accounts about Jesus. Muslims believe that God ordered Abraham, the first Muslim, to sacrifice his son Ishmael—not Isaac as the book of Genesis records. God then tells the obedient Abraham not to go through with the killing. The square shrine is said to mark the spot where God spared Ishmael's life. The thwarted sacrifice of Ishmael is celebrated each year on the tenth day of the twelfth month in the Islamic calendar. This is the end of the month-long *haj* pilgrimage to Mecca.

## A NEW FAITH

Muhammad's new religion spread rapidly throughout the Arabian Peninsula, due largely to the Koran's call for *jihad,* or "great striving," against all unbelievers, especially Christians and Jews. The Islamic holy book urges all Muslims to "make war" on the unbelievers "until idolatry is no more and Allah's religion reigns supreme" (Sura 8:39).[11] The reward for dying in a jihad struggle is instantaneous entrance into paradise, which the Koran makes clear is a place of great sensual pleasure.

Modern Muslim apologists maintain that jihad does not necessarily mean actual fighting. Jihad is also waged by nonviolent struggle through education, propaganda, and economic boycott. But it is abundantly clear from the Koran—and from the *Hadith*, the codified Islamic oral tradition of Muhammad's actions and sayings—that the *primary* meaning of *jihad* is actual fighting, "holy war." That is why Islam has long been known as the religion of the sword.

Newly converted Arabian warriors avidly obeyed the doctrine of jihad. Islam's founder certainly took it very seriously. Muhammad's many battles and victories are recorded in the Hadith. "Muhammad was much more than a prophet. He was a soldier—he took part personally in some of the early battles," wrote G. H. Jansen in his book *Militant Islam*. "He was wounded in the face and was known to have killed at least one of his adversaries."[12] Popular Muslim accounts say Muhammad personally killed many of his opponents, including some of Medina's most prominent Jews.

The early Muslim military campaigns were designed mainly to acquire booty, most historians agree. But before long the spirit of religious holy war was propelling Arab armies across the known world. Within a few years of Muhammad's death in 632, Muslim warriors were driving into the Holy Land and Syria. The corrupt Byzantine Empire could not withstand the rapid onslaught. Jerusalem was captured by Muhammad's successor, Omar, in 638. Egypt and Cyprus fell several years later. Some people, tired of corrupt Byzantine rule and frequent violent Christian feuds, welcomed the Arabs.

By 650 the fired-up Arabians, who saw their lightning victories as proof that Allah was with them, had driven deep into the territory of the other regional superpower, Persia, converting people everywhere they went. Within one hundred years, Muslim armies had conquered much of Spain, all of North Africa, the entire eastern Mediterranean region up to the Caucasus Mountains, the Persian Empire, the northwest portion of the Indian subcontinent, and were fighting their way into central Asia.

Conversion to Islam was a very simple matter, as it is today. One only had to recite three times the *Shahada*, the Islamic affirmation of faith: "There is no God but Allah, and Muhammad is the Prophet of Allah." This simple method of entering Allah's kingdom contrasted sharply with seventh-century Judaism and Christianity, which had elaborate conversion procedures. Muslim victors often forced whole communities of Christians and Jews to convert—or face execution.

The affirmation of faith is the first of Islam's Five Pillars of Faith to which every Muslim must adhere (some authorities add jihad as a sixth pillar). The others are: paying of the *zakat,* an obligatory alms tax; saying prayers five times a day while facing the Kaaba Shrine in Mecca; keeping the daytime fast during the Muslim holy month of Ramadan; and making the *haj,* or pilgrimage, to Mecca at least once in a lifetime.

These pillars are observed by both Sunni and Shiite Muslims, the two main branches of Islam (there are more than one hundred and fifty Muslim sects altogether). The minority Shiites, most numerous in Iran, Iraq, and Lebanon, are followers of Muhammad's cousin and son-in-law, Ali. Disappointed that he had not been named the leader of Islam immediately after Muhammad's death, Ali's followers engaged in a violent struggle with the Sunnis. The more powerful Sunnis came out on top, keeping control of the holy sites in Mecca and Medina. Shiite and Sunni Muslims still battle each other today, as evidenced by the long and bloody war during the 1980s between Shiite Iran and Sunni-controlled Iraq, and intermittent skirmishes in Lebanon.

Naturally, neither Christians nor Jews were too happy with either form of the Arabian warrior's religion, and especially with Islam's rapid advance in obedience to the Koran's many jihad calls, such as these in Sura 4:74 and 76: "Let those who would exchange the life of this world for the hereafter, fight for the cause of Allah; whether they die or conquer, We shall richly reward them. . . . The true believers fight for the cause of Allah, but the infidels fight for idols. Fight then against the friends of Satan."

## HOLY PERSECUTION

The "infidels" were alarmed by Muhammad's insistence that the Koran was the final revelation of God sent to correct the many distortions and untruths that had been allegedly introduced into the Old and New Testaments over the centuries. (Muslims maintain that prophecies forecasting Muhammad's advent were deliberately eliminated from both Testaments.) Adherents of the two "corrupted" faiths would either submit to conquering Muslim armies and convert to Islam or burn in hell as a consequence. The Christian nations responded to this new challenge with armed might wherever they could. That option was, of course, not open to the stateless Jews.

In Christianity, the Jews already had to endure what they considered to be a major digression from the revealed religion of the God of Israel. Now, fired-up followers of an Arabian upstart were conquering the world with an even more distorted version of Judaism's revealed truth (although in some ways Islam is closer to Judaism than to Christianity, especially in its dietary laws and emphasis on religious legislation).

The Jews were especially worried that the advancing armies would repeat the Islamic founder's killings and expulsion of their coreligionists in Arabia. In 624 Muhammad ordered the Jewish Banu Qainuqa tribe of Medina to flee without their possessions after they refused, at least for the most part, to convert to his newly revealed "final revelation from God." A second Jewish tribe was expelled in 625 after allegedly aiding Muhammad's opponents from Mecca, who defeated the Muslims in a battle just outside Medina.

After the Meccans attacked Muhammad's forces again in 626, the "Angel Jibril" supposedly told Muhammad that God was ordering him to fight against a third Jewish tribe living near Medina, Banu Quraiza. The prophet ordered every Jewish man killed (more than nine hundred were slain, according to Jewish historians) and the women and children sold into slavery. Jewish men in groups of five or six were made to kneel in front of newly dug trenches. Muslim swordsmen then came along and sliced off their heads, which fell along with their bodies into the trenches. The slaughter lasted all day and into the night.

Jewish historians insist that none of the Jews converted to Islam, despite an offer by Muhammad that their lives would be spared if they did so. After Muhammad's death, the remaining Jews of Arabia, except for some living in the Yemeni enclave in southern Arabia, were either killed, forced to convert, or expelled from the peninsula. All remaining Christians were also forced to vacate the Islamic holy land.

The widespread Islamic conquests eventually persuaded Muslim leaders of the need to moderate their minorities policy somewhat. Mass murders and forced conversions declined, and a rich Muslim culture developed in much of the Islamic world—one in which Jews and Christians were often allowed to participate, at least to a certain extent. However, some modern historians believe that it was not Arab conquerors who brought about Islam's glorious age. They say that the cultural leaders in many Muslim-dominated regions were actually local Christian, Jewish, and Persian converts to Islam and their descendants.

Those Christians and Jews who refused to give up their faith were officially subject to the *dhimmi* (non-Muslim) laws laid down by Muhammad's successor, Omar. Patterned on koranic teachings, the laws clearly defined all unbelievers as second-class citizens with restricted rights. Breaking some of the laws could mean the death penalty. Jews and Christians had to pay special head and property taxes. They could hold no position of authority over or marry a Muslim. They had to wear distinctive clothing to mark them out (the yellow patch so popular in Europe was first introduced by a Muslim *caliph,* or ruler, in the ninth century). They could not perform religious practices in public. They were forbidden to build new houses of worship. And they could not ride a horse in public (a symbol of authority).

In practice, some of these restrictions were ignored, modified, or imposed on a limited basis. Yet, when it suited the whim of a particular Muslim ruler, as it often did as the great Islamic civilization declined, the restrictions would be fully imposed—often with deadly consequences for non-Muslims. On the other hand, any Muslim attempting to convert to either Christianity or Judaism was certain to be killed, in accordance with Islamic law.

The Koran orders Muslims to "take neither Jews nor Christians for your friends. They are friends with one another. Whoever of you seeks their friendship shall become one of their number. Allah does not guide the wrongdoers" (Sura 5:51). Another reason to stay away from the *dhimmi* peoples is because they "spare no pains to corrupt you. They desire nothing but your ruin. Their hatred is clear from what they say, but more violent is the hatred which their breasts conceal" (3:118).

However, some Muslims ignored this rule throughout history, as many do today in Israel. But such kuranic teachings meant that many Jews, and to a lesser extent Christians, were forced at times to live in special marked-off areas—the precursor of the ghetto in Europe. These areas were at times attacked, looted, and burned, and their residents murdered.

Some historians argue that Christian leaders derived much of their anti-Jewish legislation from Islam's dhimmi laws, just as they basically picked up the concept of holy war from the Muslims. Others say that Muhammad borrowed the ideas from the Christians with whom he came in contact. Whatever the case, it is quite clear that Jews living under Muslim rule endured nothing like the frequent wholesale slaughters that occurred in medieval Europe. Yet Muslim oppression was often harsh, even if generally less intense than in lands further north. Anti-Jewish attacks became quite frequent in the 1800s, especially in North Africa, as European colonial rule began to wane. Violent attacks increased even further in the early part of the twentieth century as thousands of European Jews settled in the Holy Land.

A significant portion of the Arab world has experienced economic revival in the last few decades, due mainly to the "black gold" known as oil. The great Islamic culture that sprang up in the seventh and eighth centuries, and then declined sharply due to corruption and increasing European colonial power, has shown new signs of life, mainly as a result of generously flowing petro-dollars.

Saudi Arabia and other Gulf states have used their newfound wealth to rebuild their long-dormant societies. Islam itself has also experienced a resurgence throughout the region, helped along by generous gifts from Muslim Gulf treasuries. Substantial funds have also been channeled to the United States, Europe, and elsewhere, in most cases helping to spread the extreme views propagated by Osama Bin Laden and other radical Muslims. The history of the Jews in Muslim lands and the Arab world's renewed power and influence play a significant part in the ongoing Arab-Jewish struggle over the land of Zion.

CHAPTER 4

# SUFFER THE LITTLE HOLY LAND

"I'm dead," I announced to myself, as the long barrel of the tank gun came ever closer to my front windscreen. However, my self-proclaimed death notice turned out to be, to my great relief, slightly premature. At the last possible moment, the Israeli tank crew raised the long, steel gun barrel several feet above my Volkswagen roof. I said an extra prayer of thanksgiving as I slowly continued on my way to the Voice of Hope radio station.

It had already been an unusual morning drive to the station, located about a mile from the Israeli border. Most days the journey from my home in the northern Israeli town of Kiryat Shmona took only twenty minutes or so, occasionally longer if army vehicles were waiting in line before me at the border checkpoint. But previous regular routines, such as the length of my morning drive, had gone out the window several days earlier when Israeli troops began pouring across the border into Lebanon. My commute to the radio station would never be the same again.

It was providential that I spotted the tank barrel coming over the crest of the hill. I definitely would have been the loser in a battle with the Israeli-made *merkava* ("chariot"). I quickly pulled off the road to let the fifty-six-ton armored vehicle pass. But another tank was right behind it, and then another, and another! I carefully inched my Volkswagen up to the edge of the ridge to see how many more army tanks were in this convoy.

I couldn't believe my eyes! There before me, stretched out along the narrow valley road for as far as I could see, were hundreds of Israeli tanks

slowly making their way from the Golan Heights into southern Lebanon.
After waiting several more minutes, I still couldn't see the end of the long
convoy.

"I can't be late for work," I told myself, as I slowly made my way forward down the hill. The tank drivers courteously steered their armored
chariots as far as possible onto their side of the narrow road. Still, I just
barely squeezed by them. I chuckled when I considered what the crews
must be thinking of my Israeli-licensed white Volkswagen taking on hundreds of battle tanks alone in southern Lebanon!

Except for the jarring experience of almost having one of the tank bar-
rels smash into my car windshield, I made it to the station unscathed.
I signed on the air a little late, explaining to my listeners that I had got-
ten caught in heavy traffic.

Even though I suddenly had to contend with military traffic jams on
battle-scarred south Lebanese roads, there were definite benefits to having
the Israelis around. For one thing, PLO shells no longer rained down from
Beaufort Castle, situated on a strategic crest just above the road to the station. The medieval crusader fortress was captured from the PLO on June
6, 1982, the day after Israeli forces started pouring into southern Lebanon.
The battle for the ancient castle had been fierce and, I thought, a bit ironic.
Despite all the modern tanks and warplanes in the Israeli armory, and the
artillery and mortar shells the PLO possessed, they fought hand to hand in
the end, just as in the days when European Christian defenders lost the castle, and several others like it to the south, to Muslim warriors.

## THE ROMAN DESOLATION OF ZION

Warfare has been an almost constant feature of life in the land that the
Bible calls holy (Zech. 2:12) ever since the final destruction of the Jewish
state of Judea by chariot-driving Romans about A.D. 135. When Roman
warriors had vanquished the hundreds-of-thousands-strong Jewish army,
which had risen up in revolt against hated Roman rule, the emperor
Hadrian decided enough was enough. He would wipe out Judea forever.

The Jews who remained alive after the slaughter were driven out of
Jerusalem and surrounding areas. The city where David had set up his

throne was renamed "Aelia Capitolina," and a temple to the pagan god Jupiter was built on the site of the Jewish temple, destroyed by the Roman warrior Titus sixty-five years earlier. Judea was given the Latin name "Syria Palaestina"—anglicized as "Palestine"—to erase any Jewish connection to the land that the God of Israel calls his own. The Romans plainly intended to insult the Jews by the choice of a name derived from the Philistines, Israel's ancient enemies who lived on the coastal plain.

The Jews did not entirely disappear from the Holy Land, however, as many people wrongly assume. In fact, Hadrian's successors allowed a Jewish ministate to exist for several centuries in Galilee. The ruling Sanhedrin was re-established, and Jewish religious studies flourished. However, Jewish emigration increased significantly after the Roman Empire officially adopted Christianity in the fourth century. Christian ecclesiastics, now protected by the state, burned synagogues in Galilee.

After the Roman Empire was divided late in the fourth century, Eastern Byzantine rulers stepped up persecution of the Jews. The emperor Justinian tried to force remaining Jews in the Lord's land to convert to Christianity. Many Jews fled east to Mesopotamia, also known as Babylon, which rapidly became the center of Jewish life and learning.

Yet many Jews remained in the land, and others joined them during periods of less intense persecution. Official records listed forty-three Jewish communities in the sixth century: twelve along the coast, in the Negev Desert and east of the Jordan River; and thirty-one in Galilee and the Jordan Valley.[13] Local Jews even briefly regained a foothold in Jerusalem in A.D. 614 after helping the Persians to invade and conquer the Byzantines. But Constantinople was back in the saddle within a few years, and the Jews paid dearly for their "treason."

Despite renewed Byzantine persecution, many Jews survived to see Arab-Muslim warriors push out the Christian empire in A.D. 638. Islamic rulers, keenly aware of the importance of Jerusalem to Christians and Jews, were fairly tolerant of their *dhimmi* (non-Muslim) subjects, who continued to outnumber Muslims in the land until the crusaders were defeated five centuries later. Jewish and Christian communities flourished in many places, including Jerusalem.

The Muslims, however, made it quite clear that their religion was superior to the two older faiths and would rule Jerusalem until Allah's judgment day. The ancient Jewish Temple Mount would naturally be the best place to make such a statement. Although there is no evidence that Muhammad ever visited Jerusalem, Muslim clerics declared that the Islamic prophet rode at night to the city on his faithful horse, al-Burak. After tying up his horse to the Western Wall, Muhammad is said to have bodily ascended from the Mount on a short visit to heaven. The area was proclaimed a sacred Islamic site, and work was begun on a magnificent shrine—the Dome of the Rock. In 691 the shrine was completed.

Among inscriptions from the Koran that line the round dome are several ridiculing Christian belief in the deity of Jesus: "This is the whole truth about Jesus, the son of Mary, which they are unwilling to accept: Allah forbid that He Himself should beget a son!" (Sura 19:35–36); "Say: 'Praise be to Allah who has never begotten a son, who has no partner in His kingdom'" (Sura 17:111).[14]


## NO REST FOR THE HOLY LAND

The Lord's land was ruled from 661 by Umayyad Arab Muslims based in Damascus. However, Umayyad rule was increasingly challenged by the basically non-Arab Abbasid dynasty of Baghdad. In 750, Abbasid armies overcame their Damascus-based adversaries and began to rule the Holy Land from the Mesopotamian capital. Just over a century later, General Ahmed Tulun, a Turkish governor of Egypt, went to war with the Umayyads. He overcame their armies in 878. After further bloody battles, Umayyad forces recaptured Jerusalem in 904.

The tenth century saw continuous struggle for control in the area. Egyptian Ikhshidi princes overthrew Umayyad rule in 934. Twenty-five years later the Fatimid Caliphs of Cairo defeated their Baghdad rivals and began to rule the land. In a preview of the coming Crusades, Byzantine leaders took advantage of the almost constant Muslim internal battles to invade in 970. They were finally defeated by Muslim forces in 976. Just prior to the First Crusade, Seljuk Turks conquered the land in 1070, holding it until 1080.

As the war-filled centuries progressed under one Muslim ruler after another, many local Christians and some Jews converted to Islam in order to escape oppression and to better their social and economic standing. Despite such conversions of convenience, Islam was not the majority religion in the Holy Land until the large-scale slaughter of local Christians by the victorious Muslim armies at the end of the Crusades (the Jews, as noted in chapter 2, had already been largely eliminated by the "Christian" invaders).

Pope Urban's crusader forces arrived to throw out the Muslim "infidels" in 1096. Many Jews, aware of the growing persecution of their brethren in Europe, helped the Muslims in attempts to repel the advancing armies. Battles raged in the area for many decades. Untold numbers of Muslims and Jews were slaughtered by the victorious crusaders. The new European landlords defended themselves from a number of magnificent castles, such as Beaufort, which they constructed throughout the area. However, the Muslims, under the Kurdish general Saladin, roundly defeated the crusaders in a major battle near the Sea of Galilee in 1187. Islamic rule was re-established in Jerusalem. The pope's armies retreated to the coastal plain, where they suffered their final defeat and expulsion in 1291.

As Christian and Muslim armies slaughtered each other, Mongol forces from Asia swept into the area. They entered and sacked Jerusalem twice, in 1244 and 1260, and launched a full-scale invasion of the land in 1299. The Mongols were finally defeated by Muslim warriors in 1303.

Over the next several centuries, the by-now ravished Holy Land was ruled from either Damascus or Cairo. The various rulers, known as the *mamluks,* were mostly descendants of Turkish or Circassian slaves who had settled in one of those two great cities. Of course, they frequently fought each other, not allowing the decimated land to recover from its earlier, immense wounds.

The area was conquered yet again, in 1516, by the rapidly expanding Turkish-Ottoman Empire. As it had been in the past, Jerusalem was once again ruled from the ancient city of Constantinople, now under Muslim control and renamed Istanbul. Records show that there were about thirty Jewish communities in the land of Abraham, Isaac, and Jacob, mostly around the northern towns of Safed and Tiberius, when the Turkish Muslims arrived. Some of these Jews had remained over the centuries—somehow surviving the frequent wars and massacres; others had slipped in over the years, seeking refuge from persecution in Europe and elsewhere.

The Ottomans, whose renowned leader Suliman the Magnificent built the current walls of Jerusalem's Old City, treated their Christian subjects fairly well. They knew that persecution would bring the wrath of the great European powers, already quite concerned over the growth of the Turkish Empire. At first the Jews were also treated with some respect. Suliman even allowed a leading member of the expelled Portuguese Jewish community, Joseph Nasi, to set up a semi-autonomous Jewish area around Tiberius. Persecuted Jews from the papal states joined others from the Muslim world in settling in and around the town, which was one of the four Jewish "holy cities" of the time. A local textile industry was set up, employing many Jews. Jacob's children also migrated into the three other holy cities: Jerusalem, Safed, and Hebron.

However, most of Suliman's successors were not so liberal-minded. Ottoman officials several times barred all Jewish immigration to the Promised Land. Jews were sometimes allowed to slip in after paying *baksheesh* (a Turkish word meaning "bribes") to appropriate officials. Such bribes sometimes helped Jewish "visitors" from abroad to stay in the land. Turkish Muslim authorities barred Jews, even local ones, from buying property anywhere in the land of their ancestors. In 1856 this policy was reversed at the request of Sir Moses Montefiore, a wealthy British Jew. However, the ban was reinstated later in the century as increasing numbers of Jews moved to their ancient homeland.

During the second century of Ottoman rule, a most interesting and unusual character marched onto the world stage. Shabbetai Zvi was born in Smyrna in 1626. In 1648 he announced to his Turkish friends that he was the long-awaited Jewish Messiah. The follower of the Jewish mystical Kaballah sect was quickly expelled from town. After wandering for more than a decade, Shabbetai ended up in Jerusalem, where he proclaimed to all in 1665 that he was the Messiah. His "John the Baptist" was a man named Nathan, from Gaza (then another center of Jewish settlement).

Nathan and others traveled far and wide with the good tidings of the

"Messiah's" advent. By 1666, hundreds of thousands, if not millions, of Jews from all over Europe and North Africa were preparing to depart for the Holy Land to be citizens of the Jewish state that Shabbetai promised to set up (after somehow neutralizing the Muslims). Many thousands had actually begun the journey to Zion when news came that the "Messiah" had gone to Istanbul to lay his claim before Ottoman leaders. The Turks were not impressed, and they ordered Shabbetai to convert to Islam or die. He chose the former, much to the dismay of his many hopeful Jewish followers around the world.

Persecution of the Jews, particularly by local Muslim officials, was frequent and sometimes fierce during the Ottoman years, especially after the anti-Jewish Mulrad III became sultan in the mid-1500s. (This, plus savage religious wars in Europe, may help explain why so many were eager to believe in Shabbetai.) Many of the estimated twenty thousand Jews in the holy Galilee town of Safed—home of the Kaballah movement—were massacred in 1660. Mob violence against the Jews of Hebron broke out in 1775. Safed, which had been restored by a liberal Turkish ruler after the 1660 massacre, was again sacked in 1799. At this time, a sadistic Albanian-born Muslim nicknamed "the butcher" gained power in the region. He ordered the beheading of any subject who displeased him—especially dhimmi (non-Muslim) subjects.

Some historians believe "the butcher's" mistreatment of French merchants in the port town of Acre prompted Napoleon to launch his invasion of the region at the end of the eighteenth century. The French emperor tried to enlist Jewish support for his venture by promising to restore Jerusalem to Jewish control. But Napoleon's dreams of empire in the region were severely set back when his fleet of ships was destroyed by British forces during the battle for Egypt in 1798.

The following year Napoleon launched a ground invasion of the Holy Land from the Mediterranean coast of Sinai. On March 6, French forces captured the coastal town of Jaffa. Napoleon then moved north to the port of Acre, near modern Haifa. However, Turkish forces from Syria, with the aid of the British, withstood his siege of the town. Napoleon was forced to retreat to Egypt in June of 1799, his dreams of ruling the Promised Land shattered.

## LET'S GO UP TO ZION

Ever-increasing numbers of Christians and Jews made their way to the Holy Land throughout the nineteenth century. In 1831 the land was conquered once again, this time by the Egyptian ruler Muhammad Ali. He had gained control of Egypt several decades earlier after French and British forces withdrew from the area. Although Ali had waged a number of wars against rival Muslim sects on behalf of the Ottomans, he turned against Istanbul after Turkish leaders refused to hand over Syria (which included the Holy Land) to him as a reward.

Ali's military occupation, spearheaded by his son Ibrahim, was met with little opposition from local citizens since, as Holy Land historian James Parkes put it: "Turkish rule had few admirers even among the Muslim peasants."[15] After Ibrahim captured Damascus and was heading for Turkey, Russia feared that a new vigorous ruler would occupy Istanbul. Russia sent forces to stop the Egyptians' northward advance. Things settled down for a few years until Ali's forces attempted a new northern thrust. The British then intervened against the Egyptians, bombarding Ali's positions in Acre and other coastal areas. Muhammad Ali's forces were finally pushed out of the Holy Land in 1840.

The Lord's frequently fought-over land, Parkes says, suffered constant internal warfare over the centuries between clans and villages, along with frequent invasions from without. But it also had to contend with a natural disaster during the nine years of Egyptian rule: a severe earthquake struck the Galilee region in 1837. Historians believe that half of Safed's ten thousand citizens perished in the quake, along with a third of Tiberias's twenty-five hundred residents. Many villages in the area were destroyed.

It was during the short period of Egyptian rule that British, American, and other Western Christian missionary groups began to appear in Jerusalem and other parts of the Holy Land. This trend accelerated when the Ottomans regained control, with the Christian European powers wielding increasing influence over Istanbul. European consulates in Jerusalem took advantage of the situation to help the Church of England, the Lutherans, the Roman Catholics, and others set up churches, hospitals, and orphanages. The Eastern churches—Greek Orthodox, Greek Catholic, Armenian, Egyptian Coptic, and Syrian Coptic—watched uneasily as the powerful Roman Catholic Church established its first-ever patriarchy in 1847.

Despite the growing influence of Christian Europe in the Lord's land, all of the churches from East and West were constantly reminded of their "protected" position under Islam. A sword-bearing Turkish guard, or *kawass,* accompanied church leaders wherever they went, and all church activities had to be cleared with Muslim Ottoman authorities.

Visitors to the Holy Land in the 1800s described it as desolate, sparsely populated, and riven with lawlessness. Powerful local families known as *effendis* constantly fought one another. Roaming Bedouin tribesmen launched frequent attacks on the settled population, especially on villages, which were sometimes overrun and destroyed. Turkish rulers generally ignored the effendi violence since they were dependent on the powerful clans to collect taxes and help raise armies for the constant Ottoman wars in central Europe. Like everyone else, they could do little to prevent the nomadic Bedouin pillaging, since the fast-moving Arabs were usually gone almost as soon as they arrived.

After so many centuries of almost constant warfare, it was no wonder that the Lord's land was such a miserable place. The American writer Mark Twain expressed great disappointment with the sad state of the land during a pilgrimage in 1867: "Palestine sits in sackcloth and ashes . . . desolate and unlovely . . . Nazareth is forlorn . . . Jericho the accursed lies a moldering ruin . . . Bethlehem and Bethany, in their poverty and their humiliation, have nothing about them now to remind one that they once knew the high honor of the Saviour's presence."[16]

Describing the Jezreel Valley, the site of ancient battles and of the prophesied final battle of Armageddon, Twain wrote: "There is not a solitary village throughout its whole extent—not for thirty miles in either direction. There are two or three small clusters of Bedouin tents, but not a single permanent habitation."[17]

Despite the sad state of the land, things improved somewhat for the Jews as the century wore on. The European consulates, especially the British, often took up their grievances with Ottoman authorities. Still, such assistance was limited, and Jews continued to suffer humiliations at the hands of local Muslims.

Throughout the years of Ottoman occupation, a steady stream of Jews trickled into the land of their forefathers. By the middle of the nineteenth century Jews were becoming the largest single group in Jerusalem—for the first time in more than seventeen hundred years. Their numbers had grown so much in the crowded Old City that a group moved out in 1878 in order to build a new Jewish town on the coastal plain of Sharon. They named their town Petach Tikva, Hebrew for "Gate of Hope." The Baptist Village, where I spent my first weeks in Israel, is just a few miles from what is today a large, modern city northeast of Tel Aviv.

During the four hundred years of Ottoman rule and before, local Muslim leaders knew of the centrality of Jerusalem, and the rest of the Holy Land, to Judaism. As the years wore on, they observed how the Jewish "People of the Book"—treated as second-class dhimmis in Christian as well as Muslim lands—were gaining increasing influence and stature in "enlightened" Europe. They knew that European Jews were bound to re- peat Joseph Nasi's attempt to increase Jewish immigration and set up an autonomous area in Judaism's ancient heartland. They realized that reli- gious Jews in Europe and the Arab world expected that, one day, their God and his chosen Messiah would restore to them their Promised Land.

Muslim leaders in the 1600s had witnessed the fervent Jewish expec- tation of return passionately played out by hundreds of thousands of Jews desperately grasping on to Shabbetai Zvi's false messianic claim. They knew that many Jews had already come to live in the Holy Land through- out the centuries, despite the enormous obstacles put in their way by Muslim and Christian rulers. They knew that Jews around the world mentioned Jerusalem every day in their prayers as they faced in the direc- tion of the Holy City. Muslim leaders must have sensed, to their dismay, that the time was fast approaching when Jews from the four corners of the globe would seriously attempt to fulfill their long-held yearning to return to the Promised Land—the land given by the God of Jacob to their fore- fathers thousands of years before.

CHAPTER 5

# RETURN TO ZION

M y apartment in Kiryat Shmona was not elegant, to say the least. However, the rent was extremely reasonable—seventy-five dollars a month for a two-bedroom flat. There was a simple explanation for the northern Israeli town's wonderfully low rental rates: Kiryat Shmona's sixteen thousand residents had received PLO shells so many times since the mid-1970s that well over half of them had moved to other, quieter parts of the country. Nonetheless, people were returning to Israel's northernmost town when I moved there in August 1982. The shelling had stopped in June.

My teammates and I had often visited Kiryat Shmona during our year on nearby Kibbutz Hagoshrim. It was, quite honestly, a depressing experience. Few people ventured out into the town's business center for fear that a Russian-made Katuysha rocket would come crashing down on their heads. In fact, PLO gunners often waited until just after 4 P.M.—when stores reopened after the afternoon siesta—to shoot rockets toward the center of town. We often found ourselves the only customers at the few open ice cream stalls.

All of us knew there was a risk of unexpectedly meeting our Maker during one of our afternoon outings, but then again, we reasoned, bombs had landed more than once on our kibbutz. An exploding rocket had even sent pieces of metal shrapnel into a wall just inches above the heads of several sleeping Hagoshrim children, one of them the son of the kibbutz gardener whom I worked for during most of 1981.

The road I now traveled daily to the Voice of Hope radio station in south Lebanon took me right past the Tel Hai Museum located less than a mile north of Kiryat Shmona. The museum, clearly visible from the road, commemorates an earlier Arab-Jewish confrontation: an Arab attack on the Tel Hai ("Hill of Life") fortress in 1920 that killed eight Jews who defended the compound. Kiryat Shmona, the "town of the eight," is named after the victims.

Among the eight was Joseph Trumpeldor, a former Russian army officer who had lost an arm in the Russo-Japanese war of 1905. Trumpeldor came to live in Turkish-controlled Palestine in 1912. He swiftly became one of the Jewish community's main military leaders. The words Trumpeldor is said to have cried as he and his comrades were fighting off the Arab attack—"It is good to die for your country"—became a symbol for a strong defense to the fledgling Jewish community in the Holy Land.

Trumpeldor settled in the Galilee area during the "second wave" of Jewish immigration, which occurred between 1904 and 1914. Like the first *aliyah* (the Hebrew word for "immigration," which literally means "going up" to Zion), most of the immigrants came from Russia. They were fleeing the Russian and east European pogroms: the widespread, organized massacres of hundreds of thousands of Jews, which began in western Russia in 1881 and later spread to Poland, Romania, and other areas. The vicious attacks continued on and off for more than two decades. More than a million Jews left Russia and eastern Europe by the turn of the century because of the rioting, looting, and mass slaughter, which devastated the world's largest concentration of Jews.

Most of the emigrants moved to the United States. However, more than fifty thousand managed to come to the ancient land of their forefathers, *Eretz Yisrael* (the "Land of Israel"), despite Ottoman immigration restrictions. Quite a few later left because of the tough conditions they found there.

Those conditions were spelled out for me and my Project Kibbutz teammates in 1981 during a lecture by historian Arieh Avneri, a member of Kibbutz Hagoshrim. He had just written a book in Hebrew on the pre-state conflict between Arabs and Jews living in the Holy Land, called *The Claim of Dispossession: Jewish Land Settlement and the Arabs*.[18] Avneri's book focuses on Jewish immigration and subsequent land purchases between the years 1878 and 1948. Some of the information presented later in this chapter comes from his well-documented book.

## LA CHAIM!—"TO LIFE!"

As noted in chapter 4, the Holy Land was not exactly at its prime when significant numbers of Jews began immigrating during the latter part of the nineteenth century. The area had been called Palestine in the West since the Roman destruction of Judea in A.D. 135, but was usually referred to as southern Syria in the Muslim world.

Reports from the British consulate in Jerusalem echo Mark Twain and others in describing a sparsely populated, underdeveloped land riven with violent Bedouin attacks and clan warfare. The land was divided into two Ottoman districts. The border ran just north of Jerusalem and Jaffa. The northern district, divided further into two subdistricts, was administered from Beirut. Jerusalem was the headquarters for the southern district. The area east of the Jordan River was administered from Damascus. The entire region was ruled by Muslim caliphs in Istanbul, nearly a thousand miles away. Although Turkish was the language of government, few people actually spoke it, save for a few well-known phrases and words.

The Western superpowers grew increasingly interested in the region as the century wore on, mainly because of the vital Suez Canal, which the French and British were constructing in Egypt using local peasant laborers (many of whom died in the process). Other than this grand project, the Middle Eastern economy had begun to stagnate, driving many people, especially better-educated Arab Christians, to seek their fortunes in America and elsewhere.

The few departing Jews were quickly replaced by others—especially religious Jews from Europe and North Africa—who took advantage of the growing European presence to slip into Jerusalem and other towns. Arab workers from Morocco, Algeria, and Egypt and other parts of the Ottoman Empire wandered into the Holy Land, which had no clearly defined borders other than the Mediterranean Sea. They came in search of work as the economy improved during the second half of the century.

Protestant Christians came to live in the Lord's land in increasing numbers in the late 1800s. The first Protestant missionaries encountered fierce opposition from both the long-established Eastern churches and the Muslim Ottoman authorities.

An American church group, expecting the imminent return of the Lord, arrived in 1866. The American Protestants brought prefabricated houses, which they set up near the port town of Jaffa. However, official and unofficial harassment and poor living conditions pushed most of the sojourners out of the Promised Land within a few years.

Just as the Americans departed, a group of twelve German Lutherans, taking advantage of improving German-Turkish relations, arrived to await the Lord's return. They set up a colony near Nazareth. But the scourge of malaria left all twelve dead within a year. Other determined Germans soon replaced them. The German colonists bought the abandoned American prefabs and erected them in two locations: one near Jaffa and the other just outside Haifa. Additional settlements soon sprang up near Jerusalem (when I moved to the city in 1984, I lived in the "German Colony" neighborhood, located southwest of the Old City).

Other locations attracted more Germans. Before long, about a thousand Germans were living in the land. Their advanced agricultural methods were slowly adopted by local farmers. The German colonies thrived until Hitler rose to power in the 1930s. British authorities ordered the entire community to leave after several leading members declared themselves Nazi sympathizers.

The long-established Greek Christian community continued to grow in size during the waning years of the Ottoman Empire. A Greek neighborhood was built just south of the German colony as Jerusalem expanded south early in the twentieth century. Most local Greeks were connected to the Greek Orthodox Church—the main Christian body in the land since the time of the Byzantine Empire.

Arab workers migrated to the Holy Land in increasing numbers in the late 1800s, seeking jobs. Ironically, growing Arab employment opportunities were largely due to the economic activity generated by immigrating Russian Jews! A Belgian company, contracted to build local railroad lines, imported many Arab workers from Egypt, Syria, and Lebanon. Not a few of them stayed put after the projects were completed. Turkish authorities brought in Circassian workers from the Black Sea region. Hundreds of Maronite Catholics came to live in Jerusalem to escape bloody fighting going on in Lebanon. Armenian Christians, seeking to escape Ottoman oppression in Turkey, migrated to the area in increasing numbers.

A steady stream of Jews made their way to the Holy Land in the 1800s from Egypt and other North African countries. Many Syrian Jews fled to Galilee and Jerusalem in 1840 following widespread anti-Jewish rioting in Damascus. Violence broke out in Damascus and surrounding areas after rumors spread that local Jews had murdered a priest in order to use his blood in unleavened Passover bread—the same "blood libel" pinned on the Jews down through the centuries in Europe. Yemeni Jews in the southern Arabian Peninsula continued to long for Zion, and some found their way overland to the ancient homeland in the late 1800s.

In southern Europe, a rabbi in the Serbian town of Semlin was busy drawing up plans in the 1850s for a large-scale Jewish migration to Zion. Rabbi Yehuda Alkalay, a Sephardic Jew (*sephardi* means "Spanish" in Hebrew, but the term in modern Israeli usage generally refers to Jews from Muslim and other oriental countries, whether or not their ancestors came from the Iberian Peninsula), published his plan in 1857.

The rabbi's ideas caused considerable excitement among many of the millions of Jews in Eastern Europe and Russia who were confined by law to live in "the pale"—specially marked off, crowded provinces in the Russian Ukraine and occupied Poland. Jews longing to live free of persecution "beyond the pale" eagerly studied Alkalay's plans for a return to the Promised Land.

Holy Land fever was also stirring during the nineteenth century in Great Britain, but not only among Jews. Various Christian leaders and writers were speaking out on the need for a Jewish homeland. In 1839 the Church of Scotland sent out a two-man delegation to report on the condition of the Jews living in the land. Their report, detailing the discrimination and frequent persecution local Jews were forced to endure, was widely debated in Great Britain. The church then sent out a memorandum to Protestant monarchs throughout northern Europe, printed in full in the *London Times* newspaper, advocating support for a Jewish homeland in the Holy Land.

Christian associations were formed throughout Britain to help Jews return to the land. Of course, many Christian members had motives other than just helping persecuted Jews; they saw a Jewish return as a necessary, prophesied prelude to the second coming of Jesus. Meanwhile, several leading rabbis of undisputed orthodoxy began to teach that the messianic deliverance, so long hoped for and expected, would not occur before or concurrent with a Jewish return to the land, but would follow such a return.

As it became apparent that the pogroms were not just a passing phenomenon, but the worst sustained anti-Jewish violence since the Middle Ages, many east European and Russian Jews quickly searched for another home. The age-old Jewish migration was on again. Groups called "Lovers of Zion" were formed to promote Jewish emigration to the ancient homeland. Many packed their bags and fled, as their ancestors had done so many times in the past. But there was a difference this time: thousands were on their way not to another Gentile nation but to the Promised Land!

In the middle of the first aliyah wave, which brought around twenty-five thousand Jews to the land between 1880 and 1903, a young Jewish journalist from Vienna covered the trial of a French Jewish army officer in Paris. The officer, Alfred Dreyfus, was convicted of treason despite a lack of evidence against him. He was later acquitted in a retrial. The Jewish officer's trial unleashed a wave of vicious anti-Semitism in what was then considered to be the most cultured city in Europe.

The young journalist, Theodore Herzl, had already begun to despair of continuing anti-Jewish discrimination in "enlightened Europe" before witnessing this latest outbreak of hatred. Suddenly, as if inspired from above, he became a fiery advocate for a Jewish state, seeing it as the only solution for his perennially despised and persecuted people. But Herzl was not content to sit around and wait for the Messiah to set up such a state, as most Jews had been since the Roman exile. Like the Lovers of Zion, Theodore Herzl took action.

The Viennese-born Jew quickly penned a book that would prove to be the main inspiration for what became known as the "Zionist Movement."

The book was titled *The Jewish State: An Attempt at a Modern Solution to the Jewish Question.* A year later, in 1897, Herzl convened the First Zionist Congress in Basel, Switzerland. Delegates voted to establish the World Zionist Organization, with Theodore Herzl as its president, to work for the setting up of a Jewish national home in Palestine. A Jewish flag with the six-sided Star of David was adopted, along with a national anthem entitled "Ha Tikva" ("The Hope"), which lifts up the "hope of two thousand years to be a free people in our Land, the Land of Zion and Jerusalem."

Exactly fifty years later, the United Nations voted to set up a Jewish state in the land that the God of Israel gave to Abraham and his descendants almost four thousand years ago.

## COUSINS IN CONFLICT

There was one major problem facing the modern children of Abraham, Isaac, and Jacob. The Holy Land already had people living in it who also traced their ancestry to Abraham—through Ishmael, the patriarch's oldest son. These Muslims, along with most Christians, were convinced that the Jews would never again be a sovereign people in the land of their ancient forefathers. It was inconceivable that the rejected Jews would once again wield authority over the biblical holy sites, which had been in Muslim and Christian hands for close to two thousand years. The Roman Catholic and Orthodox churches had long concluded that they were the new Israel of God, and the Jews only a perpetual witness to sin and folly. The Muslims were clearly triumphant over both older religions, which had strayed from the true path of Allah. The idea that the wretched Jews would run the place once again was dismissed out of hand as a theological impossibility.

Still, alarm grew as the evidence on the ground outpaced religious certainties. The Jews *were* returning, and they were openly declaring that their goal was an independent state on the same ground where their ancient ancestral homeland stood. Meanwhile, the Turkish Empire was crumbling, and nobody knew exactly what would come in its place.

In 1858, some four decades before Herzl's Zionist Movement came into being, Turkish authorities restricted the selling of land to Jews. Local effendi families demanded a total ban in 1891. Still, as Arieh

Avneri documents, many wealthy Arab families themselves sold land to Jews, mostly at inflated prices. Much land was also purchased from absentee owners living in Beirut, south Lebanon, Damascus, and elsewhere. Death threats were issued, and sometimes carried out, against anyone caught selling land to Jews. Immigrating Jews, backed by such European millionaires as the Rothschild family, were willing to pay almost any price to have a piece of the ancient homeland. Most of the property that Jewish settlers somehow managed to purchase lay in the sparsely populated coastal plain and the Galilee region.

Tension sprang up almost immediately between Jewish settlers and their Arab neighbors. Muslim Arabs in particular could not accept the fact that dhimmi Jews were establishing independent, successful farming communities near the heart of the Islamic world. Avneri writes that the two peoples had different views of property ownership: the Jews stuck to legally defined boundaries, while Arab farmers were more interested in landmarks and long-established grazing practices. Jewish farmers thought that each community should establish and use its own water resources, while Arab farmers and shepherds insisted that freshly dug Jewish wells be open to all.

Tension also resulted from initial Jewish reluctance to hire Arab workers. These factors led to a number of armed Arab attacks on Jewish settlements, especially in the area southeast of Jaffa and near the Sea of Galilee. Other assaults were simply the usual Bedouin raids every settled town or village was subject to at the time.

As Jewish nationalism manifested itself in the continuing waves of immigrants coming from Europe, Arab nationalism also began to stir in the region. Middle Eastern Arabs had little love for their Turkish masters, even if they were fellow Muslims. They also resented British and French interference in the region. Still, most Arab leaders cooperated with the Allies against the Germans and Turks in World War I. They hoped to receive European support for the setting up of an independent state or states in the region once the crumbling Ottoman Empire was finally dismantled.

While benefiting economically and medically from the European Jewish and Christian influx into the land, local Arabs realized early on that their chances of being included in a larger regional Arab state or states were threatened by Jewish hopes to establish a homeland. Very few expected at the time that the small area known in the West as Palestine would become its own independent state. In 1914, as the First World War began to shake Europe, anti-Zionist societies were formed in Jerusalem, Jaffa, Haifa, Beirut, Cairo, and Istanbul to encourage Arab and Muslim resistance to the emerging Jewish national home.

The Great War was destined to change not only the face of Europe but also that of the Middle East. Soon after Germany and Turkey were finally defeated by the Allied powers in 1918, politicians went to work redrawing national boundaries throughout Eastern Europe. The Arabs waited patiently for the politicians to begin mapping out an independent state or states on the Arabian Peninsula and farther to the north.

In 1915 Arab Muslim leader Sharif Hussein of Mecca (the title *sharif* denotes ancestry from Muhammad) had been promised by the British high commissioner in Cairo, Sir H. McMahon, that London would be "prepared to recognize and support the independence of the Arabs" following the defeat of the Turks. However, McMahon added that any independent Arab state or states could not include the Turkish district administered from Beirut—in other words, most of modern day Lebanon and northern Israel. He also implied that the district of Jerusalem should be excluded from the proposed Arab-controlled areas.

Hussein replied that "the people of Beirut will never accept such isolation." He was, of course, referring to the Muslims of Beirut and surrounding areas, not the Christians who were eager to be isolated from their Muslim neighbors.

British insistence on the exclusion of the eastern Mediterranean coastal area made a lot of sense to the other victorious Allied powers. All were aware that Lebanese Christians had often suffered persecution during many centuries of regional Muslim domination. French Catholics were especially eager to see a French-protected area carved out for their Lebanese coreligionists. The British government was just as keen to see Christians and Jews in the Holy Land exempted from further Muslim domination. The United States generally backed these positions. It was obvious that the British and French had other reasons for wanting to protect Christian and Jewish interests in the region: both, but especially the

British, had far-flung empires to protect, and the strategic Middle East with its vital Suez Canal was of utmost importance to them. The two powers reasoned that having European-oriented enclaves in the area would add greatly to their empire-maintenance efforts.

The British had another compelling reason for proposing that the southern coastal area be excluded from any Arab state. The government in London had sought, and received, Jewish assistance during the war. In return, and in line with general sympathy for the Jewish need for a homeland after so many centuries of wandering and persecution, British foreign minister A. J. Balfour, on behalf of the government, issued the following statement to Zionist leaders during the final months of World War I:

> His Majesty's Government views with favour the establishment in Palestine of a national home for the Jewish people, and will use their best endeavours to facilitate the achievement of this object, it being clearly understood that nothing shall be done which may prejudice the civil and religious rights of non-Jewish communities in Palestine or the rights and political status enjoyed by Jews in any other country.

Soon after the "Balfour Declaration" was issued on November 2, 1917, British general Sir Edmund Allenby drove the last Turkish soldiers out of Jerusalem, ending many centuries of Muslim control. The Holy Land was in British Christian hands.

Although the wording of the Balfour Declaration was somewhat imprecise, historians such as Walter Laqueur say that the clear British intention at the time was to work for the setting up of a fully sovereign Jewish state in Palestine.[19] Laqueur records that there was some initial ambivalence and even acceptance of the declaration in the Arab world. However, the overwhelming reaction was one of rejection.

Arab leaders in the Holy Land said it would be impossible to set up a Jewish national home while at the same time guarding the civil and religious rights of non-Jews living in the land. Zionist leaders responded that the rights of local Arabs would indeed be respected in a Jewish state. They were optimistic, wrote Laqueur, that local Arabs would eventually accept the Jewish national home and live in peace with it.[20]

Jewish Zionist leaders considered "Palestine" to be the entire area that today comprises Israel, the territories captured by Israel in 1967, and Jordan. In fact, the whole area legally came under that name at the 1920 postwar San Remo Conference, where the world powers voted to give Britain a mandate to oversee the setting up of a Jewish national home in Palestine. (See maps 1 and 2 in the appendix.) The Zionists hoped they would be allowed to settle in all of what later became Israel, Judea, and Samaria (later known as the West Bank), the Gaza Strip, and the east bank of the Jordan River up to the town of Amman. The mandate given to Britain stated that Jews could settle anywhere west of the river, but not necessarily east of it.

British authorities were eager to keep their pledges to the Arabs as well as the Jews. Therefore, Jewish settlement east of the Jordan River was banned in 1921, and the area—two-thirds of designated "Palestine" under the mandate—was declared the Emirate of Trans-Jordan. Sharif Hussein's son Abdullah was installed on the throne. The British continued to play a vital role in the new state until the mid-1940s, overseeing the setting up of various political institutions and an army.

Farther to the east, Britain created the Arab state of Iraq, with Abdullah's brother Faisal enthroned as king. Faisal Hussein, representing his father and brothers, had met in 1919 in Paris with the head of the Jewish Zionist Movement, Dr. Chaim Weizmann, a highly respected British scientist. At the meeting Faisal signed a joint statement committing the Arabs to recognize "Jewish national aspirations" for a homeland in Palestine. But at the bottom of the paper he added in Arabic, "provided the Arabs gain their independence." He seemed to be saying that a Jewish state would be permissible, but only if the Arabs, long controlled by Turkey and the European powers, were finally allowed to enjoy total sovereignty in the other areas where they lived.

While these momentous political decisions were being made, about ten thousand Jews came to live in the Holy Land. Most fled a new wave of anti-Jewish violence in Russia. The latest attacks, in which some seventy thousand Jews lost their lives, broke out as Russian communists fought a bloody civil war with their noncommunist opponents for control of the country. By 1923 another twenty-five thousand Jews would join them in what later became known as the "third aliyah wave."

During this period the League of Nations—the precursor of the United Nations—endorsed the San Remo decision to give Great Britain a mandate to set up a Jewish national home in Palestine. The fifty-two nations voting in favor noted "the historic connection of the Jewish people with Palestine" and called for the establishment of a "Jewish Agency" to aid British authorities in accomplishing their mandate.

Holy Land Arabs were not thrilled with the world body's decision, as they had not been with the April 1920 San Remo declaration of support for a Jewish state, although the League of Nations also approved mandates for Britain and France to oversee the setting up of independent Arab states in the rest of the region.

Soon after the San Remo declaration, Muslim and Christian community leaders, led by the powerful Husseini clan, met in Jerusalem and issued a proclamation that totally rejected the British Mandate to set up a Jewish national home, adding that Palestine belonged exclusively to the Muslim and Christian worlds. They also poured scorn on Faisal Hussein's acceptance of Jewish nationalist aspirations in the biblical Promised Land. Their Arab brethren would eventually live in sovereign Arab states, while they would have to reside with the Jews, who were compared with "poisonous snakes" in leaflets distributed in Jerusalem and Jaffa. No nation on earth had tolerated the Jews, said the leaflets, so why should the Arabs of Palestine have to?[21]

A month before the San Remo Conference, Joseph Trumpeldor and his seven colleagues were attacked and killed at Tel Hai. While the conference was under way, a Jewish settlement east of the Sea of Galilee was abandoned after Arabs murdered a settler. Arab bands attacked eight other settlements in the area during March and April. After debating how to respond to the violent assaults, the Jews decided to establish the Hagana defense force in June. It would later evolve into the main arm of the pre-state Jewish army.

In May 1921 widespread Arab violence broke out against the growing Jewish community. Armed Arab bands attacked Jews living in Haifa, Jaffa, Petach Tikva, and two other towns. The Jaffa riots were the bloodiest—

forty-seven Jews lost their lives. Zionist leaders, still publicly speaking about their hopes of amicable Jewish-Arab relations, were beginning to realize that local Arabs were determined to do everything in their power to prevent the establishment of a Jewish state. They feared that British authorities would cave in to the growing Arab violence and go back on their pledge to set up a Jewish homeland.

Confronted by growing Arab opposition, British leaders began to redefine their mandate in terms more acceptable to local Arabs. Colonial secretary Winston Churchill issued a statement in 1922 saying that the British did not envision that "Palestine as a whole should be converted into a Jewish National Home, but that such a Home should be founded in Palestine." The statement did not placate local Arab leaders, who said the British were not adequately taking their fears or aspirations into consideration.

Many Jewish immigrants settled in kibbutz collective farms, which were established from 1909 onward in various parts of the Holy Land. The Hebrew word *kibbutz* means "ingathering." The founders of the kibbutz movement were mainly socialists who either ignored or had abandoned the faith of their fathers. Yet the name they chose for their communities had a definite biblical, prophetic ring to it. Kibbutz settlements were established throughout the Jezreel Valley—the area Mark Twain had described as virtually without inhabitants a half century earlier.

Stagnant swamps in the valley kept away most immigrants, as elsewhere in the northern part of the Holy Land. The tepid waters were breeding grounds for malaria-carrying mosquitoes. Many Jewish pioneers lost their lives in the process of clearing the swamps. But, as one of them told me when I briefly lived on a Jezreel Valley kibbutz in 1982, it was "better to die while doing something for your people than to be massacred in the Russian pogroms." A few of the settlers were immigrants from the United States. One of them, Golda Meir, later became Israel's first female prime minister.

The fourth aliyah wave (1924–28) brought sixty-seven thousand Jews to the ancient homeland. The new wave of immigrants was comprised largely of urban Polish and Russian Jews who were more inclined to settle in cities than on farming cooperatives. Many went no farther than

Tel Aviv, a Jewish town established in the sand dunes just north of Jaffa in 1909. The city rapidly became the main Jewish urban center.

Zionist leaders continued to voice hopes during the 1920s that Jews and Arabs could coexist in peace in the Holy Land, despite the 1921 riots. A Zionist congress held in Germany in 1922 proclaimed the desire of the Jewish people to "live with the Arab people in friendship and mutual respect, and together with them develop the homeland common to both into a flourishing community which would ensure to each of its peoples an undisturbed national development."[22]

There were regular political and social contacts between Jewish Zionist and Arab leaders in Jerusalem and elsewhere during the decade, and many Zionist leaders expressed optimism that the Arabs of Palestine would eventually see the growing Jewish presence in the land as a positive development leading to better living standards for all.

By 1929, about 150,000 Jews had settled in the land. More than half had immigrated since 1918. The Arabs numbered around 700,000. The overall population of the Holy Land had increased by only about 350,000 since 1880, in spite of the Jewish influx from eastern Europe and Russia.[23] Many more of the three million Jews who moved to the West during the period might have come to the Holy Land if Ottoman and British authorities had not enacted immigration restrictions at various times.

## LIFT UP THE SWORD OF ISLAM!

The relatively small numbers of Jews that came were too many for most local Arabs, who were beginning to believe that the Jews just might succeed in setting up a sovereign state in Mandatory Palestine. The generally better-educated and largely socialist or communist immigrants were seen as a major cultural threat to the conservative Islamic and Christian communities.

Although Jews had succeeded in purchasing only about 4 percent of the land by 1929, and although there was plenty of room for growth, local Muslim Arab leaders whipped up passions and fears among their followers by warning of the dangers posed to Islam by the growing Jewish presence. The Jews, so long oppressed by both Muslims and Christians, were planning to take revenge on the Arabs, they maintained. Jewish fighters would attack and destroy the Dome of the Rock shrine and Al-Aksa Mosque in Jerusalem, bringing humiliation to Islam. The fact that most of the immigrants were not at all religious did not impede the issuance of such warnings.

With such dire warnings sounded in many mosques throughout the land, Arab resistance to the growing Jewish presence took on an increasingly religious tone during the 1920s. It is no coincidence that the emerging leader of the Arab struggle against the Jews was the president of the Supreme Muslim Council in Jerusalem, the grand mufti Haj Amin Husseini. He would not echo the earlier, relatively moderate tone of Faisal Hussein or his father, the sharif of Mecca. Husseini traveled to many Arab capitals raising money to repair Muslim holy sites in Jerusalem, warning in every place of the dangers of allowing the Jews to gain any sort of sovereignty in the Holy Land.

The Holy Land Muslim leader repeatedly preached that the sinister Jews were plotting to take over all local Islamic holy sites, and especially the two mosques located on what the Jews call *Har ha Biet*, the "Mount of the House" (of God). Husseini insisted that Jews should not be allowed to pray at the Western Wall, or Wailing Wall of Haram al-Sharif. He declared the wall an Islamic holy site, since the prophet Muhammad had supposedly tied up his horse, al-Burak, to the wall just after making his night journey to Jerusalem. Jews attempting to pray at the Western Wall, a traditional Jewish prayer site for centuries, increasingly found themselves the target of stonings and other physical attacks.

On August 23, 1929, at the grand mufti's instigation, hundreds of Muslim Arabs poured down from the Temple Mount and assaulted Jews praying at the wall. Then they burst out of the Old City to attack Jews living in nearby neighborhoods. Many Jews were killed or wounded. Some Arab Christians joined in the assaults, but most stayed on the sidelines. Arab attacks quickly spread to other parts of Mandatory Palestine.

In a particularly brutal atrocity, fifty-nine Orthodox Jews, including many women and children, were slaughtered in Hebron, south of Jerusalem. Most of the dead, many of whom had been tortured and dismembered, were descendants of Jews who had lived in Hebron, where

Abraham's Tomb is located, for hundreds of years. Twenty Jews were killed in another of the four holy cities, Safed. Seven kibbutz settlements were attacked and burned. Armed Arab gangs also launched assaults in Haifa and Tel Aviv. British forces, refusing to allow the Jews to take up weapons and defend themselves, killed 110 Arabs before the rioting was stopped on August 26. A total of 133 Jews lost their lives during the three days of violence, and another 339 were wounded.

In 1930 the League of Nations sent a committee to the Lord's land to investigate the question of Jewish and Arab rights at the Western Wall. Islamic officials from various countries appeared before the committee, along with Amin Husseini. Jews must not be allowed to pray at the site, they urged, since the entire mount belongs to the Muslims. The matter was of utmost importance to the Islamic world, the committee members were told, since the Jews were openly praying for their ancient temple to be rebuilt on its original foundations, where the sacred Dome of the Rock shrine is located. Jewish representatives pointed out their ancestors had built the Temple Mount, first occupied by Muslims in the seventh century A.D. It was only right that Jews should be allowed to pray at one of the remaining retaining walls of their ancient Temple Mount.

The committee agreed that Jews should be allowed to pray at the wall, in light of the fact that they had done so for centuries and Muslims had the entire Mount to pray on, but ruled that Muslims held absolute ownership of it. However, the committee forbade the Jews to blow the traditional ram's horn, the *shofar,* near the Western Wall on Jewish holy days, a move that deeply offended religious Jews.

In order to further whip up Muslim opposition to the establishment of a Jewish state in the Holy Land, Husseini hosted a Pan-Islamic World Conference in Jerusalem in December 1931. Islamic delegates were told that they must rise up to defend the Muslim holy sites from Jewish plots to take them over. Sacred Islamic shrines such as Abraham's Tomb in Hebron (from where Jews had been banned from praying since the end of the Crusades) were under threat of being taken over by the "Zionist invaders," warned the grand mufti. Islamic leaders pledged their full support for Husseini's struggle, agreeing that everything must be done to keep a sovereign Jewish state from being formed in "sacred Palestine."

Despite growing Arab-Muslim opposition, the number of Jews immigrating to the designated Jewish homeland took a sharp upward swing in the 1930s. The main reason for the Jewish influx was the rise of the viciously anti-Semitic Nazi movement in Germany, Austria, and other portions of central Europe. There is little doubt that many, if not most, of the 250,000 European Jews who came to live there during the decade (a quarter of them refugees from Germany) would have remained where they were if not for the rise of Adolf Hitler. Long-established and successful Jews suddenly found themselves under attack simply because they were Jews. Many ended up at Haifa or Jaffa ports with little more than the shirts on their backs. But at least they had their lives—something that could not be said after World War II for six million of their fellow Jews. The British royal navy prevented many Jewish refugees from landing in Palestine between 1936 and 1939, as numbers began to exceed official quotas. Others were intercepted and interned in British prison camps set up along the coast.

European Jews fleeing Hitler's madness met with no more Arab sympathy than had those Jews who barely escaped with their lives from the pogroms in Russia and Eastern Europe. Indeed, the grand mufti Husseini was a strong supporter and personal friend of the German führer and of Italian fascist leader Benito Mussolini, who "adopted" the Palestinian leader and promised to aid his struggle against the Jews.

Haj Amin Husseini's frequent sermons in support of Hitler's anti-Jewish campaign were closely monitored by British mandate authorities. They ordered him arrested after the British governor of the Galilee district was assassinated by the mufti's men in 1937. However, Husseini evaded British forces and escaped to Lebanon. The grand mufti continued to encourage resistance to the Jews as he traveled between various regional Arab capitals.

When World War II broke out in Europe, Husseini declared a jihad against Britain. The Muslim leader spent the war years in Berlin, where he headed the Arab Office, a propaganda and espionage arm of the Nazi war administration aimed at strengthening Arab support for the Axis powers.

In the mid-1930s the head of the Jewish Zionist community in the Holy Land, David Ben Gurion, contacted various Palestinian Arab and

Syrian leaders to present a political proposal that he hoped would bridge the growing gap between Arabs and Jews. He proposed that the Arabs allow a majority Jewish state to be set up in Mandatory Palestine, which would then join in a federation with nearby Arab states. Although local Arabs would be a minority in the Jewish state, they would form part of the overall Arab majority in the federated states. Every state in the federation would pledge nonbelligerency toward the others, with freedom of travel and commerce guaranteed. Thus, the rights and security of both Arabs and Jews would be protected.

Ben Gurion's proposal was totally rejected by the Arab leaders he contacted. Again, they insisted that no Jewish sovereign state should be allowed to exist in the region.

Before Haj Amin Husseini fled to Lebanon, he helped organize an Arab general strike to protest stepped-up Jewish immigration from Europe and Zionist hopes to establish a sovereign Jewish state. Stores were closed for six months in 1936 following Arab attacks in April and May, which left twenty-one Jews dead. Jewish settlements and shops were attacked. Jewish crops were burned and tens of thousands of trees were uprooted. Jewish buses were bombed, and individual Jews were gunned down everywhere. In all, eighty Jews were killed and many more injured before the British succeeded in stopping the armed uprising in October.

British troops, who sustained thirty-three casualties, shot and killed more than one hundred Arab gunmen and rioters during the six-month revolt. Local Arab leaders met during the early part of the rebellion to demand that London stop all Jewish immigration to the Holy Land, forbid all Jewish land purchases, and set up an Arab majority government. But by the end of September, they realized that the British were not going to discuss Arab demands until all violence ceased.

After several months of relative calm, Britain sent a royal commission to Jerusalem in early 1937 to investigate the increasingly violent Arab-Jewish conflict. The commissioners ended up recommending that the mandate for a Jewish homeland in all of western Palestine be annulled. Instead, the land should be partitioned into separate Arab and Jewish states.

Although the Jews were deeply disappointed with the recommendation of a truncated Jewish state, most Zionist leaders were willing to accept it, saying it was better to have a tiny state than none at all, especially in light of the rise of the Nazi movement and the impending war in Europe.

As Jewish leaders debated the British partition plan, the Arab world moved swiftly to condemn it. Arab leaders meeting in French-ruled Syria in September 1937 declared that they would never permit the setting up of a Jewish state in any part of "sacred Palestine." Shortly afterward, armed Arab bands began a new round of attacks against British soldiers and Jewish settlements. The attacks were much fiercer than the first round of disturbances in 1936. Arab leaders again declared a general commercial strike, which was often enforced by violent means. Rival Arab factions increasingly turned on one another, leading to many Arab deaths—a situation that would be repeated in another Palestinian Arab uprising fifty years later.

By the summer of 1938 Arab gunmen had taken control of most of the hilly regions in the Judea and Samaria district. The British reacted swiftly and forcefully, entering villages and towns in pursuit of armed bands. Homes of suspected or known Arab gunmen were destroyed, and widespread curfews were imposed. Security measures were tightened even further after Arab saboteurs blew up the British-owned Iraqi oil pipeline, which ran through lower Galilee to the Mediterranean coast near Haifa.

Hundreds of Arabs and Jews were killed, along with many British soldiers, before the violent revolt was halted in early 1939. Later that same year German forces under the command of Adolf Hitler invaded Poland—then the country with the largest concentration of Jews in the world—beginning the worst war in mankind's long, bloody history. For the Jews it would be a catastrophe of unimaginable proportions.

k ✡ ✝

# JACOB COMES OUT ON TOP

I will probably never get used to it. In the middle of a conversation, while sitting next to somebody on a bus or sometimes while standing in line at the bank or post office, I see it. Maybe it strikes me more forcefully than others because of my familiarity with the prophecy in the Book of Revelation, which predicts that a world dictator will one day order everyone to have a mark placed on his or her hand or forehead. The jarring experience of having a good friend become a neo-Nazi in my own hometown heightens my sensitivity to the sight.

Whatever the reasons, I am certain I will always recoil a bit when I see the numbers tattooed on the back of the hands of Jews who somehow survived the Nazi death camps of Europe.

I have never had the courage to ask any camp survivor what it was like to be in Auschwitz, Treblinka, or one of the other extermination camps that took the lives of millions of their fellow Jews. How can I ask them to relate the unspeakable things they saw, the things they experienced? I've read a few of the tortured accounts survivors have committed to paper, and have even visited a Nazi death camp in Austria. But to ask someone to speak about these things—it is just too much.

Very few survivors of Hitler's partially successful attempt to wipe out the Jewish people made it to the shores of the Promised Land. It was not easy for Jews to get into the land in those days, despite the mandate given to Great Britain to oversee the setting up of a Jewish homeland. Mandate authorities had again placed severe restrictions on the numbers of Jews allowed to enter after the Arab revolts between 1936 and 1939. Those limitations continued during and after World War II, despite the obvious need for Jewish refugees fleeing Europe and North Africa to go somewhere, anywhere.

## THE WHITE PAPER

As the second Arab revolt was finally put down in early 1939, the British convened a conference in London to hear Arab and Jewish proposals on how to resolve the deepening crisis in the Holy Land. The Jewish delegation, headed by Zionist leader Chaim Weizmann, pleaded for the British government to honor the original mandate commitment to set up a national home for the Jews. Weizmann said it could either be part of a larger binational state in which the Jewish and Arab communities both ran their own affairs, or a small Jewish state in part of the land, as proposed in the earlier partition plan.

The Arab delegation, which included Palestinian representatives along with those of surrounding Arab states, refused to even sit in the same room with the Jews. They repeated earlier demands for a halt to all Jewish immigration and land sales and for the immediate setting up of an independent Arab state "over every inch of Palestine." The Arabs made clear that one of the first acts of such a state would be to deport all Jews who were not already living in the land at the start of the "Zionist invasion" in 1881.

After the conference ended, the British issued a document containing a proposed "final solution" of the Arab-Jewish conflict. Known as the White Paper, the document deeply shocked Zionist leaders. The Jews, facing annihilation in Europe, would pay the heaviest price for ending the conflict, although they were the targets of armed attacks from Arabs.

The White Paper called for the establishment in Mandatory Palestine of an independent Arab-dominated state within ten years. Jews would number only about a third of the overall population. Only seventy-five thousand Jews would be allowed into the land by March 1944, after which no more would be let in without Arab consent (which the British, of course, knew would not be forthcoming). Jewish land purchases would be severely restricted, and Jews could only settle in certain parts of the Arab-dominated state. At a certain point the British would withdraw, leaving the minority Jews to fend for themselves against the Arabs' openly declared threat to destroy them.

The White Paper solution was a disaster for the Jews, who saw it as a recipe for total destruction at the hands of their hateful Arab cousins. The proposed solution was also an embarrassment for many British members of Parliament, who said the British government was abandoning the Jews, along with the League of Nations' mandate to set up a Jewish homeland. One member, Herbert Morrison, who later served in Winston Churchill's cabinet, called the British White Paper proposal a "cynical breach of pledges."[24]

Although the White Paper was very much in their favor, Palestinian leaders rejected it, despite advice from Egypt and Iraq that they accept it. The grand mufti Husseini insisted that all "colonial Jews" who had "invaded Palestine" since the 1880s had to leave the land, and no more should be let in.

Jews in Tel Aviv and elsewhere took to the streets to protest the British proposal. They charged, among other things, that London was deliberately ignoring the Arab pledge to throw most Jews out of the proposed state. The White Paper solution, they maintained, would certainly lead to a bloody confrontation between Arabs trying to enforce the expulsion and Jews fighting to remain in their ancestral homeland. Outraged Jewish leaders said that Britain was selling them down the drain in order to buy Arab support during the coming war. Hitler had already invaded Czechoslovakia by this time, making war in Europe almost a certainty.

In fact, British officials quite openly admitted to Zionist leaders that securing such Arab support was indeed one of the main reasons for the White Paper solution. The Jews of Mandatory Palestine felt abandoned, betrayed. Many refugees from prewar Europe, who had barely escaped Hitler's clutches, felt that certain death now awaited them in their promised homeland . . . at the hands of Nazi-supporting Arabs.

World Jewry was already distressed by the decision of leading Western nations meeting at an American-initiated conference in Evian, France, in 1938, to severely restrict the numbers of Jewish refugees they would allow into their countries. This decision, which seems extremely cruel with the hindsight of history, was actually in line with public opinion in most Western countries. The American Veterans of Foreign Wars, for example, passed a resolution just before the conference calling on Washington to suspend all foreign immigration for ten years. Nobody wanted floods of Jewish refugees, it was clear, just as the British didn't want them entering their ancestral homeland, upsetting the Arabs on the eve of a world war.

British Mandatory authorities had let in 61,800 Jews, mostly refugees from Germany, the year before the Arab revolt broke out in 1936. But in order to help dampen the violent Arab uprising, only 12,800 immigrants were allowed in during 1938, and 16,400 in 1939, the year World War II began. The numbers dropped even further during the war, with only 4,592 immigrants permitted to enter during 1941, and 4,206 in 1942.

As many historians have noted, the British restrictions were purely political in nature. There was certainly enough room in the land to accommodate many more people than were allowed in. By the start of the Second World War, there were about one million Arabs and four hundred thousand Jews in the Holy Land. Today the land holds over eight million people—more than five times as many as in 1940—yet there is still room for development. The sad fact is that many Jewish lives could have been spared if they had been allowed to enter the land of their ancient forefathers before and during the war.

Jewish Zionist leaders were divided as to how to respond to the White Paper. Some, including David Ben Gurion, who later became Israel's first prime minister, advocated open revolt against the British. Other, more moderate voices said such a course could lead to harsh repression of the Jews, and possibly the cancellation of all further immigration.

Before the argument was settled, Hitler invaded Poland, setting off World War II. As German forces swept through Eastern and Western Europe, there was no question of open Jewish revolt against the British, who were leading the fight against the Nazis. The common enemy was so evil that the dispute over the White Paper had to be put aside.

In fact, despite the sense of betrayal that local Jews felt toward the British government, many volunteered to fight with British forces. A "Palestinian Brigade" was set up, made up mostly of Jewish men, but with some Arabs as well. The force was sent to carry out fortification work in France in 1940. Other units fought throughout the Middle East. In all, some 27,000 Jewish men and women served under British command. However, the Jewish soldiers were always carefully referred to as "Palestinians" so as not to offend the Arabs.

## NOWHERE TO HIDE

The year 1942 marked the start of Hitler's systematic campaign to destroy the Jews of Europe. The demonic campaign was outlined at the secret Nazi Wannsee Conference in Berlin. The head of the German Gestapo, Reinhard Heydrich, informed the gathering of a plan for the "final solution of the Jewish problem in Europe." He presented a document detailing how the estimated eleven million Jews of Europe and Russia were to be exterminated in Nazi-run death camps. The German SS, under the command of Adolf Eichmann, was given the task of rounding up the Jews and seeing that they were executed.

Meanwhile, in another part of Berlin the grand mufti of Jerusalem was helping to organize an Arab military unit known as Free Arabia. After proclaiming Hitler "the protector of Islam," Haj Husseini told the Arab soldiers that their mission was to lead an army that would liberate Jerusalem from British-Jewish control. In the Holy Land, Allied forces prepared for a German ground invasion from North Africa.

The Arab fighters were to join German general Erwin Rommel, known as the "desert fox," whose forces were then sweeping into British-controlled Egypt. The city of Tel Aviv and oil depots at Haifa Port had already been bombed in 1940 by Italian planes operating out of Libya. Now, the likely prospect of a Nazi ground invasion was being seriously prepared for in the Lord's land. It was not to be.

Rommel's Egyptian advance was halted on July 1, 1942, about one hundred miles east of the Egyptian-Libyan border. Three weeks later, Nazi troops in occupied Poland began gathering up Jews living in the Warsaw ghetto to send them to "work" in the Treblinka "labor camp."

Despite their joint war effort, British Mandatory forces continued to try to stop local Jews from smuggling in Jewish refugees. In one particularly notorious case, the British refused pleas by Jewish officials in early 1942 to allow the *Struma,* a ship carrying 769 refugees, to land in Haifa. The ship, stuck at Istanbul, was then ordered by Turkish officials to sail back to its Black Sea port of departure in Romania. The next night the ramshackle vessel sank, leaving all but one passenger dead. News of the tragedy produced anti-British demonstrations in Tel Aviv and elsewhere, with posters proclaiming that the British high commissioner for Palestine, Sir Harold MacMichael, was a murderer.

World War II left much of Europe in shambles. Starvation and disease threatened to kill those who managed to stay alive during the worst carnage in mankind's history. For surviving Jews the scope of the horror that had befallen their people was finally coming to light. Jews in the Holy Land at first hoped that initial reports of the extent of the Holocaust were exaggerated. No one could believe that such total devastation had overtaken their Jewish brethren in Europe. But as death camp survivors arrived in ships off the coast of the Jewish ancestral homeland, the stories they told confirmed the worst reports reaching the land.

Almost every Jew living in the Promised Land had lost relatives or friends in Hitler's hideous "final solution." The mass slaughters during the Crusades and the pogroms of the late nineteenth and early twentieth centuries were nothing compared to what had just occurred in modern, "enlightened" Europe. The seeds of anti-Semitism, planted in the public mind so many centuries earlier by several early church theologians and watered by Reformation leader Martin Luther, had finally borne their logical, if ghastly, result: a systematic attempt, led by Nazi Germany, to eliminate the Jewish people from the face of the earth.

As many surviving European Jews discovered they could not return to their homes, which had either been destroyed or were now occupied by others, their eyes turned increasingly toward Zion. Chaim Weizmann pleaded with British prime minister Winston Churchill to lift the White Paper restrictions and allow into Mandatory Palestine an estimated one hundred thousand Jews living in Allied-run refugee camps. He noted that the free nations of the world were willing to take in only a small portion of the homeless Jews despite worldwide revulsion over the holocaust.

Soviet communist forces now occupied Poland, part of Germany, and many other former Jewish centers, he noted, making resettlement in such places dangerous for surviving Jews. As if to prove his point, anti-Jewish pogroms broke out after the war in many parts of Poland, leaving more than 350 Jews dead by the middle of 1946. Among those killed in this postwar slaughter was the father of Israel's ninth prime minister, Yitzhak Shamir.

The United States, housing many of the Jewish refugees in army-run European camps, urged London to allow the one hundred thousand refugees into the Holy Land. Despite these pleas, the new British Labour Party government of Prime Minister Clement Attlee, which came to power in July 1945, refused to open the gates of the Holy Land to any but a few of the stateless Jews.

## THE JEWS FIGHT BACK

In response, many stunned and angry Jews in Palestine joined underground groups, such as the Stern Gang and the Irgun, which had earlier been set up to fight against British Mandatory authorities. One of the underground leaders was Yitzhak Shamir, who learned that most of his family had been killed in the Nazi slaughter before the death of his father in Poland. Such discoveries, of course, only increased the determination of underground group members to fight for the setting up of a Jewish state, even if they had to use terrorist tactics to do so.

The mainstream Hagana Jewish force condemned the methods of the underground groups. They argued that Irgun and Stern Gang terror attacks, even if aimed solely at British soldiers and officials, were counterproductive, driving the British even further away from keeping the mandate commitment to set up a "Jewish national home in Palestine." Jewish cooperation, such as had been displayed during the war, was the best way to change British opinion, they believed. Hagana leaders noted that Winston Churchill repeatedly promised Zionist leaders that, despite the White Paper, a Jewish state would be set up after the Allies won World War II.

However, when it became apparent that the new British government would not keep Churchill's promise, the Hagana joined forces with the two underground groups to form the Jewish Resistance Movement. The newly united Jews sabotaged the main Lydda-Jerusalem rail line on November 1, 1945. The British responded forcefully, arresting thousands of Jews. They were particularly interested in capturing Irgun leader Menachem Begin, who later became prime minister of Israel in 1977, placing a two-thousand-pound-sterling bounty on his head.

As Jewish refugees continued to languish in postwar European refugee camps, new British foreign secretary Ernest Bevin agreed to set up a joint Anglo-American committee to recommend a solution to their plight. Committee members visited the camps and took testimony in Jerusalem from Jamal Husseini, the grand mufti's cousin and postwar leader of the local Palestinian Arab community. Husseini stood firm against any further Jewish immigration and repeated the Arab demand that an independent Arab state be established over the entire area where the ancient Jewish nation was located. He maintained that the Arabs should not be made to pay for sins committed against Jews by "imperialist Western nations."

Zionist leader Chaim Weizmann acknowledged that the setting up of a Jewish state was not something local Arabs should be expected to welcome. But he added that the Jews did not intend to supplant the Arabs and, instead, hoped that the two related peoples could live together peacefully, despite past Arab violence against Jews. Weizmann told committee members that the choice was not between absolute right and wrong, but between the lesser injustice of a small portion of the world's Arabs having to live in, or next to, a Jewish-controlled state and the greater injustice of breaking the mandate promise to finally set up a Jewish homeland after so many centuries of wandering and persecution, culminating in the hideous holocaust.

The Anglo-American committee voted unanimously to recommend the repealing of the White Paper and urged the British government to admit the European refugees. Committee members suggested that a binational state under continuing overall British control be set up with Jews again allowed to purchase land. But Foreign Minister Bevin turned down the recommendations, saying their implementation would greatly offend the Arab world, whose vast oil resources were increasingly coming to light.

Five days after the recommendations were published, Britain granted total independence to Trans-Jordan, making it the seventh independent

Arab state in the Middle East. Meanwhile, the 100,000 or so Jewish refugees living in crowded European camps were joined by another 150,000 Jews fleeing the renewed pogroms in Poland and communist rule elsewhere in Eastern Europe.

After it became apparent that Britain still planned to fully implement the White Paper—setting up an independent Arab state in Palestine with a Jewish minority and no further Jewish immigration—a new round of attacks was launched by the Jewish Resistance Movement. On June 17, 1946, ten bridges linking the Holy Land with neighboring countries were blown up. The next day, the Stern Gang attacked railway workshops in Haifa, leading to a bloody fight with British troops. Two weeks later the British imposed a total curfew in the land and arrested some two thousand Jewish leaders and gunmen. Jewish Agency headquarters in Jerusalem was occupied and searched for twelve days. Weapons were seized from kibbutz settlements all over the land.

The strong British actions would leave local Jews totally defenseless if the proposed Arab state came into existence, argued many Jewish resistance leaders. Irgun commander Menachem Begin thought that the time had come to wage full-scale war against British Mandatory officials. He launched his campaign by ordering the bombing of Mandatory headquarters, located in Jerusalem's most prestigious hotel, the King David.

On July 22, Irgun members disguised as Arab porters brought milk cans full of explosives into the basement of the hotel's southern wing, just below Mandatory offices. At 12:40 P.M. the milk cans blew up, sending shock waves throughout the hotel and bringing down half of its southern wing. Ninety-one British, Arab, and Jewish bodies were dug out of the rubble.

Many Zionist leaders condemned the attack, which Begin said had been coordinated with the mainstream Hagana. Begin insisted that a telephone warning had been sent to British headquarters in the hotel before the charge exploded. The Irgun attack was only meant to destroy evacuated Mandatory offices, said Begin, not to kill anyone. Irgun member Adina Nisan later testified that she had called the Mandatory offices a half hour before the explosion to warn of the attack. She also said she had phoned the French consulate and the *Palestine Post* newspaper. However,

Mandatory officials maintained that they had received no warning from the Irgun. Hagana leaders, deeply upset over the deaths and the damage done to the Zionist cause, severed most links with Menachem Begin's organization.

British officials ordered a new crackdown as a result of the devastating blast. More than twenty-five thousand soldiers and policemen descended on Tel Aviv, which was placed under curfew, to search for Irgun members. After 787 suspects were arrested and placed in a Mandatory detention camp (some were later hanged), the mainstream Hagana announced it would revert to a nonviolent campaign to try to reverse Britain's stand against a Jewish state.

Hagana members stepped up their attempts to smuggle in Jewish refugees from Europe and increased efforts to set up settlements in areas that Zionist leaders hoped would become part of a Jewish state. The settlements were often established in one night under the cover of darkness, protected by armed Jewish guards. The other part of the campaign was not so successful. The Royal Navy intercepted most Jewish refugee ships off the coast, sending passengers to detention camps in British-controlled Cyprus.

News reports of battered Jewish war refugees being turned away from the very gates of the Promised Land and then herded into British barbed wire camps on the island of Cyprus aroused world sympathy for the latest Jewish plight. The case of the refugee ship *Exodus* was especially embarrassing for Britain. The Royal Navy used military power to intercept the ship, which was carrying more than forty-five hundred refugees, killing three Jews and wounding around one hundred in the process. The refugees were then sent to Cyprus and eventually back to holding camps in, of all places, Germany.

## REDRAWN PROPOSALS

World outrage over British handling of the Jewish refugees forced His Majesty's government to rethink its White Paper solution. As a result, it put forward a new plan that would divide the Lord's tiny land into four sectors. The Jewish portion would be only 17 percent of western Mandatory

Palestine. The sector would not be an independent state, but an autonomous area under British control. The same would be true for a larger Arab sector. Jerusalem and the Negev Desert would not be part of either the Arab or Jewish sector, but would be British-administered districts.

Zionist leaders responded to the latest British suggestions by proposing that the land be divided into separate Jewish and Arab states, as had been originally proposed by the British almost a decade earlier. The Jewish Agency put forward a plan that left Bethlehem, Hebron, Nablus, and the coastal port of Jaffa in the Arab state, with the Jewish state containing the region of Galilee, the coastal area from Haifa to Gaza, and the Negev Desert. The city of Jerusalem would be placed under international control.

The Arabs rejected both plans and announced that they would launch a jihad to prevent the establishment of a Jewish state in any portion of "sacred Palestine." Grand Mufti Amin Husseini, who escaped in June 1946 from a prison in France where he was being held as a war criminal, planned the Arab-Muslim jihad from his new headquarters in Cairo. Husseini proposed that an Arab army of one hundred thousand men be quickly established and trained to invade and take over Mandatory Palestine if and when the British withdrew. Local Arab opinion was divided as to whether or not this was the wisest course of action. Many Palestinian Christians thought that some sort of land division was possible, preventing an unnecessary bloodbath on both sides.

As the Arab-Jewish struggle grew hotter, the Arab nations decided in 1946 to launch an economic boycott against the emerging Jewish state, adding that sanctions would be enacted against any other nation or company that dealt with the Jews. Zionist leaders were not upset over the first part of the boycott, expecting to do little business anyway with hostile Arab neighbors. But the secondary boycott of countries and companies that refused to go along with the Arab boycott was considered to be potentially very damaging to a fledgling Jewish state. An office to oversee the Arab boycott was set up in Damascus. The economic boycott, still partially in existence in the early years of the twenty-first century, was stepped up after the state of Israel was established in 1948.

Despite growing Arab hostility toward the Jews of Palestine, Arab League secretary Azzam Pasha agreed in 1946 to meet with Zionist representatives

Abba Eban and David Horowitz, who tried to convince him that war would benefit no one. The Zionist representatives said that the Holy Land's Jewish community was willing to sacrifice some of its hopes and dreams in order to live in peace with the Arabs. They proposed a U.N.-guaranteed security arrangement for all parties.

However, Pasha rejected the Jewish peace overtures, saying the Muslim world was duty-bound to prevent a sovereign Jewish state from springing up in its midst. The Arab League official admitted that the Arabs might not be able to fulfill their pledge to destroy the Jewish state at birth, but that they would try nonetheless—with all their might.

While the Arabs prepared for war, the Jews intensified their struggle to drive the British out of the land. The Stern Gang and Irgun launched a new series of attacks against Mandatory targets. British authorities responded with more arrests and by hanging several leading Irgun members. Martial law was declared in Tel Aviv, cutting off the Jewish center from the rest of the land.

In Washington, President Harry Truman came out in favor of a "viable Jewish state in an adequate part of Palestine"[25] and called upon Britain to let in weary European Jewish war refugees. Even though London had hoped to keep control of at least some parts of Palestine for strategic political and economic reasons, it finally gave in to world and local pressure and handed over the intractable dispute to the United Nations in February 1947. The British, tiring of their crumbling world empire, had finally conceded that the forces at work in the Promised Land were beyond their control.

## THE REBIRTH OF ISRAEL

On May 15, 1947, the United Nations established a committee to propose a settlement of the Jewish and Arab struggle over the Promised Land. After months of deliberations, a majority of the ten nations represented on the committee recommended partitioning the land into separate Jewish and Arab states, with Jerusalem, Bethlehem, and surrounding suburbs to be an international zone under U.N. control. The partition plan was similar to the 1946 Jewish Agency plan except that the Arab state would be larger, encompassing most of western Galilee, the hilly regions of Samaria and Judea south to Beersheba and the northern shore of the Dead Sea, and south from Gaza into the northwest corner of the Negev Desert. A majority of the Jewish state's land would lie in the arid Negev Desert.

Zionist leaders expressed alarm that the proposed Jewish state would be in three separate segments connected by small, difficult-to-defend passageways. (See map 3 in the appendix.) But after much debate, they accepted the plan. Britain and the Arab states lobbied hard against it. In Washington a battle raged between pro-Arab members of the State and Defense departments, eager not to alienate Arab oil countries, pro-Zionist members of Congress, and the White House.

On October 9, 1947, President Truman spoke out in favor of the partition plan and ordered his United Nations ambassador to vote for it. The Soviet Union, apparently hoping the Jewish state would have a socialist if not communist orientation, also supported the plan. It was approved by a vote of 33 to 13 on November 29. The Jews of the world rejoiced, while the Arabs vowed that the proposed Jewish state would never see the light of day.

It was not long before Arab displeasure with the U.N. decision was registered. On November 30 a three-day general strike was declared. Arab rioters killed seven Jews on the first day of the strike, with many more injured. By the end of December, 205 Jews and more than 120 Arabs had died. Unlike in the 1930s, the Jews were now fully armed and not dependent on British forces for their protection.

Meanwhile, several Arab countries announced that they would attack and destroy the Jewish state the moment the British pulled out of the area. Violent pogroms broke out against Jews living in Beirut and in the British protectorate of Aden in the southern Arabian Peninsula, leaving more than eighty Jews dead. Jews in other Arab countries naturally feared that they would be the next targets of growing Arab-Muslim wrath. In London a date was set for the British withdrawal: May 14, 1948.

Fighting escalated in January 1948, with armed Arab bands quickly gaining control of most of Mandatory Palestine's roads (as the British frequently looked the other way). On January 20 approximately eight hundred Syrian Arabs, who entered the area as the Arab Liberation Army, attacked a Jewish settlement in upper Galilee. Three settlements south of the Sea of Galilee were attacked by more than three hundred Arab fighters on February 17. About five thousand Liberation Army irregulars, mainly from Syria and Iraq, joined the fray in March. Fighting alongside local Arab forces, they succeeded in capturing and closing sections of the main Jerusalem–Tel Aviv road. Mostly Jewish west Jerusalem was surrounded, cut off, and besieged. Jewish forces fought hard to reopen the roads into the city. Jerusalem's desperate Jewish residents were rapidly running out of food and water. Hundreds of Arabs and Jews died in other fierce clashes around Jerusalem during the spring. Egyptian irregulars quickly joined the battle, launching assaults on Jewish settlements and nearby roads south of Jerusalem and in the Negev Desert.

On the night of April 8 a combined Irgun-Stern Gang force killed more than one hundred Arabs in Deir Yassin, a village just above the road to Jerusalem.[26] The attack was in response to frequent ambushes launched from Deir Yassin and nearby villages on Jewish vehicles traveling on the temporarily reopened Jerusalem–Tel Aviv road. The Arabs called it a calculated massacre. Some Jewish participants later said they had "lost their heads" in the midst of battle and killed noncombatants, but they insisted that the killings came after Arab fighters feigned surrender and then opened fire on approaching Jews. Mainstream Jewish leaders condemned the killings of Arab civilians, with the Jewish Agency calling them "utterly repugnant."

In apparent revenge, armed Arabs attacked a Jewish convoy of doctors, nurses, and students four days later as they were on their way to Jerusalem's Hadassah Hospital near the Mount of Olives. Seventy-nine people were slaughtered. British forces stationed nearby did not intervene despite urgent Jewish calls for help.

By mid-April the fighting had intensified. Palestinian Arabs began fleeing their homes in droves. An estimated twenty thousand entered Lebanon and Syria by the end of the month. Many others went to stay with relatives in the hills of Samaria and other predominantly Arab areas. More than one hundred thousand Palestinians fled Haifa and Jaffa by the second week of May. Jewish forces captured Tiberias on April 19, and

Haifa on April 23. The Jewish holy town of Safed was captured on May 11 after fierce house-to-house combat between Jewish militiamen and some three thousand Iraqi and Syrian irregulars. Jaffa fell to Jewish forces on May 12.

The escalating fighting caused the United States and others to have second thoughts about the wisdom of the U.N. partition plan. The U.N. called for the British to delay their withdrawal until a peaceful resolution of the conflict could be formulated. Chaim Weizmann pleaded with President Truman not to hinder the setting up of a Jewish state, saying the alternative to statehood was Jewish extermination in the Holy Land. "Officials in Washington thought the chances that the Jewish state, if proclaimed, would survive, were not very good," wrote historian Walter Laqueur.[27] In light of the proclamation by Arab League countries that they would launch a full-scale attack immediately after the last British forces withdrew, the U.S. government's assessment seemed correct.

By 1948 the Holy Land had more than 1.2 million Arab residents. Some of these had come from Egypt and Trans-Jordan during the preceding decades to work in the economically booming land, where many jobs were created by the large Jewish influx. A majority lived in the area designated as an Arab state under the U.N. partition plan. Many Palestinians living in Jaffa and Haifa had moved to the two coastal towns in previous years from family homes in Judea and Samaria, taking advantage of growing job opportunities in the towns.

There were around 650,000 Jews living in the Lord's land in 1948, mostly concentrated along the coast, in the Jezreel Valley, in upper Galilee, and in Jerusalem. The Jews had inferior weapons compared to those in neighboring Arab countries. One would have thought that the Jewish state would be easily annihilated at birth by the superior numbers of Palestinian Arabs, backed by the armies of surrounding Arab countries. But it was not to be.

Historians who have conducted extensive research into the roots of the 1947–49 Arab-Israeli conflict generally agree that local Arabs at the time had little sense of Palestinian nationality, separate from their larger Arab identity. No sovereign country called "Palestine" had ever existed in history.

Having never been a distinct nation, local Arabs had developed almost none of the infrastructure necessary to set up an independent state once Britain withdrew. Some were regional Arabs who had only entered the biblical Promised Land in previous decades. Local Arabs were divided politically into various factions headed by rival families, the most powerful being the Husseini clan (from which Yasser Arafat comes). There had been frequent, bloody clashes between Haj Husseini's supporters, who totally rejected the Jewish presence, and other more moderate clans headed by the Nashashibi family. More than two-thirds of the Arabs of Mandatory Palestine lived in villages controlled by local clans. Intense rivalries often sprang up between neighboring villages (which is still occasionally the case today). Education levels were low, as was political awareness.

Most of those "Palestinians" motivated enough to resist the Jews did so mainly to *prevent* a Jewish government from gaining control of the area, not so much to *establish* an Arab state.

The Jews, on the other hand, were years ahead in terms of education, political awareness, and their sense of being a distinct people united in a shared history and destiny. A majority had fled for their lives from anti-Jewish violence in Russia and Europe. Their will to survive was, on the heels of the Holocaust, enormous. But more importantly, they had established over the years highly centralized military and political structures in preparation for an eventual British pullout. Underground arms factories worked hard to produce weapons to stave off the anticipated Arab invasion. The Jewish community knew it would have to be fully prepared for statehood—and war—on the day of the British withdrawal if it was to stand any chance of overcoming the Arab world's jihad to crush the emerging state.

Jewish Zionist leader David Ben Gurion made the official proclamation of statehood on Friday afternoon, May 14, 1948, after the national anthem "Ha Tikva" was sung by the assembled Jews at the Tel Aviv Museum: "By virtue of the natural and historical right of the Jewish people, and of the resolution of the General Assembly of the United Nations, we hereby proclaim the establishment of the Jewish state in Palestine, to be called Israel." The Jewish dream expressed in the national anthem to again "become a free people in our land, the land of Zion, and Jerusalem," had finally come true.

After almost two thousand years of wandering and persecution, the long Jewish exile from the ancient Promised Land officially came to an end. But the struggle for an independent, sovereign Jewish state was not over. In fact, in many ways it was only beginning.

On the very evening of Ben Gurion's proclamation, as the weekly Jewish Sabbath was getting under way, Egypt, Trans-Jordan, Iraq, Syria, and Lebanon made final preparations for their pre-announced holy war to annihilate the newborn state of Israel. As they did so, Palestinian Arabs continued to stream out of their homes in a refugee flight that would color and compel the Arab-Israeli conflict for many decades to come.

# CHAPTER 7

# ARABS AND JEWS AT WAR

I thought it was a rather odd assignment for an American disc jockey in the midst of war-ravaged Lebanon. Surely they had no idea what a Frisbee was! However, since my instructions were to demonstrate how the flying disc worked, off I went with a Voice of Hope coworker to throw Frisbees around Sidon's Ein Hilweh Palestinian refugee camp.

The brown eyes of the Palestinian children gleamed with curiosity as we walked into the camp, which is basically a neighborhood in the southern port city of Sidon. The youngsters curiously eyed the dozen or so white plastic discs stuffed under our arms. As we spread apart and began throwing our American-made Frisbees, with "Courtesy of the Voice of Hope Radio Station" stamped in English neatly inside, their curiosity bubbled over into great excitement. The dozen or so children who initially came out to greet us suddenly became hundreds. All of the boys wanted to be the first to try out the newfangled toy, which was rapidly becoming the latest fad at Ein Hilweh.

After coaching several of the children on the finer points of Frisbee-throwing, we walked to the nearby Voice of Hope relief truck to begin phase two of the day's excitement. Several other staff members and Voice of Hope founder George Otis were waiting there to help hand out care packages consisting of a Frisbee (which we later heard were mainly being used as plates), a blanket, some candies, and an Arabic-language Bible. Palestinian mothers and fathers soon followed their children to the truck and began clamoring for the packages. Suddenly the scene turned ugly as people started to scale the large vehicle and grab for more than one package.

Within minutes a decision was made to move the truck, now surrounded by hundreds of shouting camp residents. Israeli soldiers standing nearby fired into the air as the large relief vehicle was slowly backed out from the midst of the crowd. International television crews filmed the chaotic scene. I and several others cleared the children out of the truck's path as it was carefully driven out of the camp. To put it mildly, our small relief effort didn't exactly turn out the way we had hoped it would.

Several weeks later two other Lebanese Palestinian refugee camps became household words all over the world. With Israeli army encouragement, Lebanese "Christian" militiamen entered the Sabra and Shatilla camps in southwest Beirut on Thursday, September 16, 1982. The militiamen were supposed to go after Palestinian fighters who had battled Israeli forces from positions inside the camps.

But the Lebanese gunmen didn't just kill their Palestinian counterparts. Many hundreds of Palestinians, several hundred of them women and children, were shot and killed. While the slaughter went on, Israeli troops—allied, if loosely, with the Christian militiamen—were stationed just outside the camps. The Lebanese militiamen, full of bitterness following the assassination of their beloved leader, President-elect Bashir Gemayel, only two days before, had taken revenge on the hated Palestinians, whom the Christians largely blame for setting off the Lebanese "civil war" in 1975.

The massacre was fairly typical of the things that were occurring in Lebanon in those days. For example, Shiite gunmen attacked the very same camps three years later, killing more than five hundred Palestinians, again many of them women and children. Nevertheless, the world was shocked. Israel bore the brunt of international condemnation even though military and government leaders said they had not known in advance that the Lebanese Christian militiamen would go after civilians as well as armed PLO fighters. Local Israeli commanders said they had heard frequent shooting in the camps, but assumed that armed Palestinian gunmen were the only targets of Lebanese militia fire.

An Israeli government-ordered commission of inquiry—set up as a result of wide-scale public demand—reported in 1983 that Israeli leaders, and especially Defense Minister Ariel Sharon, should have known, and probably did, that allowing Gemayel's embittered supporters into the camps was a sure recipe for disaster.

## THE FIRST ARAB-ISRAELI WAR AND PALESTINIAN FLIGHT

That there are Palestinian refugees living in Beirut is, of course, the result of the 1947–49 Arab-Israeli war. Did these people flee their homes at the behest of Arab military and political leaders, as the Israelis basically maintain, or were they deliberately pushed out by the Jews, as the Arab world claims? This question lies at the center of the Arab-Israeli propaganda war, which has raged alongside the "hot wars" ever since 1948. My own informal research shows that Israeli Jews usually echo the popular idea that Arab leaders ordered the Palestinians out, while the Palestinians insist that the refugee flight resulted from a deliberate Jewish plot to expel the Arabs. What is the truth?

With the release of classified papers in Israel, Britain, and elsewhere in recent years, a clearer picture of what actually took place is emerging. The evidence shows that everyone had a hand in promoting the refugee flight, including the Palestinians themselves, but especially their leaders.

Based largely on previously unavailable information, Israeli journalist and historian Benny Morris has authored a controversial book on the topic, called *The Birth of the Palestinian Refugee Problem, 1947–1949*.[28] He writes that the Palestinian refugee flight basically began as a result of the Arab war launched against the emerging Jewish state. The Jews neither planned nor initially encouraged it. Moreover, the first evacuation wave was, for the most part, neither encouraged nor discouraged by surrounding Arab states and local Arab leaders.[29]

During the first few months after the outbreak of hostilities in early December 1947, the majority of those who fled were wealthy Arabs seeking temporary shelter elsewhere—until things settled down a bit. Many were Christians who were not enthusiastic about the holy war being launched against the Jews. As the fighting intensified in early 1948, most of those leaving were again seeking only to escape for the duration of the battles, believing that the Arab countries would surely be victorious in their forthcoming invasion. The flight of prominent Palestinians encouraged many other Arabs to leave their homes.

According to Morris, the picture changed somewhat after the April Deir Yassin killings, with fear of the Jews becoming a secondary motive for flight. The Arab media trumpeted and exaggerated the episode for propaganda purposes, but this also had the effect of scaring many Palestinians, even though mainstream Jewish leaders condemned the killings. Irgun and Stern Gang members were not unhappy with the growing Palestinian panic, writes Morris, believing that the Jewish state's chances of survival would increase if fewer Arabs remained within its designated boundaries. At the same time, both Arab and Jewish military commanders ordered the evacuation of towns and villages to clear the path in anticipation of major battles in mid-May as Arab armies launched their announced full-scale jihad.

Street battles between Jewish and Arab forces in several major cities, especially Haifa, Tiberias, and Jaffa, sped up the Palestinian flight. Local Palestinians felt demoralized when most of their leaders fled the scene at the first sign of a Jewish victory. This in turn led to more flight. Arab military disorganization, coupled with occasional looting and rapes committed by irregular Syrian and Iraqi forces, contributed to a general breakdown of Arab morale. Even more people then fled for safety.

On Saturday morning, May 15, Tel Aviv was bombed by Egyptian aircraft, signaling the start of the full-scale Arab assault against the newly born Jewish state. Trans-Jordanian King Abdullah, who had hopes of annexing the "Arab portion" of partitioned Palestine, attacked from the east.

To the north, Syria, Lebanon, and Iraq launched their armed assaults with the aim of throwing the Jews out of Tiberias and Haifa. The Israelis were hard pressed on every front, since the invading armies had air power, artillery, and armor, all of which the outnumbered Jews still lacked (British Mandate officials did not allow the Jews to import weapons). The Syrian army, assisted by Iraq, attacked north and south of the Sea of Galilee, capturing several settlements. In the Galilee panhandle, Lebanese soldiers briefly took control of a Jewish settlement in the Naphtali hills and surrounded another. Fighting was especially intense around the Sea of Galilee.

Cairo's forces slowly penetrated up the Gaza coast toward Tel Aviv, capturing kibbutz settlements along the way. After several weeks of fierce fighting, the Egyptian advance was halted twenty miles south of Tel Aviv with the aid of the first Israeli fighter planes, newly arrived from, of all places, Czechoslovakia.

Arab-Jewish battles raged north and south of Jerusalem and around the Old City. The Trans-Jordanian forces, known as the Arab Legion, were especially tough soldiers since the legion was set up and commanded by the British. Jewish fighters were quickly forced to abandon several settlements north of Jerusalem, and four others in the Etzion Bloc southeast of Bethlehem. Once again the Tel Aviv–Jerusalem road was closed, this time by the Arab Legion, forcing the Israelis to build a temporary bypass to reach besieged Jews in west Jerusalem. Abdullah's forces next captured the Old City, but could not overrun Jewish west Jerusalem.

To the surprise of almost everyone, the Arab offensive ran out of steam in early June. Analysts say the combination of extremely high Jewish fighting morale (the Arabs had, after all, pledged to throw them into the sea), and disorganization and low motivation among the Arab forces contributed to the change of tide. As it became apparent that they were not succeeding in their holy war of annihilation, the Arabs agreed to a United Nations–sponsored twenty-eight-day truce. It took effect on June 10.

Naturally enough, the fierce warfare in all parts of the Promised Land forced a new wave of Palestinian-Arab flight. Benny Morris writes that, contrary to popular Israeli opinion, the Arab states did not urge Palestinians to flee the offensive, except in a few instances. But such advice was hardly necessary, he notes, since Palestinian civilians, like people anywhere, were not eager to get caught up in full-scale warfare. Likewise, Morris found no evidence to support the Arab charge that the Israelis pushed out Palestinian villagers as a deliberate policy of expulsion, but in the midst of battle, "it was understood by all concerned that, militarily, in the struggle to survive, the fewer Arabs remaining behind and along the front lines, the better."[30]

At the same time, Israeli leaders began to realize that the mass evacuation would help solve one of the new state's main projected problems—

the presence of a large Arab minority that could aid outside Arab forces in future attacks upon Israel. In all, somewhere between 200,000 and 300,000 Palestinians became refugees during this period, joining many thousands who fled before April 1948.

When fighting resumed on July 8, Israel's army, which had received new equipment during the twenty-eight-day truce, went on the offensive, capturing more of the region of Galilee and the strategic towns of Ramle and Lydda, southeast of Tel Aviv. Attempts by some of the estimated 100,000 Israeli soldiers—one-sixth of the Jews of Israel (many were basically civilians who had been handed guns and quickly taught to shoot them)—to capture the Old City of Jerusalem were unsuccessful. The Arabs, again seeing that they were getting nowhere, agreed to another cease-fire, to begin on July 18.

During the ten days of fighting, another twenty to thirty thousand Palestinians became refugees. Many of them were from the towns of Ramle and Lydda (the latter located next to the strategic international airport), whose defense was suddenly abandoned by the Arab Legion. Military analysts say King Abdullah probably decided that the towns were beyond the area he could successfully conquer and annex to his kingdom. Ramle and Lydda had been central Arab staging grounds for attacks on the Tel Aviv–Jerusalem road. Convinced that control of the towns was essential to the new state, Israeli officials ordered the residents to evacuate their homes. Morris writes that this was the first and largest deliberate expulsion ordered by the Israelis during the war.

Arab irregular forces did not accept the July cease-fire, and fighting continued in many areas. In mid-October full-scale warfare resumed. The Israelis managed to cut off Egyptian forces south of Jerusalem and to open the coastal road south of Tel Aviv. The Negev Desert town of Beersheba was captured on October 21, as was the entire area of upper Galilee by October 31.

With the Arab armies clearly defeated, Egypt agreed to indirectly negotiate an armistice agreement in early January 1949. The U.N.-mediated armistice was signed in February. Agreements with Lebanon and Trans-Jordan soon followed. Negotiations with Syria, which continued to launch attacks on Israel, were more difficult, but an armistice was finally signed in July of that year.

During the final battles of 1948, another 100,000 to 150,000 Palestinians became refugees. Some of these, especially Muslims living in the Galilee region, were ordered out of their homes by the Israelis. Most Galilee Christians and Druze (a religious sect derived from Islam) were allowed to remain in their towns and villages. Israeli leaders were, by this time, eager to have as few Muslims as possible in the Jewish state since they feared that the jihad would be resumed (as it was) by the Arab nations at some point in the future, with Palestinian Arabs, especially Muslims, likely to act as an internal "fifth column" against Israel.

Benny Morris concludes that the Palestinian refugee flight was caused by a combination of factors, all of them set into motion and overshadowed by the fierce fighting initiated by the Arabs. "What happened in Palestine/Israel over 1947–49 was so complex and varied, the situation radically changing from date to date and place to place, that a single-cause explanation of the exodus from most sites is untenable."[31]

The United Nations reported that 726,000 Palestinian Arabs had become refugees before and during the war. The Israelis put the number at around 600,000, and the Arabs at about one million. Some 150,000 Arabs remained in their homes in Israel. It is important to note that nearly two-thirds of the Palestinian refugees had not left the Holy Land, but went to areas designated by the U.N. partition plan as parts of the proposed Arab state. About 38 percent fled to Judea and Samaria, according to U.N. statistics, while another 26 percent went to the Egyptian-controlled Gaza Strip. The next largest group, 14 percent, fled to Lebanon, with 10 percent entering Syria and another 10 percent crossing over to Trans-Jordan (some of these were returning to family homes). Only about 1 percent settled in Egypt.

Thousands of Palestinians counted by the U.N. as refugees, especially many who fled from coastal cities to towns and villages in Judea and Samaria, actually returned to family homes. Israeli officials said such Palestinians could not be truly considered as refugees. This is the main reason for the lower Israeli refugee estimate. U.N. officials also suspected that more than 150,000 people who registered as refugees, especially in Trans-Jordan, were actually Arab peasants who already lived outside of Palestine.

The historical evidence suggests that, while the Israelis deliberately expelled some Palestinian Arabs following months of bitter fighting, most left of their own volition or at the behest of local Arab commanders. More importantly, if the Arabs had not been certain of their ability to destroy the Jewish state—rejecting the United Nations partition plan and launching local attacks and then a four-front army assault—the plan could have been carried out with little or no violence and no forced refugees. Many Palestinians might have chosen to move to the new Arab state, and they would have most likely done so with full compensation. Various relocation schemes for those wishing to move had already been discussed at the United Nations, the Jewish Agency, and in Washington.

The Palestinian refugee flight was tragic, as is their continuing plight today. But the historical record shows that pinning the blame solely or largely on Israel, as the Arabs, communist countries, and many others have done ever since, simply is not accurate.

By the time armistice negotiations got under way in 1949 (see map 4 in the appendix), the Israelis had decided to allow only a token number, if any, of the Arab refugees to return to their homes. It was judged too dangerous to allow such a return, at least until passions cooled in the region. Israeli leaders hoped that the refugees could be permanently resettled in Judea, Samaria, and Gaza—the areas designated for an Arab state by the United Nations—or in the other countries to which they had fled. The United States and the U.N. pressed Israel to take back at least a third of the Palestinians.

However, after the loss of some four thousand soldiers and two thousand civilians, or about 1 percent of the total Jewish population of Israel (equivalent to around two million Americans in the Vietnam War), Israeli officials were not willing to let potentially fifth-column Palestinians into the now predominantly Jewish nation.

Israel quickly realized that the Arab countries, reeling from their defeat, had absolutely no intention of resettling the Palestinian refugees in permanent housing, even though the United Nations, the United States, and others offered to help them do so. The refugees were instead to become the main propaganda weapon in the ongoing Arab struggle to destroy the Jewish state. The Egyptians feared that resettling Gaza Arabs inside Egypt would lead to greater instability in their country.

On the other hand, Cairo was not willing to turn the strip over to Jordanian King Abdullah, who was strongly disliked by Egyptian leaders, or to grant the area "independence." Abdullah was dead set against allowing the Palestinians to set up an independent state along his western border in Judea and Samaria. Anyway, the Palestinian Arabs did not want a state there, holding out instead for the total destruction of Israel. The Lebanese were too preoccupied with their own problems to worry about the Palestinians. The Syrians had no intention of doing anything that might make life any easier for the hated "Zionist invaders."

Keeping the refugees in increasingly cramped camps would provide a steady stream of disgruntled young men ready and eager to fight for the "liberation of Palestine." Their continuing homelessness would also provide constant propaganda ammunition against the very existence—in the heart of the Arab-Muslim world—of mainly Jewish Israel. And besides, the United Nations would take care of the medical and food needs of refugee camp residents, lifting the burden off Arab treasuries. Despite these factors, Jordan did eventually resettle many of the estimated seventy thousand refugees who fled east across the Jordan River—the only Arab country to do so. Today, a majority are fully integrated and fairly prosperous citizens of Jordan.

In early 1950 Jordanian King Abdullah annexed the districts of Judea, Samaria, and east Jerusalem, although only two nations, Britain and Pakistan, recognized his move. In order to reduce Jewish claims to the area, the king dropped the biblical names Judea and Samaria and announced that the annexed land would be known as the West Bank of the Kingdom of Jordan, since it was located beyond the west bank of the Jordan River. At the same time, Abdullah was holding secret talks with Israeli leaders in order to try and work out a permanent peace settlement between the two neighboring countries. He was assassinated for his efforts in 1951. A Palestinian militant who opposed his "traitorous talks with the enemy" shot and killed the king as he toured the Muslim shrines on the Temple Mount.

## JEWS AT THE CENTER OF THE WORLD

As the Arab Palestinians were fleeing, thousands of Jews, mainly from Europe, Asia, and North Africa, began pouring into the newborn state of Israel. Most were temporarily housed in tent camps, others in homes and apartments that had been abandoned by fleeing Arabs. Anti-Jewish persecution and occasional rioting, which broke out in a number of Arab countries in 1947 and continued through 1948 and 1949, led hundreds of thousands of Jews to abandon their homes and flee to Israel. Many of the more than one-half million Arabic-speaking Jews who sought refuge in Israel during the late 1940s and early 1950s were forced to leave their possessions behind, arriving in the country destitute.

Although the Jewish state was financially strapped, the new immigrants, many of whom could truly be called refugees, were absorbed into the country. By the end of 1951, 690,000 Jewish immigrants had made their way to the Promised Land, more than doubling Israel's May 15, 1948, Jewish population. The number of Jewish arrivals was roughly equal to the number of Palestinian Arabs who had fled.

By 1970 nearly 600,000 European Jews had immigrated to Israel. The vast majority of them, more than 80 percent, came from six Eastern European countries which fell under Soviet-communist control after World War II. The largest group, 229,779, emigrated from Romania, the country which violently threw off its communist dictatorship in 1989. More than 150,000 came to Israel from Poland. Thousands of Jews also arrived from China, the Soviet Union, India, Iran, North and South America, South Africa, Australia, and New Zealand. Jews were literally returning to their ancient ancestral homeland from the uttermost parts of the globe. At least eighty-six countries contributed Jews to the new nation during Israel's first two decades.

Forging a united society with people from so many diverse cultural backgrounds was not easy, to say the least. Arabic-speaking Oriental Jews complained of discrimination at the hands of the European Ashkenazi "elite." Like their pre-state European cousins, most had suffered some degree of persecution before immigrating to Israel, leaving many emotional scars to overcome. The threat of annihilation was ever present, with the Arab world periodically renewing its jihad against the Jewish state. Between the "hot wars," the military threat was kept alive by frequent sniping and crossborder terror attacks from the Gaza Strip, the West Bank, and the Golan Heights. Many Jews were killed by this constant war of attrition, 967 alone between 1951 and 1955.

Despite the many obstacles, a remarkably united Israeli society has been forged in just a few decades. Much of the credit for this can be traced to shared army duty, which acts as a great force of integration among the various Jewish communities. Israel's armed forces quickly became the strongest in the Middle East, reducing fears that the Arab world would eventually succeed in its war of destruction. Mutually shared burdens helped to create a relatively stable society, free to pursue nation-building in the midst of a sea of Arab hostility.

Jews from Arab countries have slowly moved up the ladder of social success. Many of them have excelled in entertainment, business, the military, and government. Israel's most popular singer in the 1980s was Ofra Haza, of Yemeni background. For the first time ever, Jewish politicians born in Arab countries occupied two of the three senior government cabinet posts in 1996—Foreign Minister David Levy from Morocco and Defense Minister Yitzhak Mordechai, born in Iraq. A later Defense Minister, Binyamin Ben Eliezer, also from Iraq, would become the first Oriental Jew to head a major political party in 2002. At any rate, intermarriage between different immigrant groups, and time, is leading to the emergence of the truly "Israeli Israeli," a native Hebrew speaker with little or no ethnic distinction, and very much at home in the Middle East.

Serious economic problems have plagued the Jewish state since its inception, mainly because of Israel's need to maintain such a disproportionately large military machine. Fighting the various wars has severely strained Israel's economy. The fact that most Israeli men must spend at least one month a year doing military reserve duty is another serious financial drain. Israel's overly socialized and bureaucratic system of government, patterned too closely on Eastern European models, has also blocked economic progress, although a more open free-enterprise system is now coming into place.

These factors, plus the constant fear of terrorism and never knowing when the next war will begin, have caused many Israelis—estimates say more than half a million—to move overseas since the 1950s. Many so-called *yordim* (literally "those who go down" from Zion) say they intend to return after making their fortune in greener, mostly American pastures, although only a small percentage have made it back home so far.

## SINAI—ISRAEL'S SECOND WAR

Constant crossborder attacks from Egyptian-supported Palestinians in the Gaza Strip, which left more than four hundred Israelis dead in the early 1950s, and a threatening Egyptian-Syrian military alliance led to Israel's second major war, the 1956 Sinai Campaign. However, it was actually more of a superpower contest than an Arab-Israeli conflict.

The Soviet Union, fighting a rather hot cold war with the United States for regional influence, began sending arms to Egypt via Czechoslovakia in 1955. The United States and Western Europe were at least as concerned about the Soviet move as was Israel, since the strategic Suez Canal runs through Egyptian territory. After the arms deal was signed, Washington withdrew an offer to help Egypt build a dam on the upper Nile River. The move infuriated Egyptian strongman Gamal Abdel Nasser, who responded by nationalizing the canal.

The fiery Egyptian leader, whose speeches were peppered with both Marxist and Muslim slogans, was already perceived as a great threat in Israel before the decision was taken to join British and French forces in a campaign to return the Suez Canal to Western control. Nasser had ordered his navy to blockade the Israeli port of Eilat in 1954, closing Israel's outlet to the Red Sea. He also banned all Israeli shipping through the canal, effectively cutting off Israeli exports to the Southern Hemisphere. Next he signed a military pact with Syria, while telling the world in frequent, bombastic speeches that he would lead the Arab states in a renewed attempt to annihilate "the Zionist entity." All the while Nasser was massively beefing up his armed forces in the Sinai Peninsula.

Israeli forces, in coordination with Britain and France, attacked Egyptian positions on October 29, 1956. In a preplanned move, the two

European powers joined the assault the next day. Egyptian defenses quickly crumbled as Israel seized the Gaza Strip and the Sinai Peninsula. But the United States was unhappy with the attempt to forcibly retake the Suez Canal, fearing all-out war with the Soviet Union. The Soviets had threatened to use force if a U.N. General Assembly resolution for an immediate cease-fire was not heeded. Under American pressure a cease-fire went into effect on November 6. A special U.N. force was created to separate the warring armies in the Sinai. Within several months the Israelis withdrew from the conquered territory, finally pulling out of the Gaza Strip in March 1957.

Although Nasser had lost the war, he emerged as the hero of the Arab world for successfully holding on to the Suez Canal. He vowed to renew the military struggle against the "Zionist-imperialist state" at an appropriate time in the future. As the so-called "Nasserite Movement" spread across the Arab world, Israeli leaders became more and more alarmed. They responded by continuing to build up the Israeli defense forces and by beginning work on a secret nuclear weapons program, with French assistance. Meanwhile the Soviets and their communist-bloc allies stepped up military support to Egypt and Syria, who continued to sponsor cross-border raids into Israel by Palestinian gunmen known as *fedayeen*.

## THE PLO

In 1964 Nasser helped to set up an organization that would later become a major player in the Arab-Israeli conflict. The first official Arab League summit meeting, held in Cairo in January, decided to back the establishment of an organization to represent all Palestinian Arabs in "the struggle to liberate Palestine." Echoing the pre-state Zionist practice, Palestinian delegates held a congress in east Jerusalem during May to implement the Arab League decision. The result was the Palestine Liberation Organization.

The first PLO leader, Ahmed Shukeiri, pledged at the congress that the PLO would aid the Arab nations in throwing the Israelis into the sea. The PLO was to be the roof organization for various Palestinian paramilitary and civilian groups, most of them assisted by the Kremlin and its allies. Yassar Arafat, head of the largest armed group, *al-Fatah* (Arabic for "the victory" and also the name of a chapter in the Koran that celebrates Muhammad's capture of Mecca), became overall PLO leader in 1969.

The Arab states, often at each other's throats over the years, continued their frequently intense rivalries by sponsoring various subgroups within the PLO. The Egyptians backed the setting up of the Marxist Popular Front for the Liberation of Palestine, headed by George Habash. The Syrians sponsored the Palestine Liberation Front, led by Ahmed Jabril, which briefly joined forces with Habash's group. Not wanting to be left out, Iraq backed the Popular Democratic Front for the Liberation of Palestine, headed by Naif Hawatmeh. The various PLO subgroups have at times clashed violently with one another, and more often with Arafat's mainstream Fatah movement.

Israelis saw the PLO as another vehicle in the ongoing Arab attempt to drive them out of the region. They had good reason to think so. The Palestinian congress of May 1964 adopted a founding charter for the Palestinian movement that called for Israel's total destruction. Here are some of the charter's main points:

Article 1. Palestine is the homeland of the Palestinian Arab people and an integral part of the great Arab homeland.

Article 3. The Palestinian Arab people possesses the legal right to its homeland, and when the liberation of its homeland is completed, it will exercise self-determination solely according to its own will and choice.

Article 6. Jews who were living permanently in Palestine before the beginnings of the Zionist invasion will be considered Palestinians. [In other words, Jews living in the land before the first aliyah wave of the 1880s can stay after the land's "liberation."]

Article 8. The phase in which the people of Palestine is living is that of the national struggle for the liberation of Palestine. [The article then calls for unity and the suspension of internal rivalries, ending with the statement that the Palestinians "comprise one national front which acts to restore Palestine and liberate it through armed struggle."]

Article 9. Armed struggle is the only way to liberate Palestine and is therefore a strategy, and not tactics. The Palestinian Arab people affirms its absolute resolution and abiding determination to pursue the armed struggle and to march forward toward the armed popular revolution, to liberate its homeland and to return to it.

Article 10. Fedayeen action [paramilitary and terrorist attacks by armed Palestinians] forms the nucleus of the popular Palestinian war of liberation. [The article then calls on all Arabs to support groups launching such "actions."]

Article 15. The liberation of Palestine, from an Arab viewpoint, is a national duty to repulse the Zionist, imperialist invasion from the great Arab homeland, and to purge the Zionist presence from Palestine. Its full responsibilities fall upon the Arab nation, people and government, with the Palestinian Arabs at their head.

Article 19. The partitioning of Palestine in 1947 and the establishment of Israel is fundamentally null and void, whatever time has elapsed.

Article 20. The Balfour Declaration, the Mandate Document, and what has been based upon them are considered null and void. The claim of a historical or spiritual tie between Jews and Palestine does not tally with historical realities. . . . Judaism, in its character as a religion of revelation, is not a nationality with an independent existence.

The Palestinian Charter also contained assurance that the holy places of Christianity and Judaism will be protected after the "liberation"; it called for broad international support for the struggle; and it declared Palestinian neutrality in the various internal Arab conflicts.

The covenant ended with Article 33: "This Covenant cannot be amended except by a two-thirds majority of all members of the National Council of the Palestine Liberation Organization in a special session called for this purpose."

## THE SIX DAY WAR

Three years after the founding of the PLO, the Arab world, led by Gamal Nasser, renewed its jihad against Israel. The result was similar to the first attempt to wipe out the Jewish state in 1948—the Israelis ended up with more territory than they started out with. In fact, the June 1967 Six Day War left Israel in control of the entire West Bank, the Gaza Strip, the Sinai Peninsula, and the Golan Heights just above the Galilee panhandle. Of greatest importance to most Israelis, Jewish forces had also captured Jerusalem's Old City. Jewish sovereignty had returned to the area of King David's city, including the ancient Temple Mount, for the first time in more than two thousand years.

The war was preceded by a period of rapidly escalating hostile rhetoric and actions on the part of Egypt and attacks from Syria. Ever since 1948 Israeli settlements in the north had been assaulted by Syrian forces and Palestinian fedayeen. The frequency of the attacks increased during 1966, with five Israelis killed and around twenty wounded. Syrian soldiers lobbed artillery shells and fired machine guns and rifles at Israeli settlements, such as Kibbutz Hagoshrim, in the Hula Valley below the Golan Heights. Syrian infiltrators planted land mines in the fields and along roads, and Syrian artillery fire was directed at Israeli boats on the Sea of Galilee.

The attacks were stepped up even further in the spring of 1967, with frequent tank battles between Israeli and Syrian forces. On April 7 Israeli planes—most of them purchased from France, which was then Israel's main foreign source of weapons—struck at Syrian artillery positions. Six Soviet-supplied Syrian MIG jets were shot down in subsequent dogfights. The Syrians responded on April 8 by lobbing two hundred heavy mortar shells on Kibbutz Gadot, located on the Jordan River just next to Syrian front lines. The shelling completely destroyed the settlement.

Nasser was meanwhile banging the drums of war ever more loudly. On May 14 he mobilized his armed forces of around 240,000 men for what he said would be a decisive attack upon Israel. Two days later he demanded that United Nations peacekeeping forces leave the Sinai Peninsula and began moving his army across the Suez Canal. Under increasing pressure, the U.N. agreed on May 19 to withdraw its international force, while Cairo radio announced that the Arabs now had a chance to "deal Israel a mortal blow of annihilation, to blot out its entire presence in our holy land."[32] Three days later Nasser ordered his navy to repeat the 1950s blockade of the Israeli Red Sea port of Eilat, a move that Israeli officials, in accordance with international law, considered an act of war.

The entire Arab world was called upon to support the Egyptian-Syrian attempt to wipe out the Jewish state. Mutual defense pacts were signed between Egypt and Jordan on May 30, and between Egypt and Iraq on June 4. Forces were mobilized in Jordan, Saudi Arabia, Kuwait, Iraq, Algeria, and Lebanon. Israeli leaders quickly noted that they were potentially facing almost three times as many soldiers, three times as many tanks, and more than three times as many warplanes as they had at their disposal. Even more alarming was the presence of Soviet and other East Bloc forces aiding Egypt and Syria. Tension reached fever pitch during the last week of May, when Syrian, Iraqi, Jordanian, and Lebanese soldiers were moved to forward positions close to Israel's borders.

The Arab nations refused to listen to international pleas that they halt their movement toward war. With Israeli soldiers heavily outnumbered along the borders, the Israeli cabinet decided that the Jewish state's best hope for survival was to strike the first blow. On the morning of June 5 Israeli warplanes launched a lightning, yet carefully calibrated, attack on Egyptian aircraft stationed at more than fifteen bases throughout Egypt, nearly wiping out Nasser's entire air force. The Six Day War had begun.

After two days of fierce battles with Jordanian forces—who began shelling Israeli positions on June 5 from east Jerusalem despite Israeli pleas to King Hussein to stay out of the war—Israeli troops captured the walled Old City of Jerusalem. Israeli soldiers had been hampered somewhat in battling to enter the city by strict orders not to harm any Christian or Muslim holy places. With tears in their eyes, emotional Jewish soldiers touched the ancient Western Wall of the Temple Mount, which had been off-limits to all Jews since Jordan captured the Old City in 1948. Israeli leaders toured the nearby Jewish Quarter, largely destroyed during the Jordanian conquest nineteen years earlier. Officials surveyed the remains of ruined Jewish synagogues and homes, promising to begin the quarter's reconstruction immediately.

By June 10 Israeli forces had occupied the Sinai Peninsula, the annexed West Bank of Jordan, and the Syrian Golan Heights. Several hundred thousand West Bank Palestinians and some from the Gaza Strip fled east during the fighting, greatly swelling the Palestinian refugee population in Jordan proper. Some of the refugees later returned to their homes.

The overwhelming Israeli victory stunned the Arab world. The Soviet Union, deeply embarrassed by its client's disastrous defeat, broke off diplomatic relations with Israel. The Israelis, who had only one week earlier faced the real prospect of annihilation, were ecstatic over the war's outcome, and especially over the reuniting of Jerusalem. But there was much grief over the loss of 766 soldiers and the wounding of twenty-five hundred others.

The Six Day War left the Jewish state in control of land more than three times the size of Israel, with an Arab population of more than a million people. How Israel could rule such a large area with a hostile population was of immediate concern to Israeli leaders. The government of Prime Minister Levi Eshkol wasted no time in stating its readiness to hand back at least most of the captured territories, providing the Arab states finally agreed to halt their twenty-year jihad against Israel. But vanquished Arab leaders, meeting in Sudan in September 1967, declared that they would not negotiate, recognize, or make peace with the "Zionist entity."

Soon after the meeting in Sudan, the United Nations passed Resolution 242, which called on Israel to withdraw its forces from "territories occupied in the recent conflict." The resolution also called for "a just settlement of the refugee problem" and for all Middle Eastern nations to be permitted "to live in peace in secure and recognized borders." The Israelis said they would comply with the resolution only after the Arab states agreed to recognize Israel's permanent existence.

Israeli leaders soon began a limited settlement program in portions of the captured territories, to the dismay of the Arab world. The program was undertaken as part of the Allon Plan, named after Deputy Prime Minister Yigal Allon. The plan stated that Israel would eventually pull out of the Sinai Peninsula, the Gaza Strip, and the West Bank, except for certain portions considered vital to Israel's security. Israel would retain control of most of the strategic Jordan Valley and the first mountain ridge west of it, along with east Jerusalem and some areas south of the city where Jewish settlements existed until 1948. The rest of the West Bank would become a Palestinian-Jordanian state.

A large corridor located around Jericho would connect the state with Jordan proper. Egypt would regain control of the Gaza Strip and most of the Sinai Peninsula. Arab leaders rejected the plan, calling again for the complete annihilation of the Jewish state. The government then went ahead and began to construct settlements in areas the Allon Plan designated as essential for Israel's security.

## THE WARS OF ATTRITION AND YOM KIPPUR

Nasser backed up his rejectionist stand by launching renewed military attacks against Israeli forces stationed east of the Suez Canal. Hundreds of Israeli soldiers were killed in the almost daily bombardments, which lasted for more than three years. The Israeli air force responded by launching raids deep inside Egyptian territory, taking on Soviet pilots several times in the process. The so-called "War of Attrition" finally ended on August 17, 1970, with Israeli and Egyptian forces still dug in on opposite sides of the canal.

The full-scale Arab jihad was renewed on Saturday afternoon, October 6, 1973. But this time Arab leaders kept quiet about their intentions before launching a surprise attack. In Israel it was Yom Kippur, the holiest day in the Jewish calendar and a day when most people, even many who are basically nonreligious, abstain from eating food. Television and radio are off the air and private vehicles stay off the roads. The quiet of the holy day was suddenly shattered around noon as sirens began wailing throughout the country, alerting everyone that another Arab-Israeli confrontation was about to begin. Men everywhere rushed off to their military units. At 2 P.M. Egyptian and Syrian forces attacked simultaneously with all of their armed might. The Yom Kippur War was under way.

The Soviet Union had fully resupplied the Syrians and Egyptians with the latest weaponry, including close to 1,000 warplanes and more than

4,000 tanks. When the battle began, Israel had fewer than 500 planes and about 1,700 tanks. Israel's 300,000 soldiers faced a combined Egyptian-Syrian force of more than 800,000, with more on the way from Iraq, Morocco, and Algeria. Later Saudi Arabia and Kuwait sent token forces to aid the Syrians. Iraq and Jordan added more than 300 tanks to Syria's already large force of around 2,000.

For the first time the Arabs had the Israelis on the run. The Jewish army was pushed back on both the narrow Golan Heights and in the Sinai Desert. But after several weeks of bitter fighting, and despite an immediate and large-scale resupply effort by the Kremlin, the Israelis, with delayed help from America, once again overcame seemingly insurmountable odds and routed their opponents. Israeli casualties were high: 2,378 soldiers dead and many more injured.

Despite their loss, the Arabs were satisfied that they had proven that Israel was not an invincible military machine. Government officials in Jerusalem found themselves engulfed in a political storm as accusations flew as to who was responsible for not foreseeing the combined Arab attack. In Idaho I was closely following the tide of battle on radio and television, wondering what was really behind this Arab-Israeli—and superpower—struggle at the center of the world.

# CHAPTER 8

# FROM OPTIMISM TO DESPAIR

L ess than three months after the Yom Kippur War ended, I was sitting in the same stuffed pillow chair where I first heard of the war's outbreak, pondering my brother Tim's testimony of "rebirth" in the Messiah Jesus, which he had shared with me several times, the last over the Christmas holidays. Beside the pillow chair was a book I had never read: the Bible. Tim had given it to me for Christmas.

At a certain point during that January 4, 1974, evening I quietly asked the God of Abraham to reveal himself to me—if he indeed existed. I'd already experienced the reality of the "other world" through friends who engaged in certain occult practices, but it had definitely been the dark side of that world. Now I wanted to know what (or should I say who?) was on the good side.

My decision to follow the Lord helped me to get a clearer picture as to why people all over the globe were closely monitoring the latest chapter in the Arab-Israeli conflict. I hadn't realized that millions of Christians see the Jewish state as a prophetic time clock, pointing the way toward the end of the world and the return of the Messiah. I knew that most Muslims view Israel as a usurper, a stealer of holy Muslim land, but I assumed that the Islamic concept of holy war went out with the Middle Ages. It was already apparent to me that Jews all over the world, on the heels of the Holocaust, looked to Israel as a special sanctuary for Jewish people everywhere.

However, it quickly became evident that the main reasons for such intense world interest in the ongoing Middle East crisis were not religious, but economic. As the Yom Kippur War raged, Arab petroleum exporting countries decided to support the struggle against Israel by sharply reducing their supply of oil to the West. A total oil embargo was enacted against the United States and the Netherlands, and partial embargoes against other lands. European nations were hardest hit by the move, since most of them imported more than two-thirds of their oil from the Middle East. The Arabs intended to press demands that the West, especially America, put pressure on Israel to withdraw from the territories captured in the 1967 war. The United States and Canada, though less dependent than Europe on imported Middle Eastern oil, did feel the pinch.

The Arab oil nations soon discovered that they could substantially push up the price of their precious commodity by restricting supplies. The international petroleum companies didn't seem too displeased by the price increases, which left more money in their pockets as well. With long lines forming at gasoline stations in many parts of the globe, the Israelis—believing that the real Arab goal was still Israel's total destruction, as outlined in the PLO Charter—were indeed pressured to give in to Arab demands that a Palestinian state be set up in the West Bank and Gaza Strip. Israeli leaders responded as they had just after the Six Day War: They would consider going back to the pre-1967 borders only if all Arab states agreed to officially end their ongoing war of annihilation.

The Palestine National Council met in Cairo in June 1974 to discuss what moves the PLO should take in the wake of the 1973 war and subsequent oil embargo. Yasser Arafat told the delegates that the Ramadan Campaign (the Arab name for the war, which occurred during the Muslim holy month of Ramadan) was only the "beginning of the advance of the Arab nation." He compared the Arabs' relative success in the war to the Muslim warrior Saladin's victory over the crusaders, adding that the Arab advance "will only end in Tel Aviv."[33] On June 8, Palestinian delegates formally adopted a ten-point plan, known to Israelis as the "phased plan," which basically calls for the dismantling of Israel in stages. Key articles of the plan include:

Article 2. The Liberation Organization will employ all means and first and foremost armed struggle, to liberate

Palestinian territory and to establish the independent combatant national authority for the people over every part of
Palestinian territory that is liberated.

Article 4. Any step taken toward liberation is a step toward
the realization of the Liberation Organization's strategy of establishing the democratic Palestinian state specified in the resolutions of previous National Councils.

Article 8. Once it is established, the Palestinian national authority will strive to achieve a union of the confrontation countries with the aim of completing the liberation of all Palestinian
territory.

In short, the phased plan calls for the setting up of a PLO-controlled
state in the West Bank and Gaza Strip. It can either be established by military means—armed struggle—or by other means, an apparent reference
to diplomatic negotiations, whichever works best. This "independent
combatant national authority" would then work to set up "the democratic Palestinian state" over all of Palestine, in other words, over Israel
as well as the captured territories, in line with the PLO's founding charter. The Arab world would be asked to back militarily the final moves
toward full liberation.

Israel, naturally enough, did not welcome the new plan. Soon after the
phased plan was adopted, Arab leaders meeting in Morocco decided to
recognize the PLO as "the only legal representative of the Palestinian
people." In November 1974 the United Nations granted the PLO full ob-
server status.

Israelis felt increasingly isolated in the mid-1970s as billions of Arab
petro-dollars flowed back into Western economies—vastly increasing
Arab power and influence. Various African states, assisted agriculturally by
Israel over the years, broke off diplomatic relations in exchange for Arab
promises of aid, which was not always forthcoming.

The low point of this period for Israel was the passage by the United
Nations in November 1975 of a resolution equating Zionism with racism.
A majority of 72 nations, including the entire communist bloc, supported
the Arab-sponsored resolution, with 35 opposed and 32 abstaining. The

resolution was meant to delegitimize Israel's very existence by condemning the movement that had led to the Jewish state's rebirth. Israel's U.N. ambassador pointed out that despite many years of war and hostility, Arab citizens of Israel have full voting rights and almost unlimited freedom of press and speech, unlike the citizens of most of the states that supported the resolution.

A political revolution occurred in Israel in May 1977. The Labor Alignment, a coalition of moderate and left-wing political parties that had governed Israel since 1948, was thrown out of office and replaced by the right-of-center Likud Party headed by Menachem Begin. The Likud Party, which won 43 seats to Labor's 32 in the 120-member Israeli parliament, the Knesset, was able to form a government with the support of several centrist parties, plus two religious parties that had earlier supported Labor-led coalition governments. Begin's election victory came on the heels of several scandals that rocked the Labor movement. The Likud Party either led or was a part of every Israeli government until Labor swept back into power in June 1992.

Defeated Labor Alignment leaders prophesied that the chances of peace with the Arab world would be further reduced under Begin, who opposed any Israeli withdrawal from the territories captured in 1967. However, such predictions proved to be premature. One Arab leader had already decided that his country's future would best be served by ending the state of war with Israel.

## CAMP DAVID PEACE ACCORDS

Egyptian President Anwar Sadat had kicked out his Soviet patrons in the mid-1970s and was looking for Western aid to help rebuild his economy, shattered by the 1973 war. His sudden arrival at Ben Gurion Airport in November 1977 was like a dream come true for most Israelis. Sadat's historic decision led to the first peace treaty between an Arab state and Israel. It also led to his assassination by members of the Egyptian Islamic Jihad group, an offshoot of the Muslim Brotherhood movement (an Islamic fundamentalist group to which Yasser Arafat belonged while a student in Cairo). The Brotherhood continues to this day to support the abrogation of the peace treaty and a resumption of the holy war against Israel.

Egypt, Israel, and the United States signed the Camp David Peace Accords on September 17, 1978, after thirteen days of grueling negotiations at American President Jimmy Carter's Maryland retreat. One accord spelled out the peace settlement between Egypt and Israel, while the other dealt with the larger Arab-Israeli conflict. The latter said that regional peace talks should be based on United Nations Resolution 242. It called for implementation of a plan giving Palestinians self-governing autonomy in the West Bank and Gaza Strip while a final overall peace settlement was negotiated by Israeli, Palestinian, Egyptian, Jordanian, Syrian, and Lebanese representatives. An elected Palestinian council would have full self-governing authority in the territories, except in security matters, while a final settlement was negotiated.

The Arab world reacted harshly to the Camp David Treaty, as did the Soviet Union. Every Arab state severed relations with Cairo, which was kicked out of the Arab League. Sadat was charged with treason for having made peace with "the Zionist enemy." The PLO totally rejected the autonomy plan, saying it would settle for nothing less than a fully independent PLO state in every inch of "liberated Palestine."

Although Jordan's King Hussein quietly signaled that he would dearly love to follow Sadat's example, his hands were tied by warnings from his powerful northern neighbor, Syria, that he would be overthrown if he made peace with Israel. The Jordanian leader undoubtedly vividly remembered the Jerusalem assassination in 1951 of his grandfather, Abdullah, which he personally witnessed.

Sadat and Begin didn't even try to reach agreement on the crucial issue of Jerusalem, recognizing that their respective positions were miles apart. Instead, at Jimmy Carter's suggestion, Begin handed Sadat a letter declaring that Israel considered all of Jerusalem to be its permanent, indivisible capital city. Sadat in turn gave Begin a letter declaring that east Jerusalem, including the Old City and its Temple Mount, was an indivisible part of the Muslim world that must be returned to Arab sovereignty. The exchange of letters kept the Camp David peace talks from collapsing at a critical juncture.

## TERROR FROM THE NORTH

The Israeli people were in an optimistic mood when I arrived in the country in November 1980. Finally there was some light at the end of what had so far proved to be a long, dark tunnel. The peace treaty with Egypt had just been signed two years before, and many were hopeful that a formal accord with Jordan was not far off. The absence of the Arab world's most powerful nation from the war camp might mean the end of the constant cycle of Arab attacks. True, I didn't meet one Israeli who wasn't pained to see the barren, but beautiful, Sinai Peninsula revert to Egyptian control as part of the settlement, but most thought its loss was more than worthwhile in exchange for lasting peace.

There were just a couple of flies in the optimistic ointment—the Palestinians and Syria. Everyone knew that an explosion would probably occur one day in Judea, Samaria, and the Gaza Strip, where Israel's growing presence and often squalid living conditions, made worse by a high birth rate, produced hundreds of thousands of young, disgruntled soldiers for the Palestinian cause.

The chances that Jordan would resume full control over its self-declared "West Bank" as part of a future peace treaty with Israel seemed remote after the Arab decision to recognize the PLO as the sole representative of the Palestinians. There was little evidence that either Jordan or Egypt was eager to take on the Gaza Strip with its teeming refugee camps. Syria was supremely hostile to the Egyptian peace move, declaring it would continue the military struggle against Israel until the Jewish state was obliterated. At any rate, the chances that Israel would give back the small but strategic Golan Heights to Syria seemed to disappear after the Knesset extended Israeli law to the area in 1981.

However, it was in Lebanon that the flies in the ointment were most apparent. The Syrians had entered the troubled country as "peacekeepers" after fighting broke out between various Lebanese factions and Palestinians in 1975. Syria now controlled two-thirds of the country. Syrian strongman Hafez Assad resisted calls from fellow Arab leaders and most Lebanese Christians to pull his soldiers out of the Land of the Cedars. Assad also heavily backed several PLO militia groups operating in southern Lebanon, although he was hostile toward Arafat's mainstream Fatah group.

The most pressing problem facing Israel in the early 1980s was the frequent rocket attacks on its northern towns and settlements, launched mainly by the PLO from south Lebanon. The attacks originated in the PLO's south Lebanon ministate, which stretched from southern Beirut to the ports of Sidon and Tyre and east to the Syrian border. The PLO zone was established after the organization was thrown out of Jordan in the early 1970s following an unsuccessful PLO attempt to overthrow King Hussein. The ever-worsening internal fighting in Lebanon left the south's mostly Shiite Muslim residents powerless to prevent the PLO from taking over their towns and villages, even though few wanted to see the Palestinian fighters in control of the area.

Israel responded in 1978 to the growing PLO presence by helping south Lebanese Christians and Shiites set up an Israeli-patrolled border enclave—the south Lebanon "security zone"—sandwiched between the Israel-Lebanon border and an area to the north patrolled by United Nations peacekeeping forces. The U.N. forces had been sent to the area in the mid-1970s to help prevent terror squads from penetrating into Israel. Still, such squads occasionally pushed through, and many PLO rockets fell on northern Israel. This led to the idea of setting up a buffer zone that would increase protection for the Jewish state, and for south Lebanese residents who were also becoming frequent targets of attack by the PLO and its allies.

As I mentioned in chapter 2, I was personally well acquainted with the fear and disruption caused by the sometimes heavy PLO shelling of northern Israel. I also knew of another, even deeper fear that shaped the lives of Israel's Galilee citizens—the fear of a Palestinian terrorist attack.

My Hagoshrim "kibbutz parents" (everyone on my Project Kibbutz team was assigned a family to visit with regularly during the year) told me about one such attack that affected them personally. Close friends lived on nearby Kibbutz Misgav Am, located in the Naphtali hills near the border with Lebanon. Their two-year-old daughter was killed when PLO terrorists crossed the border on April 7, 1980. After sneaking into the kibbutz under the cover of darkness, the five heavily armed Palestinians took over a building housing four young children, two babies, and their adult female companion. The terrorists ordered the woman to calm down the frightened, weeping youngsters. But she was unable to comfort one of the young girls, who kept on crying. At that point the leader of the terrorist band used the butt of his gun to club the child to death. The PLO terrorists, who belonged to Arafat's Fatah group, announced that they would release their kibbutz hostages only if fifty Palestinian prisoners were immediately set free from Israeli jails.

At mid-morning Israeli soldiers stormed the house, killing all five terrorists. One soldier lost his life in the assault, but the remaining five children and the adult hostage were unharmed.

The Misgav Am attack was just the latest in a series of violent terror assaults launched by Palestinian squads from Lebanon. Since 1974 the attacks had left nearly one hundred Israelis dead. On April 11, 1974, three terrorists penetrated the border and attacked an Israeli apartment building in Kiryat Shmona—in the same neighborhood where I later lived. The terrorists slaughtered sixteen civilians, eight of them children, along with two soldiers, before being killed by Israeli security forces.

Just over one month later, another three-man terror squad belonging to Naif Hawatmeh's PLO faction slipped over the border in the middle of the night, this time into the town of Ma'alot. The terrorists sneaked into an apartment building and murdered an Israeli family in their beds. Later they killed two Arab women passing by on their way to work. Finally, the Palestinian squad seized the Ma'alot high school. They held nearly one hundred Israeli teenagers and several adults hostage for most of the day until soldiers stormed the school, shooting to death the three Palestinian terrorists. As they were being attacked the terrorists lobbed hand grenades at their youthful prisoners, killing twenty teenagers. About seventy others were wounded. In all, ten terror attacks in the north and center of Israel during 1974 left fifty-nine people dead and hundreds wounded.

The Jewish state suffered its worst terror assault on March 11, 1978. Thirteen Fatah commandos set sail from south Lebanon and landed on Israel's Mediterranean coast near Kibbutz Magen Michael, south of Haifa. There they seized control of a taxi and two civilian buses after shooting dead a female American tourist on the beach. Eleven terrorists were eventually killed, a few when one of their comrades set off an incendiary bomb in the bus. The lives of thirty-three Israeli civilians and two soldiers were taken by Arafat's men. A year later four Fatah terrorists seized hostages in an apartment in the coastal border resort of Nahariya, which was also frequently shelled by the PLO from Lebanon. Three Israeli civilians and a policeman were killed before police shot and killed two of the terrorists. Another attack was launched against the town during 1979, leaving three more Israelis dead.

Undoubtedly the most widely reported terrorist attack outside of Israel occurred at the 1972 Summer Olympic Games in Munich, West Germany. The building housing Israeli athletes was taken over by eight heavily armed PLO terrorists, all members of Arafat's Fatah faction. Two Israelis, a coach and a weightlifter, were killed in the process. Viewers around the globe were glued to their television sets as the PLO gunmen, demanding the release of two notorious German terrorist leaders and more than two hundred Arab inmates incarcerated in Israeli jails, held nine Israelis hostage for seventeen hours.

After the kidnappers and their hostages were transported to a nearby air base, German snipers opened fire. In the ensuing melee, five terrorists and all nine Israeli hostages were killed. The three captured Fatah terrorists were released from jail one month later, after Palestinian gunmen demanding their release hijacked a German Lufthansa airplane.

Arafat's Fatah group, splinter PLO factions, and several Palestinian breakaway groups conducted many other terror attacks along the Israel-Lebanon border, elsewhere in Israel, and abroad. The overseas attacks usually had international communist and Arab backing, along with occasional support from non-Arab terror groups like the Japanese Red Army, whose members had killed twenty-six people at Ben Gurion Airport in a 1972 operation coordinated with the Popular Front Palestinian group. Most of the attacks were planned in Lebanon.

Ironically, almost all of the overseas casualties were neither Israelis nor Jews. The U.S. ambassador to Sudan and his deputy were gunned down in 1973 on what American intelligence officials said were orders from Arafat. Planes were hijacked, airports shot up, restaurants and synagogues blown up. Hundreds of people were killed in these attacks, which the terror groups said were legitimate nationalist acts in line with the Palestinian Charter declaration that armed struggle is the only way to liberate Palestine. Inter-Palestinian killings between rival group members left many Arabs dead as well.

## THE LEBANON WAR

By 1982 most Israelis had had enough of Palestinian terror attacks around the world, not to mention infiltrations and bombings of northern Israel from Lebanon. Israeli leaders decided to launch a "clean-out" operation against the PLO ministate in southern Lebanon, from where most of the terror assaults were either planned or launched.

After a Palestinian terrorist belonging to the PLO-breakaway Abu Nidal group shot and critically wounded Shlomo Argov, Israel's ambassador to Britain, on June 3, 1982, Prime Minister Menachem Begin convened his cabinet. After a brief discussion Begin decided to order air strikes against Palestinian targets near Beirut. The PLO responded by renewing full-scale shelling of northern Israel, halted the previous summer after American mediation. The Israeli premier then asked his cabinet ministers to authorize "Operation Peace for Galilee," a military campaign designed to dislodge the PLO from south Lebanon.

I wasn't aware of Argov's shooting, or that Israeli jets had struck Palestinian positions, when I arrived at Kiryat Shmona's nearly empty central bus station on the evening of June 4. I did note that the few Israelis who rode with me into town closely followed news reports over the radio. But the reports were in Hebrew, which I still did not understand very well, and I didn't bother to ask anyone what was going on. I caught another bus to the small border town of Metulla, where I was to spend the night at the home of Voice of Hope manager Chuck Pollack before crossing over into Lebanon to work at the station the next morning.

Before too long I discovered—with a bang—what was happening. As the nearly empty bus passed an apple grove just outside Metulla, a loud explosion filled the air. The sound was quite familiar to me. Stunned, I looked up at my fellow passengers to catch their reactions. They seemed calm even though all realized a Soviet-built Katuysha rocket had just landed not far from the bus. As we entered Metulla, rockets began falling like hailstones all around us. (We later learned that the PLO was using a newly delivered North Korean multiple launcher that could fire forty rockets at a time.) Due to the heavy shelling, the bus driver kindly let me off right in front of Chuck's house. As I disembarked, a rocket landed on the sidewalk only fifty feet in front of the bus—in fact, probably just next to where it would have been if we had not stopped.

I found Chuck alone at home, busy talking via two-way radio to the station across the border. "Why don't you join the others in the bomb shelter?" he suggested, as calmly as if he were directing me to the bathroom.

"Not until you tell me what's going on!" I demanded.

"Oh, it's just the war we've all been expecting," he replied, turning his attention back to the radio conversation.

The first Israeli war casualty occurred within an hour. A local man, driving on the very road I had just traveled on, died when shrapnel from an exploding PLO Katuysha struck him in the neck.

Prime Minister Begin thought he was authorizing a limited operation to push the PLO out of southern Lebanon. His defense minister, Ariel Sharon, had other ideas, which were apparently soon accepted by Begin. The former general and hero of the Six Day War wanted the PLO entirely out of Lebanon, followed by the installation of a friendly Christian government in Beirut that would sign a formal peace treaty with Israel. Of course, such goals would mean the Israeli operation would have to be much larger than originally conceived, pitting the Israeli defense forces against the Syrians, as well as the PLO. And so it was.

Fortunately, I wasn't yet news director at the Voice of Hope when Israeli forces poured across the border the first week of June. There was a lot of news to report—too much, in fact, to properly keep up with. And much of the news happened literally just outside our doorstep. However, we didn't necessarily report everything we saw. It was, after all, wartime.

The main Israeli route into the Bekaa Valley, where Israeli forces took on the Syrians, ran right past the station. During one of my evening newscasts I reported that "Beirut radio stations say Israel is reinforcing its tank and armor forces in the southern Bekaa Valley." I wondered with amusement how clearly my listeners could hear the loud rumble in the background as Israeli tanks and armored vehicles slowly made their way past the station on their way to the Bekaa Valley!

Many of the air battles between Israeli and Syrian jet fighters took place in our neighborhood. One would suddenly hear a loud explosion and glance up to see smoke pouring from a warplane—most of them Soviet-built Syrian MIGs—which would then come tumbling out of the sky. The remains of one such jet landed just a few hundred yards behind the station. Charbel Younis, the Voice of Hope's Lebanese chief engineer, ran out with several other staff members to see if anything could be salvaged. They found the tail-end of the plane still very much intact and hauled it up to place on display in the radio station's foyer. A picture of the station's Syrian trophy later appeared in *Newsweek* magazine.

Charbel was especially pleased to discover certain parts inside the tail that he needed to repair the station's radio transmitter. "I ordered these parts a long time ago from the States," announced the portly engineer with a big grin stretched across his face, "and finally they've arrived—via air mail from Moscow!"

Charbel's comment struck me as a bit odd in light of the fact that someone had obviously just lost his life in the shoot-down. Yet I soon discovered that the only way many Lebanese could cope with the ugly violence and intense hatred in their country was to try to keep their sense of humor alive.

The original Israeli goal of expelling the PLO from south Lebanon was accomplished with lightning-like speed, with the Israelis pursuing the PLO up the coast toward Beirut. The leader of the Israeli-funded and trained Free Lebanese Forces militia, Major Saad Hadad, who spoke regularly over the Voice of Hope to friend and foe alike (to the latter in words not usually heard on a religious radio station, which led to some moral qualms among us Westerners at the station), was welcomed with roses and kisses as he toured local Christian and Muslim villages and towns—finally freed from the hated PLO grip.

By mid-June the battle had moved to Beirut, with quiet prevailing in the Bekaa Valley after a cease-fire went into effect between Israeli and Syrian forces on June 11. Peace had come to the south for the first time in many years. Israeli tour buses quickly appeared on south Lebanese roads taking excited visitors to see the sights of the recent fighting. Joyous south Lebanese residents who had not ventured very far from their homes since the mid-1970s were busy visiting friends and relatives all over the area. Lebanese friends invited me to join them in festive meals. How good it was to eat the traditional, elaborate Lebanese dishes free of worry that PLO shells might come raining down at any moment! Lebanese families north of the border enclave—frequent recipients of return Israeli and south Lebanese militia shelling—also undoubtedly enjoyed their newfound peace.

## MANY VERSIONS OF THE TRUTH

But the situation was anything but a picnic in the rest of Lebanon. As fighting continued around Beirut, world opinion turned sharply against Israel. For the first time in her short history, Israel appeared to be the aggressor, surrounding and cutting off one of the Arab world's leading cities. Widespread media reports describing "indiscriminate" Israeli shelling of Beirut brought international condemnation, even from Washington. Menachem Begin's government in turn charged that much of the press coverage was one-sided or exaggerated, coming from journalists living under the thumb of the PLO and Syria.

Having spoken to many people who were in the Lebanese capital at the time, I believe Begin had a fair basis for his charge, even though Israel was certainly besieging west Beirut in order to flush out PLO, Syrian, and other anti-Israeli forces. For example, colleagues from Jerusalem relate that they were with a group of Christian journalists and others who visited Beirut during the fighting. While at a Maronite monastery on a hill overlooking the city, someone in the party turned on his radio to hear the BBC correspondent report that "Beirut is in flames as a result of indiscriminate Israeli shelling." However, the visitors could clearly see that very few fires smoldered in the city, which had been calm for many hours.

Had the BBC correspondent recorded his report while sitting in the Commodore Hotel, where most journalists hung out, based on information fed him by young Palestinian stringers who had an obvious interest in exaggerating reports of Israeli shelling? Or did he just *think* he saw flames everywhere, not having the clear view that the Jerusalem visitors had? Or was it an old report, being played over again by the BBC? Whatever it was, it did not reflect the reality the group saw with their own eyes that day in Beirut.

*New York Times* correspondent Thomas Friedman, who was stationed in Beirut during the siege, admits that intimidation played a role in shaping what foreign journalists reported. "No discussion about the reality of Beirut reporting would be complete without mentioning a major reporting constraint journalists there faced: physical intimidation," wrote Friedman in his book *From Beirut to Jerusalem*.[34]

He adds that, in his opinion, Syria and its Palestinian allies posed the biggest threat, noting that agents operating for them shot and killed several Western and Arab journalists during the 1970s and early 1980s. "The situation got so bad that many Lebanese were afraid to even mention the word Syria in public."[35] Friedman doesn't add the obvious: Journalists must have had the same reservations in their news reports—if they valued their own skins!

The award-winning American journalist reports that "the main PLO factions, the Phalangists (the main Christian militia), and the various Muslim militias were less direct, and much less touchy than the Syrians, but no one had any illusions that they would tolerate much seriously critical reporting."[36] Although Friedman mentions the east Beirut-based Christian forces in the same breath with the PLO and Muslim militias, he earlier notes that most foreign journalists were based in west Beirut, controlled by Syria and its Muslim and PLO allies. Therefore, the greatest intimidation reporters faced obviously came from anti-Israeli groups.

Friedman tells his readers very candidly that "for any Beirut-based correspondent, the name of the game was keeping on good terms with the PLO," after admitting that "the Western press coddled the PLO and never judged it with anywhere near the scrutiny that it judged Israeli, Phalangist, or American behavior."[37] And no wonder! The *Times* bureau chief recalls that he asked for an interview with Yasser Arafat in the midst of the Israeli siege in July 1982. Arafat's spokesman insisted that Friedman's colleague Bill Farrell conduct it, since Friedman is Jewish. The spokesman finally changed his mind, but not before telling Friedman that "I have asked our office in New York for a complete assessment of all your reporting on us."

The young correspondent admits that the remark caused him great paranoia, as it would anyone who values his life! After receiving the assessment, the PLO spokesman told Friedman that his reporting was not good enough. The tense encounter between the two men ended with the spokesman telling a Palestinian stringer who worked for the *Times* that "we know he's not bad. We just need a little more from him."[38]

As a journalist working in southern Lebanon during the war, I often read and heard what I knew to be one-sided or exaggerated reports on the fighting, none of which were ever in Israel's favor. Naturally I had sympathy for my colleagues in west Beirut, having faced some intimidation myself from leftist Lebanese and PLO groups. Yet I also had to empathize with Israeli frustration over exaggerated media coverage. I knew that the average reader and listener overseas had no way to verify fairly accurate Israeli charges that the Beirut press often slanted the news in order to please Syria and its PLO, leftist, and Muslim allies.

Still, unfair reporting does not change the by-now-obvious fact that Israel not only lost international prestige by besieging Beirut but also failed to make any long-term political or military gains as a result. While Sharon's goal of expelling the PLO from the entire country was widely supported in Israel, even by many in the Labor Party, his confidence that a lasting peace treaty was achievable between Israel and Lebanon was a pipe dream at best, since "Lebanon" was by 1982 basically two countries: one dominated by Maronite Christians and the other by Syria through its Palestinian Druze, Shiite, and Sunni Muslim allies.

While the Christian side might—and in 1983 did—sign an American-mediated peace treaty with Israel, the Muslim side, under Syria's thumb, would obviously oppose it, which it did, leading to the treaty's abrogation several months later. Had Israel pushed the Syrians entirely out of Lebanon, as Sharon wanted to do, a lasting peace accord might have been possible. The Israeli defense minister probably would have pursued this goal if not for United States opposition. From day one America pressured Israel to refrain from attacking Syrian positions, apparently afraid that an all-out Israeli assault could drag the U.S. into a confrontation with Syrian President Assad's Soviet backers.

As the siege of Beirut continued, Israeli public support for the war weakened. Charges flew that Ariel Sharon had deceived the government and the people about his ultimate intentions in Lebanon. Prime Minister Begin admitted that his cabinet had not originally envisaged a total PLO expulsion from Lebanon when it approved Operation Peace for Galilee. Still, he went along with Sharon's move to Beirut, agreeing with his defense minister that prospects for peace in the region would improve if the PLO were no longer dominating any part of the country. Most Lebanese whom I spoke with at the time, including many Muslims, were hopeful that the PLO would indeed be pushed out of their homeland, along with the Syrians, whose ongoing and overwhelming presence was increasingly resented.

Palestinian fighters and Syrian troops began evacuating Beirut in late August after several months of heavy artillery exchanges with Israeli forces. Portions of the once-great capital city lay in ruins. Palestinian refugee camps from which PLO fighters had operated were largely destroyed. PLO gunmen fled to Syrian-controlled territory north of Beirut (the Israelis basically let them escape).

A multinational force made up of American, French, and Italian Marines oversaw the separation of hostile Lebanese forces in the city after the PLO evacuation. Finally, following several months of intense battles and many casualties, relative calm returned to Beirut, and the process of repairing the war damage got under way.

In Washington the Reagan administration, upset that its ally had sunk so deep in the Lebanese mud, was busy all summer devising new proposals to end the Arab-Israeli conflict. The Reagan Plan was unveiled on September 1. It proposed a Palestinian "entity" in the West Bank and Gaza Strip, linked to Jordan. Jewish settlement activity would be frozen, with the final status of the settlements to be determined by negotiations, along with the future of east Jerusalem. The plan did not support the establishment of an independent Palestinian state, and it opposed Israeli annexation of the territories.

Prime Minister Begin was not exactly thrilled with President Reagan's plan, still hoping local Palestinians would negotiate on the basis of his

Camp David autonomy plan. He rejected the Reagan Plan on September 2. Arab leaders, meeting in Fez, Morocco, one week later, also rejected the proposal. They called for three conditions: a total Israeli pullout from all areas captured in 1967, including east Jerusalem and the Golan Heights; the complete dismantling of all Jewish settlements; and the establishment of a PLO-controlled Palestinian state with Jerusalem as its capital. The Fez resolution was the death knell of Israeli hopes that Jordan would once again play a governing role in the territories as part of an overall peace settlement. The PLO welcomed the Fez summit statement.

As political moves intensified, Israeli forces were busy digging in opposite the Syrians in the Bekaa Valley. The Kremlin was busy doubling the number of Soviet "advisers" in Syria to about five thousand. To compensate for not actively backing its ally in the earlier fighting, the Soviets also delivered substantial quantities of new missiles and planes. Occasional skirmishes took place over the next several years in the Bekaa, but both well-equipped armies seemed eager to keep away from renewed full-scale fighting. With a fresh show of Soviet support, Syria was not about to budge from Lebanon. Assad had long maintained that Lebanon was part of "greater Syria." The Syrian strongman did not accept the French mandate creation of Lebanon out of "western Syria," nor for that matter the existence of either Jordan or Israel, in what had traditionally been known, especially to Muslim Arabs, as "southern Syria."

Heavy clashes broke out around Tripoli, north of Beirut, in 1983 between Arafat's gunmen and Syrian-backed Palestinians headed by Abu Musa. President Assad had apparently decided that he, too, would like to see Arafat's PLO fighters out of Lebanon, with only Palestinians loyal to him remaining behind. He was upset that Arafat had dared to discuss the Reagan Plan with his foe to the south, King Hussein. The PLO leader was becoming too moderate for Assad, but unfortunately not nearly moderate enough for Israel. With strong Syrian support, Abu Musa's men defeated Arafat's fighters in late 1983. Hundreds of rival Palestinian gunmen and civilians were killed in the clashes. On December 23 Arafat left Tripoli for Tunis, his new headquarters.

A growing number of Israelis wanted, like Arafat, to get out of Lebanon as quickly as possible. The perception was rapidly spreading that little could be done to bring stability to the fractured, medieval-like country. Internal political pressure to withdraw increased substantially after Israeli military headquarters in Tyre was blown up by suicide bombers in November 1983, leaving sixty-one soldiers dead. Syrian-supported saboteurs claimed responsibility for the attack. This left Israeli military morale at an all-time low in the increasingly hated land of Lebanon.

United States Marines, meanwhile, made final preparations to leave Lebanon after suffering a great tragedy in October. I was on an airplane returning from a two-week vacation in London when a truck packed with explosives blasted the Marines' main barracks in Beirut, killing 241 American servicemen. U.S. officials said the attack was most likely carried out by Syrian and Iranian-supported Lebanese terrorists. I arrived at the station to discover I would be broadcasting details of a horrible terror attack involving my own countrymen. We spent the next few days reporting the sad news and trying to minister some good news to survivors who had lost buddies in the explosion. It was especially at such times that I was grateful to have the opportunity to broadcast the Lord's message of hope to hurting people in war-torn Lebanon.

## UP TO JERUSALEM!

Not long after the Marines withdrew from Lebanon, I decided it was time for me to pull out as well. My last day on the air was in February 1984. Although I had grown to love the country, I felt it was time to pursue an earlier goal: to study Hebrew in Jerusalem. I had already been offered a job in the Holy City as an overseas correspondent for IMS News, a Christian news network based in Washington, D.C. No longer would I see the Golan Heights from my living room window or get caught in traffic jams with Israeli tanks and army trucks heading north to the Lebanese border. The constant background tension always present along Israel's northern border would be exchanged for the bustle of city life in Jerusalem. I arrived on April 1, eager to unload my Volkswagen and begin a new chapter of my life in the Promised Land.

It was not long before I realized that the Arab-Israeli conflict is also played out violently in Jerusalem, the City of Peace. On April 2 three

Palestinian terrorists suddenly rushed out of a sporting goods store on Jaffa Road and King George Street—Jerusalem's busiest downtown intersection—tossing hand grenades and shooting pistols at people walking and driving nearby. One Israeli was killed and fifty-nine people were wounded, including four Palestinian passersby and ten European tourists. Police killed one of the terrorists at the scene and captured the other two.

Although my debut radio report for IMS was about terrorism, most of the stories I sent during 1984 and 1985 were related to the Israeli army pullout from Lebanon and the rapidly deteriorating Israeli economy, hit hard by the war.

As the months wore on, popular opinion in Israel increasingly supported an immediate withdrawal from what had commonly become known as the "Lebanese quagmire." The cost of keeping soldiers in Lebanon helped fuel the inflation rate, which soared to an incredible 450 percent during 1984. Although a majority of the six hundred Israeli soldiers who had been killed by October of that year died during the first few months of the war, roadside bombs and other acts of sabotage continued to take their toll.

The Israeli National Unity Government, a coalition formed after Israel's two main parties, Labor and Likud, came out basically even in elections held during the summer of 1984, voted to withdraw Israeli forces in stages. The last remaining soldiers said farewell to the area north of the security buffer zone in the spring of 1985.

Another major story that I covered during this period was an extremely controversial Arab-Israeli prisoner exchange. On May 20, 1985, Israeli leaders announced to a stunned nation that they had agreed to swap 1,150 Arab terrorists imprisoned in Israeli jails for three Israeli soldiers being held captive in Lebanon. Among the 1,150 were perpetrators of some of the worst terror attacks against Israel. The lopsided exchange—an expression of the high value Israel places on each and every soldier's life—was denounced by many politicians as a blatant surrender to terrorism, even though all welcomed the soldiers' release.

Charges of sellout were repeated just over a month later when Lebanese Shiite terrorists hijacked an American TWA jet and forced it to land in Beirut. The hijackers demanded the release of an additional 766

Arab prisoners being held in an Israeli detention center. Israeli leaders complied with the demand, prompting more charges that they had lost their will to fight terrorism. Possibly as a result of the outcry, Israel refused to release fifty Arab prisoners as demanded by terrorists belonging to Abul Abbas's PLO faction, who seized the Italian ship *Achille Lauro* while it was cruising the Mediterranean during October.

The TWA hijacking story, naturally of great interest to Americans, prompted CBS-affiliated Boston radio station WEEI to ask if I would send regular reports on the drama. I also supplemented WEEI's network reports of the *Achille Lauro* seizure and continued to send reports on other Middle Eastern happenings until 1987.

## BUILDUP TO BREAKDOWN

The longer I lived in Jerusalem, the more Palestinian Arabs I became acquainted with. Among them were Christian and Muslim shopkeepers in the Old City. Palestinian moneychangers helped me exchange my hard-earned dollars for daily deteriorating Israeli shekels (one changed money frequently, but in as small an amount as possible during those days of hyperinflation). Good friends of mine, an American Christian couple who worked at a Bethlehem evangelistic center, introduced me to quite a few Palestinian young men, both Christians and Muslims, including one who became my new Volkswagen mechanic.

The young Palestinians I befriended described in detail some of the difficult problems they had to wrestle with. Although officially Jordanian citizens, they were basically stateless people—surrounded by Israelis and yet not citizens of Israel; using Jordanian currency and passports, and yet not living any more in Jordanian-controlled territory. I understood their frustration at having to get Israeli approval for almost any act of consequence, including travel abroad. I felt their anger and hurt at being the objects of constant suspicion in the eyes of soldiers who frequently patrolled the town where Jesus was born almost two thousand years ago. I sympathized with them over the humiliation they felt when stopped and questioned while driving or riding into their own hometown—often by soldiers not exactly the epitome of politeness. I listened quietly as they expressed grief over the death and imprisonment of loved ones participating in the often-violent struggle to break away from Israeli control.

While fully appreciating their dilemma, I nonetheless urged my Palestinian friends to consider the evidence that violence only leads to more violence. I pointed out that their personal stories, while painful and sad, are also a part of the wider Arab-Israeli conflict, which has led to loss of life and hardships for many Jews as well. Root responsibility for their bad situation should not necessarily be pinned only on the Israelis, I suggested. While some of my Palestinian friends, especially Christians, did agree that violence is not the answer to their perplexing problems, I found very few who would entertain the notion that internal Palestinian and external Arab actions over the years might have contributed to their stateless situation.

Most Palestinians and Israelis, along with local and foreign journalists, sensed that an explosion was coming in the West Bank and Gaza Strip long before the Palestinian uprising broke out in December 1987. The Palestinian population of the areas was mushrooming, largely because of the high Muslim birth rate. The areas captured by Israel twenty years earlier (excluding the Golan Heights) had also become home to almost 75,000 Israeli Jews living in more than two hundred settlements, a majority of them built since 1977.

Most of the West Bank settlers were living in what amounted to urban suburbs of Tel Aviv and Jerusalem. The vast majority had not moved to the new bedroom communities for ideological reasons, but because housing was more affordable than in the big cities. Clashes occurred frequently between Jewish settlers—especially the 15 percent or so who lived in outlying settlements—and Palestinians.

Labor leaders had allowed settlement only in certain areas in accordance with the Allon Plan, despite the belief most of them held that Israel had a legal right to settle in all portions of what was Mandatory Palestine.[39] But Likud leaders promoted Jewish settlement throughout the territories, although heavily populated Arab areas were usually avoided. Despite the fact that the settlers were only a small percentage of the overall population, and for the most part living on hilltops and other areas that had been empty of Arab inhabitants, local Palestinians realized that any

Jewish presence strengthened Israel's hold on the territories and made a future total withdrawal unlikely. While Labor leaders spoke of territorial compromise and at least a partial pullout, the Likud Party clearly had no intention of evacuating any portion of the Gaza Strip or Judea and Samaria—as most Israelis called the hilly areas even before "West Bank" became a misnomer when Jordan in effect rescinded its annexation in 1988.

Likud leaders, along with many in the Labor Party, believe that the Arabs forfeited any legal claim over the territories when they rejected the United Nations partition plan in 1947. Israel's legal right to remain in the areas is strong, they maintain, since Jews were permitted to settle throughout Palestine, including in the hills of Judea and Samaria, under the original British Mandate, approved by the League of Nations. Several places, especially east Jerusalem and Hebron, have long held Jewish communities, they note, adding that Jerusalem, Bethlehem, Hebron, and Nablus (biblical Shechem) were Jewish towns long before Arabs settled in them.

Another factor that strengthens Israel's right to hold on to Judea and Samaria, say Likud leaders and others, is that the hilly areas were captured during the Six Day War after Jordanian forces launched attacks from there upon the tiny Jewish state, as they had in 1948.

Israeli government legal experts reject the term *occupied territories* since the West Bank and Gaza Strip did not legally belong to sovereign nations when they came under Israeli control. The areas were under Turkish control until the British pushed out the Turks in World War I, they point out. Britain then controlled the Holy Land until Israel assumed sovereignty over part of the area in 1948. The other portions are disputed, they note, with Israel's claim over them quite strong since it is based on historic rights, the League of Nations Mandate, and on the Arab rejection of the partition plan. Jordan's annexation of Judea and Samaria was not recognized by the Arab states or the larger world community. Egypt didn't even attempt to claim sovereignty over the Gaza Strip, which it controlled at the time of the Six Day War.

Referring to the areas as "occupied territories" implies that they will someday revert to the previous nations that held sovereignty over them. Does that mean Turkey will regain control, they ask, or possibly Great

Britain? Since the answer is obviously no, the areas should at most be referred to as "disputed territories."

Palestinians obviously reject these Israeli positions. They insist that Zionism was an illegitimate movement from the beginning, as stated in the PLO Charter and confirmed by the 1975 U.N. equation of Zionism with racism. Judaism is a religion with no nationalistic traits, and therefore Jews have no claim on the soil of Palestine. Every inch, not only the West Bank and Gaza Strip, is Arab territory.

Despite these widely held views, many Palestinians gradually came to accept that Israel does in fact exist, if not that it has a right to exist, but certainly not that Jews have any right to settle in the West Bank, including east Jerusalem, or the Gaza Strip.

It was from east Jerusalem that King Hussein launched the 1967 Jordanian attack that led to the capture of his "West Bank." The subsequent Israeli annexation of east Jerusalem did not automatically convey citizenship on Arab residents of the city, but did entitle them to choose that option and to vote in municipal elections and travel freely throughout Israel (their vehicles have the same yellow license plates as Israeli Jews and Arabs, while the Palestinians in the territories have blue plates).

After Menachem Begin came to power, several new Jewish suburbs were built around the city, mostly on land captured from the Jordanians. The growing Jewish presence naturally upset many Palestinians, especially those living in villages adjoining the new suburbs. By 2003 some 180,000 Jews resided in neighborhoods constructed on land captured from Jordan in 1967.

By the time Israelis were making final preparations for their state's fortieth birthday celebrations in May 1988, the Arab population of the West Bank and Gaza Strip had swollen to around 1.5 million. Another 140,000 lived in annexed east Jerusalem. Out of the estimated 850,000 people in the West Bank (the last official census was taken in 1985), some 90,000, about 12 percent of the population, were living in nineteen United Nations-run refugee camps. Most Palestinians resided in usually comfortable, but often crowded, homes located in the many towns and villages that dot the hills. Farming was the largest single occupation, followed by services and construction.

The economy of these areas was heavily tied to Israel's, with many people working in Israel or for Israeli companies operating in Judea and Samaria. The situation was similar in the Gaza Strip, except that a much higher percentage of the population, around 200,000 out of 650,000 people, were living in eight crowded and run-down refugee camps.

Israeli attempts over the years to improve the refugees' living conditions had met with both Palestinian and international resistance. The Israeli government launched a discreet camp rehabilitation program in 1972 aimed at resettling Palestinian families in new, modern apartment buildings and houses built near the camps. The United Nations, the PLO, and various Arab countries attacked the program, charging that Israel was only trying to upgrade housing and ease overcrowding in the camps in order to lessen political pressure on it to withdraw from the territories.

Israeli leaders admitted that this was one motivating factor, but said the camp residents would at least have better living conditions until an overall Arab-Israeli peace settlement could be worked out.

World resistance to the Israeli resettlement plan—coupled with PLO warnings to local Palestinians not to take up the offer—meant the program barely got off the ground. Some eight thousand families did move from Gaza Strip camps to new Israeli-financed housing between 1976 and 1978. However, most of the area's refugees continued to live in squalid, overcrowded camps. The largest camp, Jabalya, housed some sixty thousand people. It was there that hundreds of angry Arabs clashed with Israeli soldiers on December 9, 1987, signaling the start of a new phase in the holy war for the Promised Land.

# CHAPTER 9

## HOLY WAR OF STONES

I found myself increasingly bored with my work as a radio correspondent for IMS News after the Israeli withdrawal from most of Lebanon. Economics never interested me at all, yet Israel's dreadful financial situation forced me to focus almost exclusively on this very topic (although the 1984–85 Israeli Operation Moses airlift of thousands of black Ethiopian Jews to Israel provided some relief). As my boredom grew, I began thinking that it would be nice to go back to the United States for half a year or so to get reacquainted with family and friends. After nearly seven years in the turbulent Middle East, I definitely needed a break.

Just as I started to make travel arrangements, a former coworker at the Voice of Hope told me that his employer, the U.S.-based Christian Broadcasting Network, was looking for an additional newswriter for their nightly English-speaking newscast. The program was broadcast over CBN's Middle East Television (METV), located in southern Lebanon. The offer, which included training in video editing, seemed challenging. I had never before worked in television. I joined the METV Jerusalem news bureau in June 1987, deciding I would put off my visit to America for at least a year.

The METV bureau employed Americans, Canadians, and other Westerners who produced the nightly news in English. Lebanese Christians, along with a number of Israeli Arabs, Druze, and Palestinians, turned out an Arabic-language newscast. As I prepared my first news report for METV in early July, my mind kept wandering back to the early years of the television station and the role I played in keeping viewers glued to their sets in anticipation of the next . . . index card! Chuck Pollack had asked our Project Kibbutz team to come up with some nicely lettered index cards announcing the name of the new station (then under Voice of Hope ownership and called the "Star of Hope"), along with other pertinent information, such as where local Lebanese citizens could get their teeth fixed!

My teammates and I had labored over the project with great love and care, knowing that our cards could potentially build up a great audience, ready for the soon-coming day when facilities were completed to actually start broadcasting television programs! Huddled together in Hagoshrim's recreation room, we were thrilled when our own personal index card made its debut on the TV screen.

Six years later my voice was about to be heard nightly on the former Star of Hope, which had in the meantime become one of the most popular television stations in the region, reaching several million viewers in Lebanon, Syria, Israel, and Jordan.

As 1987 wore on, METV's nightly news reports contained increasing evidence of an impending explosion in the West Bank and Gaza Strip. The program carried details in April about the Palestinian firebombing of a Jewish car from the Samarian settlement of Alfei Menashe. The bomb left an Israeli woman dead and two of her children severely wounded, one of whom died in July. In response to the incident, angry Jewish settlers called for greater army protection along the roads. On August 2 we covered the slaying of a high-ranking Israeli military policeman, shot and killed by Palestinian gunmen who surrounded his car while it was stalled in heavy traffic in Gaza City. The entire Gaza Strip was subsequently sealed off for several days while a massive search was conducted for the killers.

Our main story during September was the formal ending of a nearly three-year state of war between Yasser Arafat's PLO fighters (who had slipped back into Lebanon—without their leader) and Lebanese gunmen belonging to the Shiite Amal militia. More than twenty-five hundred people, many of them Lebanese and Palestinian civilians, had been killed in the savage struggle, and some three thousand others wounded. The so-called "Camp Wars" began when the Lebanese Shiites, who felt threatened by the PLO's return to its former military positions in Beirut and south Lebanon, attacked Fatah outposts in several Palestinian refugee camps. The cease-fire agreement was a major psychological boost for the Palestinians, deeply embarrassed by the fierce inter-Arab bloodletting.

Also during September we reported on a border infiltration attempt by a coalition of leftist Lebanese and Palestinian groups backed by Syria. Three Israeli soldiers were killed when their patrol came upon the infiltrators not far from Kibbutz Hagoshrim. Soon afterward an Israeli soldier, a Dutch convert to Judaism, was brutally murdered in the area of Galilee. In early October an Israeli secret service agent was shot and killed in the Gaza Strip by members of the Islamic Jihad movement. Within a week of the Gaza killing, a Jew walking through Jerusalem's Old City was stabbed to death by Palestinian assailants.

The most important pre-uprising morale booster for the Palestinians occurred on November 24. An airborne hang glider, piloted by Syrian-backed Palestinians, sailed over the Israel-Lebanon border and quietly landed not far from Hagoshrim. The Palestinians made their way to a nearby army base where they killed six Israeli soldiers and wounded eight others before being killed themselves. The attack was hailed as a great victory by Palestinians both inside the territories and abroad. The once seemingly invincible Israeli army, whose image was so badly tarnished in Lebanon, was proving to be quite vulnerable even inside the Jewish state.

## THE PALESTINIAN UPRISING

By early December almost any spark could have set off the violent explosion that occurred in the Gaza Strip on December 9. Three days before, an Israeli shopper was stabbed to death in Gaza City. The strip had been a favorite shopping area for many Israeli bargain seekers, especially for those needing auto repairs and spare parts. The following evening, December 7, a private Israeli vehicle was involved in a traffic accident with a van carrying Palestinians from the Jabalya refugee camp. The accident left four of the van's Arab passengers dead.

Rumors soon spread that the Israeli vehicle had deliberately collided with the van in order to kill Palestinians in revenge for the December 6 stabbing (a charge the Israeli driver called absurd). Disturbances broke out on December 8 and large-scale rioting a day later. Israeli army reinforcements rushed in to join the vastly outnumbered soldiers who regularly patrolled the camp. One Palestinian was killed and sixteen others wounded before some semblance of calm was restored. The following day, December 10, violence spread to other parts of the Gaza Strip, and then to the West Bank. The uprising's flame had been lit.

The Palestinian revolt, often referred to as the *intifada* (an Arabic word meaning "shaking off" of Israeli rule), caught the army off guard. Israel's highly trained fighters, who fourteen years earlier had proved capable of repulsing a two-front surprise attack backed by the Soviet Union, suddenly found themselves confronting not enemy soldiers, but young adults, teenagers, and sometimes even preteens armed mainly with stones, broken bottles, and an occasional firebomb.

Such objects, along with building blocks and sharp metal objects, injured many Israeli soldiers and civilians, and even killed a few. Yet it was still morally and militarily impossible to fight Palestinian civilians as one would the Syrian or Egyptian armies. This fact frustrated both the soldiers and their commanders—all the way up to Israeli Defense Minister Yitzhak Rabin, an old soldier himself who had served as prime minister in the mid-1970s.

Rabin knew that Syria's Hafez Assad had not hesitated to brutally murder some fifteen to twenty thousand of his own citizens in 1982 when Muslim fundamentalists staged a revolt in the northern Syrian city of Hama. He remembered that King Hussein had ruthlessly crushed a PLO rebellion against Jordanian rule in 1970, leaving untold thousands of Palestinians dead. The defense minister publicly recalled that thousands of Palestinians had died in intercommunal and PLO-Shiite battles in Lebanon during the 1980s.

But none of these previous examples of how the Arab world deals with its internal disputes mattered, said Rabin, because Israel was a democracy, and a state heavily influenced by the moralistic principles of Judaism. The ways and means of Israel's neighbors would not be applied by Rabin or his superior, Prime Minister Yitzhak Shamir.

Shamir's mid-December prediction that the uprising would end soon failed to materialize. In fact, the rioting intensified, and Palestinian casualties mounted. Few world leaders called for the Palestinians to end their violent revolt; many apparently felt it was justified. But almost all condemned Israel for sometimes using live ammunition against the protesters.

In the face of growing international criticism, Rabin ordered new, less lethal riot-control measures in early January 1988—measures he hoped would reduce Palestinian deaths. The death toll from army gunfire did indeed drop. But to many observers, including Israeli critics, the new measures, which permitted beating stone throwers and petrol-bomb throwers caught running away from pursuing soldiers, seemed to partially resemble the methods used by Israel's Arab neighbors.

Whatever his intentions, Rabin's "might and beatings" policy only led to a greater worldwide outcry against Israel, particularly after several Palestinians were beaten to death. The defense minister and senior army officers quickly realized that they had not sufficiently spelled out the limits of permitted physical force, leaving it up to young, often frustrated soldiers to decide how many blows were enough. The beatings policy was modified, and a number of soldiers were court-martialed for excessive use of force, with most claiming that they were only obeying orders. However, isolated cases of Palestinians being physically abused by soldiers and security personnel continued long after the policy was changed.

Within several weeks of the uprising's outbreak, the PLO was taking charge of the popular rebellion by means of the Unified Leadership of the Palestinian Uprising, a coalition of Arafat's Fatah movement, the Syrian-aligned Popular and Democratic Front PLO groups, and the outlawed Palestine Communist Party. But it was apparent to Israeli leaders that the divided PLO was not the primary force behind the uprising, which had spread to all parts of the West Bank and Gaza Strip by mid-December. The main propellant was the Palestinians' own pent-up frustration and anger over their continuing statelessness, directed primarily at Israel, but also, at least privately, against the always-feuding PLO and Arab states that had failed over two decades to make any progress toward pushing the Israelis back into their unofficial, pre-1967 borders.

## ISLAM LEADS THE REVOLT

The first Palestinian groups to harness and direct these emotions were two Gaza Strip–based Muslim fundamentalist movements: Islamic Jihad and the Muslim Brotherhood movement. The groups quickly declared the spreading revolt to be the latest phase of the jihad against Israel and began mobilizing support for the rebellion from mosques throughout the strip.

The small but militant Islamic Jihad, founded in 1979 in the wake of the Islamic revolution in Iran, openly engaged in terror attacks against Israelis. The more moderate Muslim Brotherhood movement, active in the Holy Land since the 1940s, had actually been aided by the Israeli government in its campaign to bring Islam to Gaza's Palestinians. The number of mosques in the strip had doubled to approximately 180 in the three years prior to the uprising, partially due to financial assistance from the Israeli government's Religious Affairs Ministry. Israeli analysts say the aid was handed out largely in an attempt to strengthen the Islamic movement in the area, thus hopefully weakening support for the Soviet-backed PLO. The Israeli action reflected the Reagan administration's strong support for Islamic groups fghting Russian forces in Afghanistan.

Several Israeli experts on Islam warned officials that they were playing with fire in aiding the Muslim fundamentalists. In the end, they predicted, Islam would prove to be a more potent and intractable force than the PLO or other mostly secular Palestinian groups. The Islamic element had always loomed large in past Arab resistance to the state of Israel and could become the dominant force once again, especially in light of the Khomeini-inspired Muslim fundamentalist resurgence. They said Islamic militancy had been on the rise throughout the Middle East ever since the 1967 Six Day War. Nasser's humiliating defeat at the hands of Israel had dealt a severe blow to the Egyptian leader's basically secular pan-Arab movement and to the idea that secularist governments could crush the Jewish "infidels."

The experts noted that the Egyptian-based Muslim Brotherhood movement, founded in 1928 and suppressed by Nasser, had never renounced its aim of destroying the Jewish state. The group had only declared a "truce" with Israel in order to educate the masses for the day when full-scale jihad was formally resumed.

Even though almost all Palestinian Muslims belong to the dominant Sunni wing of Islam, the Israeli experts warned that the Iranian Shiite Muslim revolt was having a deep impact on many Palestinians, who admired the fervent religious devotion shown by Khomeini's followers. Palestinian Muslims were also thankful for the Iranian leader's frequent pledges to confront the "Zionist occupation of the Muslim holy land"— with special mention always given to the sacred mosques in Jerusalem.

Many Palestinians were also encouraged by Khomeini's support for the Hizbullah, or Party of Allah, movement, which frequently attacked Israeli forces and their Lebanese allies in Israel's security zone. The movement, whose members are mostly poor Lebanese Shiites from the Bekaa Valley and south Beirut, had been set up after the 1982 war under the supervision of Khomeini's Iranian Revolutionary Guards. To show their support for the uprising, hundreds of Hizbullah fighters, backed by Shiite gunmen from the Amal movement, simultaneously attacked eight South Lebanese army outposts on December 21, 1987, the same day that one of the first uprising general strikes was being observed in the territories. Hizbullah and allied groups are widely believed to have been behind the kidnapping in Lebanon of several dozen foreigners, including Americans, during the latter half of the 1980s.

By mid-1988 the Fatah-dominated "Unified Leadership" realized they had strong competitors in the Islamic groups. They launched a campaign to convince local Palestinians that the PLO was as dedicated to Islamic values, including holy war, as any other liberation movement. Uprising leaders pointed out that many PLO officials, including Yasser Arafat, were observant Muslims in good standing. Arafat was one of the first foreign visitors to fly to Tehran after Khomeini seized power, they noted. On top of this, the PLO, at a 1981 Islamic summit conference held in Saudi Arabia, had enthusiastically endorsed a thirty-eight-nation proclamation of "full jihad" against Israel, with Arafat personally urging a "general mobilization for jihad."

The PLO leader repeated his support for jihad in a fiery, anti-American speech given in Khartoum, Sudan, on October 15, 1985 (just after the seizure of the *Achille Lauro*), saying that "the will of the Arab nation is the will of Allah, and therefore, the Arab nation will be victorious."

Islam had always played an important role in the PLO's struggle to liberate Palestine, argued uprising leaders, noting that Islamic teachings were the soil from which much of the PLO's thinking and policies sprang.

## AN ISLAMIC COVENANT

PLO leaders were particularly worried over the growing power of a militant offshoot of the Muslim Brotherhood movement called the Islamic Resistance movement. The group, formed shortly after the uprising began, is popularly known by the acronym *HAMAS*, Arabic for "zeal." And zeal the group has indeed displayed! HAMAS leaders formally adopted jihad against Israel as their central tenet. Islamic Resistance leaders stated clearly that they considered the Palestinian uprising the first step in the renewed Islamic holy war to "liberate every part of Palestine," not just the West Bank and Gaza Strip.

In August 1988 HAMAS published its founding charter. The forty-page document, which many saw as an Islamic Palestinian alternative to the PLO's official charter, was widely distributed in the territories. An audiocassette version was also handed out, mainly to illiterate Palestinians.

The HAMAS covenant begins with several verses from the Koran that condemn the Jews because they do not believe in Allah. Former Egyptian Muslim Brotherhood leader Imam Hassan al-Bana is then quoted: "Israel will exist and continue to exist until Islam eliminates it, just as it eliminated what preceded it" (a reference to the defeat of the crusader kingdom).

Next comes the covenant's main introduction, spelling out the structure and goals of the Islamic Resistance movement, which "links arms with all warriors of the jihad for the liberation of Palestine." It calls for "Arab and world Islamic assistance, support and commitment" in the effort to destroy Israel, because "our war against the Jews is a great and serious undertaking which requires mobilization of all resources . . . until the enemy is overthrown."

The covenant's thirty-six articles detail the movement's holy war program. Following are some of the HAMAS covenant's main points:

Article 6 says HAMAS is "working to unfurl the banner of Allah over every inch of Palestine." It then goes on to promise that total Islamic control will not hurt non-Muslims, who will be "protected" by the Muslim authorities as they were down through the centuries.

Article 7 states that HAMAS is a "link in the chain of jihad against the Zionist invasion." It "looks forward to the fulfillment of Allah's promises in the not-too-distant future." The article ends with a well-known Islamic *hadith*, or Muslim oral teaching, attributed to the prophet Muhammad: "The day will come when Muslims will fight the Jews and kill them, to the degree that the Jew will hide behind the rocks and trees which will call out to the Muslim and tell him, 'Servant of Allah, a Jew is hiding behind me. Come and kill him!'"

Article 8 endorses martyrdom in the name of the holy jihad: "Allah is the ultimate objective of HAMAS, his messenger Muhammad its touchstone, the Koran its constitution, jihad its path, and death for the sake of Allah its chief interest."

Article 11 spells out the official HAMAS position regarding the present and future status of the Holy Land: "The Islamic Resistance Movement considers that Palestine is Islamic *Waqf* (religious trust) land assigned to the Muslims until the end of time. It may not be renounced or conceded, whether in whole or in part. . . . This is stipulated in the Islamic Shira (law). Palestine is to be treated like all lands forcibly conquered by the Muslims."

Article 13 states that "initiatives, so-called peaceful solutions, and international conferences to solve the Palestinian problem contradict the principles of the Islamic Resistance Movement. Renouncing any part of Palestine is equivalent to renouncing part of the religion. . . . There is no solution to the Palestinian problem except through jihad. Initiatives, proposals, and international conferences are a waste of time and entirely useless. Such conferences are no more than the appointment of infidels as judges over Muslim land. When have infidels ever dealt justly with the faithful?" The article then paraphrases a relevant passage from the Koran: "The Jews and Christians will never be satisfied until you join their communities" (Sura of the Cow, 120). Israeli analysts say Articles 11 and 13 are direct condemnations of the PLO's phased program, which calls for a Palestinian state in the territories as the first step in the overthrow of the Jewish state.

Articles 14 through 19 call upon Muslim educators to instruct the Muslim masses about the need for all-out jihad against Israel. The articles also detail the role of women in the Islamic jihad. The Islamic mother is encouraged to stay home and "educate her children to obey the religious precepts, as preparation for the task that awaits them in the holy struggle."

Articles 20 and 22 reveal the deep prejudices and anti-Semitism that form the basis for much of the continuing widespread Palestinian opposition to the existence of Israel in any part of "sacred Palestine." The former begins with a call for the "Islamic spirit" to "prevail throughout Muslim society, to counteract the scheming enemy with his Nazi conduct." It says that "Jewish Nazism" does not "spare women or children" and aims to destroy Palestinian livelihood.

Article 22 echoes more traditional forms of anti-Semitism, ironically in terms that mirror the very Nazi movement HAMAS tries to equate with modern Israel: "The enemies . . . have labored to amass astounding and influential material wealth, which has been exploited to realize their dream. They have used their wealth to gain control of the world media, news agencies, the press, broadcasting stations, etc." The Jews are said to have been "behind the French and Communist revolutions" and have "used their wealth to set up clandestine organizations to destroy society and serve the interests of Zionism." Such groups are said to include "the Freemasons, the Rotary, Lions Club, and B'nai B'rith. All these organizations engage in espionage and destruction."

After gaining control of the "imperialist states," the Jews are said to have "instigated World War I" in order to secure the Balfour Declaration from Britain. Next they "set up the League of Nations in order to rule the world." The "world Jewish conspiracy" also "caused World War II" as a "prelude to setting up their state." After the war they "gave the instructions to establish the United Nations," again "in order to rule the world." The Jews "pull the strings of any war that is waged anywhere in the world," but will finally be overthrown when "Islam comes into its own." The fact that Jews were singled out as victims by Hitler's Nazi regime, that Israel was barely getting by financially in the 1980s, and that the United Nations regularly censures the Jewish state seems to have somehow escaped the authors of the Islamic Resistance covenant. They also ignored the fact that the "Jewish-controlled world press" has been quite critical of Israel ever since the 1982 Lebanon war.

The final fourteen articles pledge HAMAS support for all "sister organizations" struggling to "liberate Palestine," including the PLO, which is called the movement's "father, brother, kinsman and friend." Surrounding Arab states are urged to "open their borders to the warriors of the jihad." The Jews must be defeated because they seek to "destroy society and values, to annihilate conscience and virtue, and to liquidate Islam." Egyptian leaders are condemned for making peace with Israel under the tutelage of the "imperialist, crusader West," and Palestinians are warned that they shall "incur the wrath of Allah and end up in hell" if they do not fully support the jihad struggle.

During the first few months of the uprising, the PLO and Israeli authorities virtually ignored the HAMAS and Islamic Jihad movements. However, by mid-1988 the Unified Leadership was forced to take notice as the two movements, especially HAMAS, proved to have the support of many Palestinians in the Gaza Strip, along with growing numbers in the West Bank.

Several general strike days called by HAMAS were widely observed, and HAMAS pamphlets giving "guidance" to the uprising began to appear regularly alongside frequently issued Unified Leadership communiqués. Tension mounted between Islamic militants and PLO supporters, some of whom were secular Marxists, leading to violent clashes in Bethlehem and other locations. As HAMAS continued to increase in strength, Israeli officials banned the organization in May 1989 and arrested many of its leading figures.

Although a devout Muslim himself, Yasser Arafat probably was not very pleased by the results of a poll conducted by Bir Zeit University, situated near Ramallah, that was published in the *Jerusalem Post* newspaper on April 14, 1988. Pollsters asked a scientifically selected cross section of Palestinians what sort of state they wished to see established in place of Israeli military rule.

The results showed that 59 percent of West Bank Palestinians wanted to be citizens of an Islamic theocratic state. Only 33 percent supported the establishment of a democratic state, while the remaining 8 percent favored a state based on communist or socialist principles. The results would undoubtedly have been much more pro-Islamic if the poll had also been conducted in the heavily fundamentalist Gaza Strip.

The poll reflected a fact that I had long known: The average Palestinian Arab is a religiously observant Muslim who has little interest in democratic values—generally seen as Western, foreign concepts. Academic, business, and other leaders hold a more prodemocracy view. They have seen Israel's free-wheeling democracy in action, and many of them would like to emulate it.

The results of the Palestinian poll didn't surprise me. Western-style democracy is not practiced in any other Arab nation. An attempt at free elections in Algeria was thwarted by military leaders in early 1992 when antidemocratic Muslim fundamentalists appeared to be on the verge of victory, although controlled elections excluding fundamentalist candidates were held in 1997, amid much bloodshed. Why assume that democratic values will prevail in any future Palestinian state that the PLO pledges to establish?

It is true that most Arab countries have legislative bodies whose members are elected by the people, but the governments are actually run by unelected kings, sheiks, presidents, or elected leaders who run unopposed, such as Egyptian President Hosni Mubarak. Indeed, Yasser Arafat brooked no true opposition when he ran for Palestinian Authority "president" in early 1996. Why expect this will change if a Palestinian state is created?

Even if Palestinian leaders somehow broke the Arab world mold and established a true democracy, it is possible that Muslim fundamentalist groups and radical PLO supporters could sooner or later win power and then abolish the democratic system—if mainline Fatah politicians did not do it first.

## ALL EYES ON ISRAEL

Media interest in the Palestinian uprising peaked in March and April of 1988, just as I began working as a regular reporter for the CBS radio network. I was on the job only one day when Khalil al-Wazir, widely known as *Abu Jihad,* or "father of the holy war," was assassinated at his seaside home in Tunis. Wazir was said to have been the "military commander" of the uprising. The April 16 death of the second-ranking PLO leader—undoubtedly gunned down by Israeli agents—led to widespread and heavy Palestinian rioting. More than a dozen Palestinians lost their lives that day, and scores more were injured.

The number of violent protests dropped substantially in the weeks following the killing, causing Israeli leaders to predict that the Palestinian revolt was coming to an end. However, violent clashes increased after King Hussein declared on July 31 that Jordan would no longer play any role in its West Bank, in effect canceling his grandfather's annexation of the area. The move revived Palestinian hopes of establishing an independent state there and in the Gaza Strip.

Clashes escalated even further after Palestinian schools in Judea and Samaria, closed in January as the uprising spread to all parts of the territories, were reopened by Israeli officials in the fall. Within several months the schools were shut once again. Israeli officials said they were being used by PLO-trained youth activists, the *Shabiba*, to recruit youngsters for violent anti-Israel activities. Palestinian teachers conceded that this was indeed often the case. The schools gradually reopened in 1990 after many Palestinian parents pressured uprising leaders to order the Shabiba to do their recruiting somewhere else.

Although world attention was shifting to the American presidential elections, ongoing *glasnost* reforms in the Soviet Union, problems in China, and other topics, the Palestinian uprising against Israeli rule continued to receive substantial coverage by the world press throughout 1988. My reports for CBS Radio were almost exclusively about the ongoing revolt.

Violence at the Temple Mount in Jerusalem's Old City was of special interest to my editors in New York. Many Fridays were spent with media colleagues on top of a building overlooking the Temple Mount plaza. The rooftop afforded us a clear view of the frequent demonstrations staged by Muslims who gathered for Friday prayer services at the Islamic holy site. Our pictures and reports of Israeli police and paramilitary soldiers shooting tear gas, and occasionally rubber bullets, at protesting Palestinians featured prominently around the world.

As we waited each week for the prayer service to let out, I often felt like a spectator at the ancient Roman Coliseum—waiting to see if blood would flow. If it did, we had a story. If not, we went away feeling that we had wasted our time.

As the uprising moved into its second year, many increasingly weary Palestinians demanded that the PLO negotiate some sort of settlement to the Palestinian-Israeli dispute, despite the HAMAS warning that talking to Israel about peace was traitorous. This sentiment was echoed by many Israeli Jews, distressed by reports of soldiers who seemed to be losing their cool in putting down the ongoing rebellion. On the Arab side the pressure came mainly from middle-class Palestinian businessmen who were suffering great financial loss as a result of the ongoing conflict.

Many shopkeepers secretly defied the uprising leadership's order to close down their businesses every day at noon. Like my Old City money-changer, they quietly received customers in the afternoons and on general strike days behind shuttered exteriors, despite occasional threats and fire-bombings from young Shabiba activists. Several businessmen said privately they suspected that communist elements in the uprising leadership were out to crush the "merchant class" because it was "too close to Israel."

Some Palestinian shop owners were forced to sell out as the intifada, with its frequent general strikes called for by the Unified Leadership and HAMAS, continued. Their shops, including many in the so-called "Christian Quarter" of Jerusalem's Old City, were often sold to Islamic fundamentalist businessmen offering generous sums of money. Most of the Christian Quarter's businesses are now owned by Muslims, who comprise more than half of the quarter's resident population.

The Reagan administration was obviously not pleased that its main Middle Eastern ally was portrayed nightly on American television screens as an apparently oppressive military regime ruthlessly killing and wounding unarmed women and children. While continuing to pledge basic American support for Israel, the State Department nonetheless joined Britain, France, China, the Soviet Union, and many other nations in frequent denunciations of Israeli anti-uprising practices. At the same time, Secretary of State George Schultz rushed off to the Middle East to try to get Palestinian-Israeli peace negotiations off the ground. But everyone knew that such talks would have to wait until after the November 1988 U.S. and Israeli general elections.

## "PEACE . . . PEACE . . ."

As election victors George Bush and Yitzhak Shamir busily put together their new governments, Yasser Arafat convened the Palestine National Council in Algiers. The PNC meeting was attended by several of Arafat's main PLO rivals, including George Habash and Naif Hawatmeh. Despite some bitter arguments between members of the Syrian-backed factions and Arafat's Fatah supporters, a declaration was approved proclaiming the "establishment of the State of Palestine in the Israeli-occupied territories, with holy Jerusalem as its capital."

Representatives of the "state" would negotiate peace with Israel based on "all relevant United Nations resolutions," presumably including Resolutions 242 and 338, which call for an Israeli withdrawal from areas occupied in 1967. However, the negotiations would be "based on Resolution 191," the original 1947 U.N. partition plan. In other words, the peace talks would begin with the Palestinians demanding that Israel withdraw not only from Judea, Samaria, and the Gaza Strip, but from adjacent areas allotted to the proposed Arab state that were captured by Israel in 1948. The proclamation added that all Palestinians who fled their homes in 1948 and 1967, and their offspring, should be allowed to return to them.

Exactly forty-one years after local Palestinian leaders and the larger Arab world completely rejected the United Nations partition plan and launched a war of annihilation against the newly declared Jewish state, the PLO was finally ready to accept the two-state solution. The move, said Arafat, signaled a Palestinian recognition of the existence of Israel. Habash disagreed, telling reporters that no such recognition was intended by PNC delegates. He pointed out that no move had been initiated to amend the PLO's founding charter, which calls for Israel's total destruction.

Speaking to reporters in Paris one month later, Arafat declared the charter to be "inoperative." However, Habash and other PLO leaders again demurred, denouncing the statement as so much hot air. They pointed out that article 33 states only a two-thirds vote by PNC delegates can change any part of the PLO's charter.

The Palestine National Council's acceptance of negotiations based on U.N. resolutions was welcomed throughout the world, although most Western democracies were not enthusiastic about the statehood declaration. Arafat's subsequent announcement in December that he would order a halt to all PLO terror attacks—which led the Reagan administration to begin official talks with the PLO—was also hailed by governments everywhere, many of whom had already "recognized" the nonexistent Palestinian state.

The reaction to these events in Israel was hardly enthusiastic. Prime Minister Shamir was joined by his coalition Labor Party colleagues in denouncing the PNC declaration of Palestinian statehood. Shamir said the declaration was designed to put a halt to the Arab-Israeli peace process, since the Palestinian side had declared a final outcome in advance that was totally unacceptable to Israel. The prime minister maintained that if *Israel* did the same thing—by announcing, for example, that it would annex the territories no matter what was decided during peace negotiations—the world would be in an uproar. But when the *Palestinians* declare statehood as the final outcome, the world overwhelmingly accepts and even welcomes the move.

Israeli leaders also rejected the restatement of the official PLO position that all Palestinian refugees and their progeny have a right to return to Israel. Most Israelis agree that an influx of even a portion of what could be several million Palestinians would spell the end of the Jewish state.

Israeli officials and political analysts said the PNC declaration did not necessarily mean that the PLO had given up its goal of destroying Israel. In fact, Arafat's second-in-command, Salah Khalaf, better known as Abu Iyad, said on December 18, 1988, that the PLO's phased plan was still operative. He told the Kuwaiti newspaper *al-Anba* that the PNC statehood declaration meant "first a small state, and then with the help of Allah, it will be made large and expand to the east [i.e., Jordan], west, north, and south." He told the paper that he was "interested in the liberation of Palestine, step by step."

Khalaf reiterated this position on January 1, 1991, during a news conference in Amman, Jordan, saying, "We accept the formation of the Palestinian state on part of Palestine, on the Gaza Strip, and the West Bank. Now we must start from that part, and we will liberate Palestine inch by inch."

Arafat's statement on terrorism was received skeptically by Israeli officials, and even by many left-wing politicians who supported negotiations with the PLO. Government leaders pointed out that Arafat pledged to continue the armed struggle against Israel, meaning that armed terror bands would not halt their frequent attempts to try to penetrate Israel's borders from Lebanon and elsewhere. The PLO leader maintained that such assaults were not terrorism but legitimate acts of self-defense. Attacks by PLO underground cells against Jews both inside Israel and in the territories would also continue, said Arafat, as would the PLO-led uprising. Israeli officials stated that these positions would wreck any chances of moving the peace process forward.

The "armed struggle" did in fact continue during 1989. Palestinian gunmen, mainly from Syria-backed PLO factions, repeatedly tried to infiltrate into Israel from Lebanon, with several attempts also made from Jordanian and Egyptian territory. Several of the actions were undertaken by Arafat's Fatah group. A heavily armed, five-man Fatah squad was intercepted after crossing into Israel from the Negev Desert on December 5. A number of Israeli soldiers were killed during the various infiltration attempts, as were most of the Palestinian infiltrators. Underground PLO cell members killed or wounded several Jews inside Israel, and others in the territories. Bombs were placed in various places, injuring a number of Jews, and forests were burned by PLO-paid arsonists.

The worst terror attack inside Israel since the 1978 coastal road bus massacre occurred on July 6. A Palestinian man from the Gaza Strip forced an Israeli bus off the main Tel Aviv–Jerusalem highway, killing sixteen Jews, including two Canadians, and wounding himself and more than two dozen other passengers. The Palestinian saboteur said he was a supporter of the fundamentalist HAMAS movement and had decided to steer the bus down a steep ravine in order to contribute to the jihad struggle.

Meanwhile, the Palestinian uprising went on, with the total Arab death toll reaching five hundred by mid-summer. More than ten thousand had been wounded, many by rubber or plastic bullets. Palestinians had killed several dozen Israeli Jews, a majority of them civilians. Hundreds of others had been injured, many of them badly burned by petrol bombs. Thousands of Palestinians had been jailed, and more than sixty deported to Lebanon. Many of those imprisoned had not been formally charged with a crime or undergone trial. Israeli officials said public trials would lead to the revelation of sensitive security information. Palestinian leaders shot back that many prisoners were jailed for purely political reasons, claiming that some had even been tortured.

Israelis residing in the disputed territories could often be found in the news as the uprising rumbled along. Many took the law into their own hands to counter what they charged was inadequate protection by the Israeli army. Settlers' cars were often the target of stones and petrol bombs, leaving hundreds injured and several dead. The Jewish residents' reactions—or what the government and army leaders at times termed over-reactions—became a hot Israeli political topic, especially after some settlers went on the rampage in Arab villages to avenge local Palestinian attacks.

Yasser Arafat was not the only one talking about peace in the midst of the continuing violence. The new Israeli National Unity Government put forward a Four-Point Peace Plan in May 1989. The proposal, drawn up largely by Defense Minister Rabin, featured Palestinian elections to choose representatives who would negotiate peace with Israel. Only Palestinians who lived in the territories would be eligible to run, meaning the PLO could not field candidates from abroad. The elected Palestinians would also play a part in governing the territories while peace talks continued.

The Israeli initiative also called for a public reaffirmation of the Camp David Peace Accords by the United States and Egypt, an official end to the formal state of war and economic boycott against Israel by all other Arab nations, and an international effort to resolve the Palestinian refugee problem.

The PLO basically rejected the Israeli plan, which was endorsed by the new Bush administration. The move was part of a growing PLO shift back to more hard-line positions that prevailed before the November 1988

PNC conference. In August 1989 Fatah delegates convened in Tunis to discuss the ongoing uprising and the PLO's "peace strategy." Fatah delegates approved a final resolution that called for "intensifying and escalating armed action and all forms of struggle to eliminate the Zionist Israeli occupation of our occupied Palestinian land." The State Department said the resolution raised "questions about the PLO's commitment to accommodation, understanding and peace."

Prime Minister Shamir's Likud Party concluded that the PLO was officially withdrawing from the comparatively moderate positions espoused by Arafat the previous winter. Several Likud leaders, including Housing Minister David Levy and Industry Minister Ariel Sharon, said that the "occupied Palestinian land" mentioned in the Fatah resolution undoubtedly included *all* of present-day Israel, along with the West Bank and Gaza Strip. If so, the largest and most moderate wing of the PLO was apparently openly embracing again the PLO charter's call for the total destruction of the Jewish state. The two ministers pressed Shamir to abandon the government's Palestinian election proposal, saying it would only lead to a sovereign state headed by Arafat.

To many observers, including myself, the Palestinian uprising didn't seem to be bringing the prospects of a Palestinian state any closer, as most Palestinians originally hoped it would. In fact, just the opposite was the case as far as I could tell. Every bullet that entered a Palestinian body created much more hatred for Israel. The destruction of several hundred homes where Palestinians charged with various crimes lived; the deportation of more than sixty intifada leaders; the frequent curfews and "search and arrest" operations; the armed Jewish settlers who sometimes seemed to be aching for a fight with their Arab neighbors—all this and more were reducing Palestinian "goodwill" toward Israel, which wasn't exactly bubbling over even before the uprising began.

Israeli endearment toward the Palestinian Arabs was certainly not reinforced by such acts as the firebombing of an Israeli bus near Jericho, which left a mother and several of her children burned to death; the slaying of three elderly Jews in downtown Jerusalem by a knife-wielding Palestinian yelling, "*Allahu akbar!* Allah is great!"; the knifing to death of at least ten other Jews, mostly in Jerusalem; the torching of forests, fields, factories, and hundreds of automobiles; or the destruction of the Jerusalem-bound bus. Such violent actions left people on both sides much more polarized, with Israelis less willing to hand back land to the Palestinians than they were before the uprising began in December 1987.

## HATERS AND HEROES

Many Israelis argued that a major bloodbath would result if their army simply pulled out of the territories, leaving rival Palestinian factions to fight it out. This contention seemed to gain credibility as the uprising entered its second year.

Internal Arab bloodletting, widespread in the Arab revolts of 1936–39, surfaced once again. In fact, by the middle of 1989 one out of every two Palestinian deaths was at the hands of fellow Arabs. More than one hundred Palestinians, or about one in five killed during the uprising up until then, had been slain by Arab executioners. The number jumped up to around 150 by the end of the year and 250 by mid-1990. The deaths were for the most part extremely brutal, with axes and knives the usual weapons used. Hands and heads were often severed, along with other body parts. Decapitated bodies, some naked, were strung up on telephone poles to act as a warning to anyone who would dare cooperate with Israel. By 1990 a majority of Palestinian uprising deaths were from intercommunal killings.

The dead, in what journalists quickly dubbed the "intra-fada," were usually accused of collaborating with Israeli authorities. My own research and that of other journalists found that only a portion actively cooperated with the authorities to help put an end to the uprising. A few were killed because they expressed reservations over the direction the intifada took; others were murdered by personal enemies using the cover of the popular revolution to mask their crimes. Still others were slain by members of rival Palestinian groups waging a war to gain local hegemony. For some, "collaboration" meant they sold drugs or engaged in prostitution, crimes said to weaken the Palestinian community and thus strengthen Israeli control. Several Christian pastors in Bethlehem and elsewhere were accused of collaboration because they refused to endorse Palestinian violence. Toward the end of 1989 the local uprising leadership, which had earlier echoed

Arafat in applauding "collaborator" killings, issued new "guidelines" in order to reduce the number of killings.

Media coverage of the uprising during its first two years often focused on the many Palestinian children and teenagers killed or injured by army gunfire. Human rights groups said more than 150 children, most of them in their teens, were shot dead or killed by tear gas by the end of 1989. The army put the number at less than half that, saying many of those counted as having died from tear gas inhalation were not even exposed to such gas.

Army investigators pointed out that since all those killed in the uprising, especially children, were hailed as "martyrs and heroes," with their pictures plastered all over local walls, the incentive to blame any death on Israel was great, even if they had resulted from illnesses or other causes. Another incentive, said Israeli analysts, was the money which the PLO paid to any family who "offers up its sons and daughters to the glorious cause," as one uprising leaflet put it.

Israeli army commanders insisted that children were often deliberately put in the front lines of violent demonstrations, since intifada leaders knew that soldiers had orders to try to avoid hitting them. Several uprising leaflets did encourage children to join in the fray, and Palestinian youngsters usually seemed to be in the forefront of violent confrontations that I witnessed.

Israeli officials charged that human rights groups and Western aid agencies operating in the territories naively believe anything told them by Palestinians. Such groups should realize that the uprising is another form of Arab warfare against Israel, they said, adding that propaganda is a vital part of any modern conflict.

I can't judge the accuracy of accounts about incidents of which I have no firsthand knowledge. But I have found over the years that many Palestinians are aware that published or broadcast reports of alleged Israeli brutality harm Israel whether the charges are completely true, exaggerated, or totally false.

Beyond this, Arab society as a whole is inclined toward hyperbole, as noted by many Westerners who have closely studied the Arab world. Certainly Palestinian terror groups have shown this tendency. Attacks that end in the deaths of most or all of the terrorists are usually labeled

156 / HOLY WAR FOR THE PROMISED LAND

as huge successes, with the number of victims killed greatly exaggerated. An example of overstatement was Abul Abbas's claim that his men killed five hundred Israeli soldiers during a raid on Israeli beaches in 1990, when in fact no Israelis were killed.

As the 1980s came to an end, the Arab-Muslim–Israeli dispute seemed as intractable as ever. Syria, Libya, and non-Arab Iran continued to speak of the total destruction of the "Zionist entity." Syrian president Assad was busy building up his formidable army—and reportedly stockpiling chemical weapons capable of devastating the tiny state of Israel. Iraq had tested a new long-range missile in December 1989 and was known to be producing chemical weapons with the help of Western, and especially German, companies—and seeking to acquire or produce nuclear bombs. Iran was waging war against Israeli forces in Lebanon through its Lebanese Shiite Hizbullah proxies. Libya, also reportedly producing nerve gas and acquiring long-range missiles, was pouring money into various terror groups operating in Lebanon and elsewhere.

Jordan, Saudi Arabia, and other more moderate Arab nations spoke of the possibility of accommodation with the Jewish state, but did so while acquiring the most advanced weapons systems available on the world market. Only Egypt had actually made peace with Israel, but it was a cold peace, at best. Some Palestinian groups spoke of a "two-state" solution to the conflict, but many others—both secular Palestinians and Islamic fundamentalists—said the destruction of Israel was, and would always be, their only goal.

As the decade ended, war, not peace, seemed to be on the horizon. And all agreed that the next major Arab-Israeli war would probably feature ballistic missile attacks, making all previous conflicts look like mere military exercises.

# CHAPTER 10

# BAGHDAD TO BIBI

The first year of the 1990s strongly reinforced the perception I had at the end of 1989: the Middle East was moving more in the direction of war than peace. An attack in February by Palestinian Islamic Jihad members on an Israeli tour bus in Egypt left nine Jews dead, several of them well-known professors from Jerusalem's Hebrew University. Attempts to implement Israel's peace plan stalled after the collapse of the National Unity Government in March 1990.

The emergence in June of a right-wing coalition government headed by Yitzhak Shamir seemingly further reduced the prospects of peace between Palestinians and Israelis. America's dialogue with the PLO was suspended following Yasser Arafat's refusal to denounce a raid onto Israeli beaches in May by heavily armed gunmen belonging to Abul Abbas's PLO faction. American secretary of state James Baker expressed frustration with both the PLO and Israel, telling Congress that the parties could "call us" when they are "serious about peace."

My growing concern that another Middle East war was brewing—which some friends believed was overblown—began to be shared by many people after Iraqi leader Saddam Hussein threatened in early April 1990 to wipe out half of Israel with chemical weapons. "I swear to Allah that we will let our fire eat half of Israel if it tries to wage anything against Iraq," Saddam said on Baghdad radio, after charging that Israel was planning to use nuclear weapons against him. Since Israel had threatened to do no such thing (although government leaders had several times warned all

Arab countries that a chemical attack upon Israel would be met by a response "one hundred times greater"), officials and military analysts began to worry seriously about what Saddam was up to.

The ruthless "Butcher of Baghdad" had used chemical weapons against his own Kurdish citizens and Iranian soldiers. He had also personally killed or ordered dead some of his opponents and a number of his closest friends and advisers. Was he actually preparing to launch deadly chemical missiles at Tel Aviv and other Israeli cities? Did Saddam really believe that Israel was planning to attack his chemical weapons and rocket-making facilities? Did he fear a repeat of Israel's 1981 air force raid that destroyed a nuclear reactor under construction near Baghdad?

Several days before issuing his threat, the Iraqi strongman stood beside Yasser Arafat in Baghdad, reviewing a military parade in honor of "Land Day," which annually commemorates the killing of six Arabs by Israeli policemen in 1976. At the parade Saddam pledged to help secure the "liberation of Palestine," telling Arafat, "I can see the day when I and you, hand in hand, march to victory in Palestine." The PLO leader responded enthusiastically, telling Saddam that "we will enter al-Quds [the Islamic name for Jerusalem, meaning "the holy"] victorious and will raise our flag on its walls. You will enter with me, riding on your white stallion."

More ominously for Israel, Arafat pledged that Iraqi Scud missiles, modified to hit Israeli targets, would be used to "liberate holy Palestine." The PLO leader was no longer uttering the moderate-sounding peace pronouncements of 1988; they were now replaced with more traditional calls to war.

Saddam stepped up his war rhetoric in June 1990, saying he would launch his missiles if Israel bombed targets in any Arab country, not only his own. The chances of an armed clash were enhanced by a growing military and political alliance between Iraq and Jordan. The two countries set up joint ground and air squadrons in the spring. Israel warned that any significant movement of Iraqi forces into Jordan would be considered an act of war.

Israeli leaders expressed alarm over the increasingly hostile Arab rhetoric, saying it was ominously reminiscent of statements made just before the 1967 and 1973 Arab-Israeli wars. The Israeli government took the repeated Iraqi war threats quite seriously, with Defense Minister Moshe Arens noting that "what the Iraqi dictator has threatened to do in the past, he has done."

Saddam's war rhetoric sent renewed shivers down Israeli spines when Iraq invaded its southern neighbor, Kuwait, on August 2. Israeli analysts said the move proved that the ruthless "Butcher" was not afraid to use his enormous military power against perceived regional enemies, be they Arab, Iranian, or Israeli.

Saddam attempted to divert attention from his invasion and annexation of Kuwait by linking his actions to the Arab-Israeli conflict. In particular, he maintained that Israel had stolen Arab land during the 1967 Six Day War and yet had not encountered the same level of international condemnation that Iraq was subjected to. This allegation was widely accepted in the Arab world, especially after seventeen Palestinians were shot dead by Israeli security forces on the Temple Mount in October, as detailed in chapter 1.

Israeli officials responded to Iraq's "linkage" strategy by pointing out that Israel had captured the West Bank, Gaza Strip, Sinai Peninsula, and Golan Heights in a war of self-defense. The Arabs had used the areas since 1948 to launch repeated attacks against Israel, they noted, and were massing large armies and equipment there when the Six Day War broke out. Kuwait, on the other hand, posed no territorial threat to Iraq. They also noted that part of the territory Israel captured in 1967 was the heart of the Jewish ancestral homeland.

By popular demand, a decision was made in early October to distribute gas masks and other protective equipment to all Israeli citizens—Jewish and Arab—and to foreigners living or studying in Israel. Masks were later distributed to Palestinians in Jerusalem and surrounding areas. The widely publicized campaign helped calm fears of an Iraqi gas attack, while virtually killing off what remained of dwindling tourist traffic to Israel.

The Palestinian uprising continued during 1990, but at a more subdued pace than in the previous two years. There was a brief upsurge of clashes between Israeli soldiers and Palestinians in May after an apparently deranged Israeli civilian shot and killed eight Palestinian workers near Tel Aviv, and in October following the Temple Mount tragedy.

The overall Palestinian death toll from Israeli army gunfire reached around seven hundred by the end of 1990 (figures varied depending upon whom you asked), with more than forty dead from Israeli civilian fire. Palestinians had killed about forty Israeli civilians and twenty-two soldiers and policemen. The Associated Press said 324 Palestinians had been killed by fellow Arabs by the end of the year as the "intra-fada" intensified.

The HAMAS movement picked up additional Palestinian support as the year wore on, especially after Saddam's calls for holy war against Israel and the West in August and September, and after the violence at the Temple Mount in October. In April HAMAS leaders demanded that their movement be allotted up to half of the seats in the Palestine National Council. PLO leaders rejected the demand. Following clashes in the summer between PLO and HAMAS supporters, the PLO was forced to recognize HAMAS's growing appeal by agreeing to honor all HAMAS-called general strike days.

Widespread popular Palestinian support for Saddam Hussein dealt further heavy blows to the already dwindling prospects for progress in the Arab-Israeli peace process. Israeli peace activists expressed open shock at the depth of Palestinian support for the Iraqi leader, with some saying that the clock apparently had been turned back to the days when Israel's total destruction was the Palestinians' chief goal.

Yasser Arafat said on September 3 that it was natural for the Palestinian masses to support Saddam. "To those who ask about the Palestinian position, we ask, 'Where is Israel in this war?' We can only be in the camp hostile to Israel and its imperialist allies who have mobilized their sophisticated war machine," said Arafat in an interview with the PLO's news agency in Tunis.

## SADDAM SHOOTS HIS SCUDS

Jews and Arabs in Israel spent the first two weeks of 1991 preparing for war. The United Nations had given Saddam Hussein until January 15 to pull his forces out of Kuwait. Very few Israelis believed that the Iraqi dictator would risk losing face by obeying the U.N. command. Most felt that

Western and allied Arab armed forces, led by the United States, would have to push Saddam's army out of the tiny oil-rich sheikdom.

Israeli leaders prepared for the worst. They were almost certain that Saddam would fire his missiles at the Jewish state if fighting broke out. Some analysts warned that Iraq might even let loose a surprise barrage in the days leading up to the mid-January deadline, in an attempt to rally Arab and Muslim world support. But Saddam did not shoot his Scuds before the Gulf War began, despite reported advice by several of his top generals that he do so.

As January 15 drew near, a palpable gloom descended upon Israel. I often looked down from the fifth-floor CBS office window at Jaffa Road, Jerusalem's main street, below. Serious-looking Israelis scurried about making last-minute preparations for war. Only once before—in May 1948—had Middle Eastern Jews known the likely date of an announced Arab attack against them. It was like waiting for the plague to strike. Everyone knew that death was lurking just over the eastern horizon, eager to meet its Israeli victims.

President Bush informed Israeli leaders that he was preparing to order an attack against Saddam's forces. In an attempt to keep Israel from launching a preemptive air strike on Iraqi missile sites, the American leader promised that Allied forces would do everything in their power to quickly destroy any Scud missiles aimed at the tiny Jewish state.

On the evening of January 15 Prime Minister Shamir went on state television to reassure his nervous nation that it would survive anything that Saddam could hurl at it. Sitting at his official desk and looking like everybody's grandfather, the soft-spoken Israeli leader recalled that the Jewish people had faced many serious attacks, and even attempts at annihilation, down through the centuries and yet, with the help of God, had always pulled through.

At 2 A.M. on January 16 the telephone rang in my Jerusalem apartment, waking me out of a fitful sleep. It was the CBS-affiliate station in Seattle calling to ask what I knew of late-breaking news that the Allied operation against Iraq had been launched. Within minutes live CNN reports from Baghdad were being broadcast on Israel Army Radio, confirming that the Gulf War had indeed begun.

Despite the fact that it was the middle of the night, news of the U.N.-backed attack spread like wildfire throughout Israel. Aware that they might become part of the action at any time, most Israelis immediately went to their *heder atoum* or sealed room—where plastic sheeting and masking tape had been carefully placed around windows and doors to prevent the entrance of gas or chemicals released by Iraqi bombs—and donned gas masks. Israeli television came on the air and began showing films explaining how to put on the German-made masks properly and how to place children in other protective equipment. The instructions, given by smiling female soldiers, were subtitled in Russian for new immigrants.

No attempts were made by Saddam Hussein on that first night of the Gulf War to "eat half of Israel" with Scud missiles. But the harbingers of death came crashing down on the Ezra neighborhood of south Tel Aviv the following night, not far from the mixed Jewish-Arab town of Jaffa. As we in Israel huddled in sealed rooms, people around the globe huddled next to televisions and radios to learn if the "Butcher of Baghdad" had indeed kept his promise to use nonconventional warheads against the "Zionist entity." It soon became clear that such weapons were not used, although this was of little comfort to the several hundred Israelis whose apartments were destroyed or seriously damaged by the Scud blasts.

Thirty-eight additional missiles were fired at Israel during the forty-two-day Gulf War. Most landed in Tel Aviv or the nearby town of Ramat Gan, although some fell on the northern port city of Haifa, on the Negev town of Dimona (site of Israel's nuclear reactor), or into the Mediterranean Sea. One almost destroyed a major electric power station near Tel Aviv. Another landed in a field not far from Jerusalem. American-manned Patriot antimissile batteries—rushed to Israel in the first week of the war—helped to intercept and destroy some of the incoming Scuds, although it was later admitted by Israeli leaders that the Patriots were largely ineffective. Hundreds of apartments and homes were destroyed in the almost nightly attacks, and thousands more were damaged. But Saddam's threats to use nonconventional warheads were never carried out.

Miraculously, only two Israelis died as a direct result of the Iraqi Scud attacks, although hundreds were injured, mostly lightly. The Israeli

National Insurance Institute reported in early 1992 that seventy-two people had died as a direct consequence of Saddam's terror-raising missile strikes, mostly from heart attacks and improper use of gas masks. Still, the death toll could have been much worse. In one case, a missile struck close to a bomb shelter packed with more than two hundred adults and children. Officials said that if it had hit the shelter, most of the Israelis inside probably would have died.

Many people throughout the world considered it even more miraculous that Israeli leaders did not order their air force pilots into action as the Scuds kept falling (it was later learned that officials were on the verge of doing so three times). Israeli armed forces chief Dan Shomron said that army commandos were even ready at one point to land in western Iraq, to conduct ground operations against Iraqi Scud positions.

After the war Israeli leaders expressed private, and later public, regret that they had kept their pilots out of the battle. They insisted that the Scud launchers would have been more rapidly destroyed by Israeli bombers. They said Israeli jets would have taken greater risks and flown much lower than Allied warplanes, whose high-altitude bombing raids were only partially effective. This opinion was strengthened in 1992 when Western intelligence reports revealed that only 3 percent of Allied bombing missions were directed at taking out Scud missiles aimed at Israel.

Many Israeli politicians and military analysts also believe that their country's deterrence posture against any future Arab attack was seriously eroded by the failure to respond to Saddam's missile strikes on civilian centers. They noted that in previous wars Israeli forces had always been able to transfer the battle into enemy territory. But this time Israel's largest metropolitan area, Tel Aviv and its suburbs, became the front line rather than the Golan Heights or Sinai Peninsula, and the armed forces were ordered—under heavy American pressure—to simply sit on their hands.

## SADDAM, HITLER, AND HAMAN

Covering the war for CBS Radio while wearing a gas mask was not easy. My colleagues and I soon discovered we would have to place our protective masks above our faces if we were to be understood by our American listeners. For me, at least, it was also difficult at times to keep from displaying emotion, especially when working long hours without much sleep.

The most unsettling moment came the first Friday of the war when air raid sirens sounded while I was eating a Sabbath meal at the home of Lance Lambert. I immediately phoned CBS in New York to relay the news that another missile attack was apparently under way.

It was difficult to keep my composure when I entered Lance's sealed basement room carrying his portable telephone, only to find my well-dressed dinner companions wearing weird-looking gas masks. As my eyes met Lance's, I immediately remembered that his father, an Italian Jewish nobleman, had been murdered in Hitler's Auschwitz death camp. Now almost half a century later, Lance, who had lived as a child through the Nazi blitz of London, was wearing a gas mask in his Jerusalem home because another Jew-hating madman was threatening to slaughter Israelis with gas-tipped missiles—the deadly gases having been mainly produced with the aid of German companies.

Forty days after the first missile attack on Tel Aviv, U.S. general Norman Schwarzkopf announced that the war was basically over, with only a little "mopping up" left to do. The next day, President Bush officially declared that "Operation Desert Storm" had come to an end. Within hours the state of emergency enacted throughout Israel just before the war was lifted.

Dressed in all sorts of costumes—particularly Saddam masks—Israelis soon took to the streets to celebrate the war's end, along with the festival of Purim, which officially began at sunset. Purim marks the victory of the ancient Jews of Persia over the tyrant Haman, whose attempt to wipe out the Jewish people was turned upon his own head following the timely intervention of Queen Esther. Many Israelis saw it as more than coincidence that the Iraqi dictator, who had boasted that he would wipe out half the Jews of Israel, was officially declared to be vanquished just hours before the onset of Purim.

In the run-up to the Gulf War, many of my foreign journalist colleagues expressed strong doubts over Saddam's ability and/or desire to lob missiles at Israel. Some were convinced that the Iraqi dictator was too afraid of Israel's potential reaction if he launched his Scuds, while others simply thought his threats were mainly posturing meant for internal consumption. I was among the minority who were convinced he would attack the Jewish state. After all, having threatened Israel so repeatedly and boisterously, his credibility in the Arab world was on the line. And I knew that public image means a great deal to vainglorious despots like Saddam.

Some Israeli military analysts doubted that Saddam's modified Scuds could actually reach Israeli targets. But as the missiles came crashing down on civilian centers, the specialists joined government leaders and the Israeli media in thanking former Prime Minister Menachem Begin for ordering the destruction of Iraq's French-supplied nuclear reactor ten years earlier. Had he not done so, they said, nuclear-tipped missiles might have landed on Tel Aviv and Haifa, potentially wiping out a large segment of Israel's Jewish population.

Despite the 1981 Israeli air strike, it became clear after the Gulf War that Saddam was far closer to developing nuclear weapons than had previously been thought. United Nations inspectors uncovered evidence that highly skilled Iraqi nuclear technicians were only eighteen months to two years away from producing nuclear bombs when the war began.

Israeli officials—unhappy that Saddam had survived the war, possibly to fight another day—expressed concern over American intelligence reports that large amounts of Iraqi enriched uranium remained intact after the U.N. campaign came to an end, along with secret underground nuclear installations and hidden caches of Scud missiles. They were skeptical that special U.N. teams, acting in accordance with Gulf War cease-fire terms, would successfully find and destroy all of Iraq's weapons of mass destruction. Officials also took note of Western intelligence predictions that Iraq would make further attempts to build nuclear, biological, and chemical weapons and Scud missiles in the future. Israeli apprehensions were reinforced when Saddam said on the first anniversary of the war that he would rebuild his military machine so that the jihad against "the cursed Israel" could continue until "Allah's victory is finally attained."

## SOVIET FLOODGATES SWING OPEN

Largely as a result of fast-moving changes in the Soviet Union, Jewish immigrants began pouring into Israel in large numbers during 1990—to the great dismay of Yasser Arafat, Saddam Hussein, and the rest of the Arab world. About 185,000 arrived in Israel during the year, another 145,000 in 1991, and close to 200,000 in 1992, increasing Israel's Jewish population by nearly 10 percent. More than 1 million Russian-speaking people had moved to Israel from the former Soviet Union by the end of 2000.

The immigrant tide, which alone increased Israel's Jewish population by more than 20 percent in just ten years, produced much-needed human resources for the country's armed forces. It also resulted in an unprecedented economic surge, especially since many newcomers were highly skilled scientists, academics, and other trained professionals. The aliyah wave also produced not a few headaches for officials trying to find suitable housing and jobs for them.

While Russian immigrants were streaming into Israel, more than 14,000 black Ethiopian Jews, most of them impoverished, were flown to the country in May 1991. In a remarkable twenty-four-hour airlift, Israeli air force jets and commercial El Al planes made more than forty sorties to bring the beleaguered Ethiopians to the Jewish homeland.

Arab leaders, including Egypt's Hosni Mubarak, met in Baghdad in May 1990 and issued a statement condemning "the transfer of Jews to Palestine and the other occupied Arab territories." Israeli leaders said less than half of 1 percent of immigrating Soviet Jews were settling in the territories (around 2 percent if east Jerusalem Jewish suburbs are included). They said the summit statement reflected Arab anger that any Jews at all were immigrating to Israel, or to "Palestine," as the Arab leaders put it.

The original "Zionist invasion" began with Russian Jews moving to Palestine, said various Arab leaders as the new aliyah wave gathered momentum.[40] Rising Jewish numbers will lead to stepped-up Israeli attempts to extend Zionist control over the entire Middle East, they maintained, and therefore the Arabs must prepare for war to oppose "expansionist Zionist threats." Yasser Arafat "proved" this point after a special U.N. debate held in Geneva in May 1990, by holding up an Israeli ten-agorot coin (worth about five U.S. cents) that he claimed featured a "map" outlining Zionist plans to conquer Jordan, Lebanon, parts of Syria, Iraq, and Saudi Arabia. Israeli coin-makers said the supposed map was in reality the eroded contours of an ancient Jewish coin surrounding a seven-branch menorah.

## ARAB-ISRAELI PEACE TALKS

As Israelis celebrated Iraq's overwhelming defeat, most Palestinians and Jordanians were anything but cheerful. They shared a sense of humiliation with many regional Arabs that Saddam's "Mother of All Battles" had turned out to be nothing less than the mother of all defeats. To be sure, Saddam's missiles did hit the Zionist state, to the cheers of many Palestinians, Jordanians, and even Arabs in such faraway places as Yemen, Sudan, Algeria, and Morocco. But Yasser Arafat's boast that Iraqi Scuds would be used to "liberate Jerusalem" did not come true.

The Iraqi defeat led not a few Palestinians to conclude that the "armed struggle" against Israel was getting nowhere and that only peace talks could eventually succeed in giving some sort of a victory to the Arab-Muslim world. Many argued that the PLO should let Palestinian leaders in the territories attend such talks even if they were mainly sponsored by Israel's ally, the United States.

Such sentiments fit right in with the thinking of George Bush and James Baker, who had pledged to their Arab Gulf War partners that continuing Israeli control over the territories captured in 1967 would be the next Middle East topic tackled by the U.S. government. They set out to get an Arab-Israeli peace conference—jointly sponsored by the Soviet Union—off the ground as soon as possible. Although none of the Middle East participants were happy with all of the conditions proposed by the Americans, Israel, Syria, Lebanon, Jordan, and the Palestinians showed up for the grand ceremonial opening of Arab-Israeli peace talks at Madrid's Royal Palace in late October. Saudi Arabia and Kuwait expressed basic support for the peace talks.

The mood was tense as Arab and Jewish delegates sat down together around a huge table, under the glare of international television lights.

Spanish premier Felipe Gonzalez officially opened the conference by greeting the delegates in the name of King Juan Carlos, a direct descendant of Holy Roman Emperor, Charles V.

President George Bush delivered the main keynote address, telling the delegates that "peace in the Middle East need not be a dream." He said the conference sponsors "seek peace, real peace. And by real peace I mean treaties. Security. Diplomatic relations. Economic relations. Trade. Investment. Cultural exchange. Even tourism." The U.S. leader predicted that "these negotiations will not be easy," but added that "the alternative to peace is a future of violence and waste and tragedy."

Soviet president Mikhail Gorbachev, whose country had done so much to fuel the conflict in past decades, told the delegates that the conference was an "event of major importance in new world politics," adding that "it would be unforgivable to miss this opportunity for peace." However, the Soviet leader—who would declare the dissolution of his crumbling union two months later—devoted much of his speech to a plea for world aid to shore up his disintegrating nation.

Egyptian Foreign Minister Amr Moussa, representing the only Arab country to have made peace with the Jewish state, raised the thorniest issue in the way of an overall Israeli–Arab-Muslim peace settlement by calling for a "complete Israeli withdrawal from all Arab territories occupied in 1967 . . . including east Jerusalem."

The sparks began to fly on the second day of the peace conference as Middle Eastern delegation heads delivered their addresses. Israeli prime minister Shamir called on the Arab world to put a final end to its state of war against Israel: "We appeal to you to renounce the jihad." He also presented a detailed account of the history of the conflict, mixing in references to the Holocaust and the Bible. Quoting Psalm 137, the Israeli leader noted that the Jewish connection to Jerusalem goes back more than three thousand years, adding that the Jews are "the only people whose holy sites are only in Israel." He said the Arabs "possess fourteen million square kilometers" of land compared to Israel's "twenty-eight thousand square kilometers," and thus, "the issue is not territory, but our existence." Shamir said Israel wanted to sign peace treaties with its neighbors and to "reach an agreement on interim self-governing arrangements with the Palestinian Arabs."

Arab delegates called the speech insulting, noting that Shamir did not even refer to an Israeli withdrawal from the areas captured during the Six Day War.

Jordanian Foreign Minister Kamel Abu Jaber warned of "extremists . . . lurking in the wings" who want to see the peace talks fail and said that "Arab sovereignty must be restored in Arab Jerusalem." However, he was the only Arab delegation head who hinted that a peace treaty might eventually be signed with Israel.

Palestinian Chief Delegate Haidar Abdul-Shafi paid homage to the PLO and called for an immediate end to Israeli settlement building. He said, "Palestinian Jerusalem, the capital of our homeland and future state, defines Palestinian existence," adding that "Israel's annexation of Arab Jerusalem remains both clearly illegal in the eyes of the world community, and an affront to the peace this city deserves." He called Jerusalem "the cradle of three world religions," despite the fact that the Holy City is not even mentioned once by name in the Islamic Koran.

Lebanese Foreign Minister Faris Bouez called for a complete Israeli withdrawal from south Lebanon. But he did not mention the anti-Israeli militias operating in the area, nor the estimated forty thousand Syrian troops occupying most of the rest of Lebanon.

Not surprisingly, the harshest speech of the day came from Syrian Foreign Minister Farouk al-Sharaa. He called Israel "the aggressor" in the 1967 war and said it must give up "every inch of occupied Arab lands," including Jerusalem. He maintained that Syria had "never been an aggressor" in the Arab-Israeli conflict—ignoring the 1947 Arab declaration of war against the emerging Jewish state and the surprise Soviet-backed joint Egyptian-Syrian attack on Israel in 1973—and condemned Zionism and the continuing immigration of Jews to Israel. The Syrian minister said that "Israeli intransigence should never be rewarded," implying that Syria would not agree to sign a full peace treaty in exchange for an Israeli withdrawal from the Golan Heights.

Direct Arab-Israeli negotiations began in Madrid in early November, followed by sessions in Washington, D.C., in December. Further bilateral sessions took place in the American capital in 1992. The most acrimonious negotiations were, as expected, between Syria and Israel. Syrian delegates again blamed Israel for the Six Day War and said the Israelis should immediately pull out of "all occupied Arab land" without expecting a peace treaty in return. Israeli negotiators voiced concern over a continuing Syrian arms buildup—which actually escalated with the collapse of Syria's longtime ally, the Soviet Union. Special alarm was expressed over Syrian acquisition of North Korean Scud-C missiles, along with equipment to build them, since the advanced Scuds were far more accurate than the older Scud-Bs fired by Iraq.

As the peace talks got under way in the American capital, Islamic countries were holding their annual summit in Senegal. Syria insisted that the twenty or more nations present pass a resolution condemning Israel as a racist state. Yasser Arafat, whose PLO was widely acknowledged to be calling the Palestinian shots at the peace negotiations, demanded that a recommitment to jihad against Israel be made by the Muslim delegates. Israeli analysts said Arafat's move was an apparent attempt to show Palestinian fundamentalists that talking peace with Israel did not mean that the PLO had abandoned its founding charter's stated goal of destroying the Jewish state.

On December 16, 1991, the United Nations voted 112 to 25 to rescind the 1975 resolution equating Zionism with racism. Israeli delight at the move was tempered by the fact that its negotiating partners—Jordan, Syria, and Lebanon—voted against the rescission, along with Saudi Arabia, Libya, and Iran. Egypt and Kuwait stayed away from the vote. Despite the positive outcome, Israeli leaders noted that the U.N. remained highly critical of the Jewish state, pointing to no less than thirty-four anti-Israel resolutions passed in 1991 alone, several of them on the morning of the rescission vote.

Many nations, including China and Japan, took part in the opening round of multilateral Middle East peace talks in Moscow in late January 1992. More importantly, nine Arab countries, including Saudi Arabia and Morocco, also attended, although Syria stayed away. Separate working groups on Middle East arms control and regional security issues, economic development, environment, water resources, and refugees began meeting in North America, Europe, and Japan in May.

In late February 1992 the Israelis presented their self-government autonomy proposals—patterned after the Camp David Accords—to

Palestinian negotiators. Israel said it was prepared to turn over most functions of government in the disputed territories to Palestinian control. A freely elected Palestinian administration would replace Israeli army rule, draw up its own budget and collect taxes, oversee an Arab police force, and have full authority over education, commerce, agriculture, transportation, and other areas of government. Israel would retain control of the borders and overall security. The final status of the territories would be negotiated no later than three years after the interim self-government began to function.

Palestinian spokeswoman Hanan Ashrawi condemned the proposals as "nothing more than an Israeli desire to consolidate the occupation," charging that Israel wanted to "implement de facto annexation and apartheid." An Israeli spokesman replied that apartheid's main aim was to keep apart two peoples inhabiting the same land—exactly what the Palestinians were demanding in calling for a separate state in east Jerusalem and the disputed territories.

True to their founding charter, the Palestinian HAMAS movement condemned the talks, calling them an affront to Islam. PLO leftist groups, led by the Popular Front, also denounced the "American imperialist-sponsored talks." Popular Front leader George Habash showed his disapproval by freezing his group's participation in the PLO executive committee. To help pacify opponents of the peace talks, Yasser Arafat and Hanan Ashrawi called for an escalation of the Palestinian uprising, while strongly condemning a stepped-up Israeli building program in the disputed territories (the Israeli Peace Now movement said more than 13,000 apartments and homes were constructed in 1991).

Tension between Arab supporters and opponents of the talks spilled over at times into violence, contributing to a further rise in inter-Palestinian killings. In the twelve months following the Gulf War, more than two hundred Palestinians were killed and more than a thousand wounded by fellow Arabs. Less than one hundred Palestinians were shot dead during the same period by Israeli soldiers as the uprising continued to wane (although the army said armed attacks against Israelis jumped from 390 in 1990 to 447 in 1991).

Several Arab and Islamic countries also expressed strong opposition to the peace talks. Iraq, which more than adequately proved it was still a party to the conflict, vowed to do everything in its power to scuttle the peace process. The Libyan government sponsored marches in Tripoli and other cities and towns, with demonstrators carrying placards calling for perpetual war against "the Zionist enemy." Iranian leaders denounced the talks, with Ayatollah Ali Khamenei warning that "those who participate will face the wrath of nations." At an anti-peace talks conference in Tehran, President Rafsanjani pledged to send Iranian troops to "fight alongside Palestinians against the Zionist regime." Conference participants, who included PLO factional leader Ahmed Jabril, passed resolutions calling for an "all-out jihad against the Zionist regime" leading to "the elimination of the Zionist existence."

Some Israelis were also skeptical that the Americans had succeeded in getting the peace negotiations rolling. They feared that the Bush administration—considered by many to be the least friendly toward Israel in more than thirty years—would put extreme pressure on the Jewish state to pull out of the strategic territories captured in 1967. These Israelis saw such a pullout as a potentially suicidal act. They pointed to a U.S. "letter of assurances" given to Palestinian leaders prior to the Madrid conference, which stated that America "believes there should be an end to the Israeli occupation," and that "we do not recognize Israel's annexation of east Jerusalem."

Predicting that the Bush administration would force Prime Minister Shamir to make dangerous concessions, two small right-wing political parties angrily withdrew from Shamir's coalition government, forcing early Israeli elections in June 1992.

Another source of Israeli skepticism was continuing terror attacks in late 1991 and 1992. As the Madrid conference was set to get under way, two Israelis, one a mother of seven, were killed when terrorists opened fire on a civilian bus north of Ramallah. Five people were injured in the attack, including four boys. The following day, three Israeli soldiers were killed when a roadside bomb went off in south Lebanon. The Iranian-backed Hizbullah militia said it had set off the charge to protest the peace conference in Spain. Three soldiers were axed to death as they slept in their tent-camp barracks in northern Israel in February. Four Arab-Israeli Muslim fundamentalists were later charged with committing the brutal murders.

The Israeli embassy in Argentina was blown up by terrorists in March, leaving four Israelis dead and scores of Argentinians killed and wounded. The assault, claimed by the Islamic Jihad movement in Beirut, followed Israel's interception and killing in February of Hizbullah leader Sheik Abbas Musawi. More than one hundred Palestinian knife attacks were reported against Israelis in the year following the Gulf War, leaving several dead and dozens wounded.

## RABIN TO THE RESCUE

In February 1992 the opposition Labor Party held a nationwide primary to choose its candidate for premier. With opinion polls consistently showing Labor trailing the Likud by around five points, many wanted to see party leader Shimon Peres replaced by the more conservative Yitzhak Rabin. Indeed, the seventy-year-old Rabin easily won the primary—the first in Israel's history.

Shamir faced a similar challenge in his party. The gauntlet was thrown down by two of his cabinet subordinates, David Levy and Ariel Sharon. Although they lost the leadership battle, the two later joined Defense Minister Moshe Arens in a bruising fight to determine who would win the prestigious second spot on the Likud's list of Knesset candidates. Levy was shocked and humiliated by the early March vote, which left him in fourth place. Claiming he had an automatic right to the number two spot due to his cabinet role as deputy premier, Levy threatened to take his mainly Sephardic supporters and bolt the party. Harsh words followed between him and other Likud leaders, including Shamir. The bitter dispute caused many traditional Likud voters to declare that they would either sit out the election or cast their ballot for the popular Rabin.

Labor took full advantage of the right-wing infighting. Aware of opinion polls showing that a majority of Israelis thought security issues should take precedence over the peace process, Rabin was portrayed in campaign ads as a tough-minded alternative to Shamir. The affable Labor candidate worked hard to woo more than some of Levy's angry Sephardic supporters. Campaigning in traditional Likud strongholds, he promised to be firm in negotiations with the Palestinians and Syria. He said his goal was to secure a Palestinian autonomy accord that would leave Israeli forces in overall control of the disputed territories.

The former army commander took a similar unrelenting stand during campaign appearances on the Golan Heights and in the Jordan Valley. He promised to retain control of the strategically important areas. However, the Labor Party platform spoke of the necessity of "territorial compromise in the West Bank, Gaza Strip, and also on the Golan Heights." It said a Labor-led government would quickly grant self-rule to the Palestinians, acting unilaterally if necessary. Construction would be frozen in all Jewish settlements, apart from those in the Jordan Valley and near Jerusalem. Likud leaders called the Labor platform a "defeatist document" that would lead to disaster if fully implemented.

With the Likud Party in disarray and Labor reinvigorated under its new-old leader, Yitzhak Rabin easily won the June 23 election. His party captured forty-four seats in the Knesset to just thirty-two for the Likud. More importantly, Labor's left-wing Meretz Party ally took twelve seats, and two small Arab parties won five, meaning that the center-left bloc had a bare, but sufficient, sixty-one to fifty-nine edge in the Knesset. However, final election results revealed that a majority of votes were actually cast for right-wing parties. Three small parties fell short of the minimum amount needed to enter the Knesset, one of them by only a handful of votes.

"The new government intends to give away the future," charged Shamir in his final Knesset speech as prime minister. He added that Rabin would "strive for peace now at the expense of fundamental national aims, which will cost us dearly in the long run." He predicted that the Labor-led leftist coalition would negotiate "according to the thesis that peace is unattainable without dangerous concessions."

The jubilant Rabin pledged that he would reach an autonomy agreement with the Palestinians within one year. He said he would replace sporadic negotiations in Washington with "continuous talks until an interim peace solution is reached, based on the Camp David framework." He also announced an immediate end to all economic subsidies for what he termed "political settlements" in the disputed territories, although he said money would still flow to "strategic settlements." He explained that the latter were those communities that Labor deemed vital to Israel's security, particularly around Jerusalem. While welcoming Rabin's election and accelerated peace talks, the Bush administration repeated its contention that "all settlements are obstacles to peace."

Although the new premier did cut off financial aid to all "political settlements" (which just happened to be those established under Likud governments), he did not succeed in reaching an autonomy deal with the Palestinians within one year of assuming office. In fact, his first months in power were marred by the same sort of Palestinian terror attacks that plagued the previous government. When a border policeman was kidnapped in December and then killed by HAMAS terrorists, he ordered the immediate expulsion of more than four hundred Muslim activists to southern Lebanon. Palestinian negotiators condemned the move and broke off the Washington peace talks with the new Israeli government.

## THE OSLO ACCORD

While PLO leaders in Tunisia were publicly fuming over the Palestinian expulsions, they were secretly embarking on a path of direct negotiations with Israel. The hidden peace process began after Rabin's foreign minister, Shimon Peres, convinced his boss that the suspended Washington talks were hardly worth resuming, since all Palestinian positions were actually being formulated in Tunis. Instead, Peres advocated opening a clandestine dialogue with the PLO. Although skeptical that direct bargaining would produce results, Rabin authorized the back-channel negotiations, which began in January 1993. Warren Christopher, secretary of state in the new Clinton administration, was made aware of the talks.

The first-ever face-to-face Israel-PLO negotiations were held in Norway, since the original offer for a surreptitious dialogue had come from the director of a government-linked think tank in Oslo, Terje Roed-Larsen. Along with Foreign Minister Johan Joergen Holst and other Norwegian officials, Roed-Larsen acted both as facilitator and mediator in fourteen secret meetings. The talks were mainly held in an old country mansion sixty miles east of Oslo. Uri Savir, director-general of Israel's foreign ministry, led his country's small delegation to the talks. Mahmoud Abbas, who reported directly to Yasser Arafat, usually represented the PLO.

When the going got rough, as it frequently did during eight months of strenuous give-and-take, Holst would sometimes invite his guests for a contemplative walk in the garden. He later explained that this usually calmed them down enough to proceed with their covert discussions.

Just as the secret negotiations were nearing a breakthrough, Syrian-backed Muslim forces in south Lebanon launched concerted attacks on Israeli troops in the buffer security zone. Six soldiers were killed in a mid-July ambush, prompting Rabin to order sustained shelling of Hizbullah positions. The Muslim militia retaliated by firing around fifty rockets into northern Israel, killing several civilians. Realizing that he could never sell his emerging deal with the PLO unless he kept up his tough image, Rabin then ordered a major military operation in south Lebanon. Thousands of Lebanese civilians fled north to escape the fighting, which ended on July 31 with an American-brokered cease-fire.

Having reestablished his hard-line credentials, Rabin prepared to drop his Oslo bombshell on an unsuspecting nation. The explosion came on August 29 when a cabinet statement was released announcing that Israel had reached a preliminary "Declaration of Principles" for a peace accord with Arafat's mainstream PLO. The deal included mutual recognition between Israel and its longtime foe, the withdrawal of Israeli troops from most of the Gaza Strip and the Jordan Valley town of Jericho, and the setting up of a Palestinian self-government authority and security force in those areas. Israel would retain jurisdiction over Jewish settlements in Gaza and near Jericho.

The Israeli army pullout, to begin by mid-December, would be followed by phased withdrawals from much of Judea and Samaria. An overall "final status" peace accord would then be negotiated over such divisive issues as Jewish settlements, a Palestinian state, refugees living abroad, and the question of Jerusalem. The final peace accord would take effect before the end of the century.

The incipient withdrawal pact came as a total surprise to most members of Rabin's own cabinet and party, with some leaders expressing anger that they had not been informed of the covert peace talks. Although most cabinet ministers strongly supported the deal, two sharply questioned the wisdom of doing business with the wily Arafat.

They noted that the PLO chief was suddenly being portrayed not as Israel's arch-terrorist enemy, but as its trusted peace partner, adding that this dramatic metamorphosis was extremely difficult for many people to swallow. Others maintained that Rabin should have announced and explained the astonishing deal in a speech before the nation, instead of through an impersonal cabinet statement.

Understanding what was most important to the average citizen, Rabin insisted that Arafat agree to end all Palestinian violence against Israelis, including a formal halt to the nearly six-year-old uprising, and to annul the PLO charter's many clauses calling directly or indirectly for Israel's destruction. The Palestinian leader promised to do so, although the commitments were made in a September 9 letter handed to Rabin, and not in the formal agreement itself. Arafat's promises paved the way for the signing of the Oslo Accord. The preliminary peace pact was sealed with historic handshakes at a White House ceremony on September 13, even though President Bill Clinton had played no part in securing the deal.

Binyamin Netanyahu, who had been overwhelmingly elected as the new Likud Party leader in March, denounced the fact that the signing ceremony was held before the Knesset was given a chance to vote on the far-reaching accord. He told his fellow legislators that Rabin and Peres "are worse than Neville Chamberlain, who threatened the security and freedom of another country, while you are threatening your own nation." He said Arafat could sell the withdrawal agreement to his own people only by making them understand that it was an initial fulfillment of the PLO's 1974 phased plan to destroy Israel in stages. Netanyahu reminded Knesset members that the Palestinian document stated that "any portion of land liberated from the Zionist occupiers, whether by peaceful or military means, will be used as a staging ground for the complete destruction of Israel."

The forty-three-year-old Likud leader said Rabin well understood that Arafat viewed the preliminary accord as a crucial first step toward a Palestinian state, with east Jerusalem as its capital. Citing Israeli intelligence reports that the PLO chief was at the point of being ousted as head of his financially bankrupt and fractured organization when the agreement was concluded, he questioned why the government had "rescued

Arafat with this dangerous accord." Netanyahu noted that the deal permitted the influx from abroad of thousands of elite PLO gunmen, warning that "this so-called police force will turn into an army that will ultimately fight against us."

Replying for the government, Foreign Minister Peres insisted that "we are not bringing any proposal for a Palestinian state." His contention was met by outraged catcalls from opposition politicians. In the end, the Oslo Accord was approved in the Knesset by a vote of sixty-one to fifty.

The veteran PLO chairman likewise faced stiff internal opposition to the peace pact. His unofficial "foreign minister," Farouk Kaddoumi, blasted the framework agreement as falling far short of Palestinian goals. PLO splinter groups based in Damascus and elsewhere vowed to wreck it, as did the fundamentalist HAMAS and Islamic Jihad groups. Syria expressed anger that Arafat had entered into a solo deal after promising to coordinate all peace moves with Damascus. Iran and Libya condemned the accord, as did Sudan and Iraq. Despite the boisterous opposition, Arafat secured the approval of sixty-three members of his PLO central council, although forty-four voted against and others either abstained or boycotted the special meeting.

## TORRENT OF TERROR

The popular axiom that "the devil is in the details" seemed to be confirmed as Israeli and Palestinian negotiators struggled to arrange the scheduled Israeli army withdrawal from the Gaza Strip and Jericho. Indeed, the pullback did not begin as scheduled on December 13. Several issues held up the evacuation, including disagreement on where the borders of the enclave should lie, whether or not Israeli troops could pursue fleeing terrorist suspects into the autonomy zones, and Arafat's demand for the immediate release of all Arab prisoners from Israeli jails. Palestinian negotiators stormed out of the talks in November, insisting that Rabin's proposals fell far short of their expectations.

However, the main impediment to the army redeployment was a sharp escalation in terror assaults, which followed a meeting in October of ten militant PLO and Islamic groups in Damascus. The ten, including the second and third largest PLO factions, vowed to step up attacks in order to thwart Arafat's "sellout to the Zionist enemy." A Jewish seminary student was murdered in early November in an assault traced to dissident members of Arafat's PLO Fatah faction. The car of a prominent National Religious Party politician was riddled with bullets soon afterward, wounding him and killing his driver.

Angry Jewish settlers responded to the escalating terrorism by stoning Arab cars and shops. Rabin then empowered the army to "use reasonable force" against the settlers, who charged that they were being abandoned by their own government.

With passions soaring both for and against the Oslo Accord, Palestinian terror groups stepped up their atrocities. A young female kindergarten teacher was killed in early December. Another Israeli was slaughtered when a civilian bus was ambushed by Islamic Jihad terrorists near Tel Aviv, and a father and son died in a shooting near Hebron. Two more civilians were gunned down near the town of Ramallah just before Christmas. The terror strikes led to Jewish civilian revenge killings of several Palestinians.

Negotiations to implement the Gaza Jericho withdrawal pact made little progress in the early part of 1994. Israeli officials thought they had secured a detailed agreement several times, only to find that Arafat had scuttled it. While the talks dragged on, so did the terror. By the end of February thirty-three Israelis had been killed in violent attacks since the festive Oslo signing ceremony in Washington.

However, the worst single terrorist assault was not by Palestinians, but upon them. Fed up with treating, and sometimes losing, friends who were victims of Arab attacks, a young Jewish doctor wearing an army uniform strode into Abraham's Tomb in Hebron. There, amid hundreds of praying Muslim men, Dr. Baruch Goldstein opened fire with an automatic rifle, killing twenty-nine and wounding many others. Even though the slayings were planned and carried out by the lone doctor, who was overpowered and pummeled to death, they deeply shocked the Israeli public and government. Financial compensation was quickly offered to the victims' families. Two small radical Jewish groups that expressed support for the killings were outlawed and their leaders jailed.

Naturally, the horrific February 25 shooting spree outraged Palestinians, who responded with sustained rioting throughout the disputed territories. Massive army reinforcements were rushed in to quell the violence, which spread like wildfire to eastern Jerusalem and Arab towns inside Israel. The PLO suspended peace talks with Rabin's government and demanded an emergency meeting at the United Nations, which voted to condemn Israel for the mass murder even though it was clearly carried out against the wishes of the government and nearly all Israelis. Likud leader Netanyahu condemned the brutal murders, but also decried the U.N. vote, noting that the world body had never found it appropriate to censure Arab terror even though it was clearly supported by several Muslim nations and many Palestinians.

Israeli anger grew when Arafat refused to condemn a series of Palestinian revenge attacks in March and April, and instead actually justified them. The worst atrocities were launched by Islamic suicide terrorists who blew up civilian buses in two northern Israeli towns, leaving twelve people dead and more than sixty wounded. Prime Minister Rabin insisted that the Palestinian leader speak out against the bus attacks, as did the Clinton administration. In the end, Arafat expressed "regret" over one of the attacks, which hardly satisfied most Israelis in light of his peace commitment to halt all Palestinian violence. Saying that the PLO chairman was apparently too weak to control the terrorist groups, Rabin accepted the statement and renewed peace negotiations. Opposition politicians charged that Arafat actually allowed some of the atrocities to take place as part of a carrot-and-stick approach to the withdrawal talks.

Despite the violence, a Gaza-Jericho pullback agreement was finally reached in May. However, it nearly collapsed when Arafat characteristically refused to sign an accompanying map at a ceremony in Cairo. After backstage crisis talks involving embarrassed Egyptian, American, and Russian officials, the PLO chief relented and the deal was sealed. The accord empowered Arafat to establish a twenty-four-member Executive Council to rule with him in the two autonomy zones and gave him control over Gaza Strip coastal waters. Several other trappings of statehood were also agreed upon, including the right to issue passports and postal stamps, establish radio and television stations, and build airports in the two zones. Likud leaders denounced most of these provisions, saying they would lead to an independent Palestinian state next to Israel's main cities, eventually controlled by Muslim extremists.

Soon after Israeli troops left most of the teeming Gaza Strip and the biblical town of Jericho in mid-May, Warren Christopher began what would turn out to be a series of fruitless excursions to the Middle East to try to secure an Israel-Syria peace accord. His first visit came after Syrian leader Hafez Assad rejected Rabin's offer to withdraw from the Golan Heights plateau in a three-stage pullout stretching over five years. The Syrian dictator said Israel must hand back "every inch" of the area in one fell swoop. Many Labor Party members felt betrayed by the proposal, recalling that Rabin had pledged to "never go down from the heights" during the 1992 election campaign. Opposition leaders condemned the offer as a sellout of vital security interests and a threat to Israel's fresh water supply.

While talks went nowhere with Assad, a breakthrough occurred with King Hussein. The Jordanian monarch affixed his signature to a "Declaration of Peace" document at a White House ceremony on July 25. This was followed on October 26 by the signing of a formal peace accord with Rabin along the Israel-Jordan border north of the twin Red Sea resorts of Eilat and Akaba. Unlike the controversial autonomy pact with the PLO, the agreement was welcomed by the opposition Likud Party, although some questioned the government's commitment to supply Jordan with fifty million cubic meters of fresh water a year, mainly from the Sea of Galilee.

Negotiations between Israel and the Palestinians over the second-stage army withdrawal from much of Jordan's former West Bank, which was supposed to have taken place by June 13, made little progress during the hot summer months. Meanwhile, Arafat continued to solidify his rule in his Gaza Strip and Jericho autonomy zones. He did so with the help of some of the more than 3 billion dollars in economic aid pledged by thirty countries, including half a billion from the United States. But his words still troubled many Israelis, especially remarks linking the Oslo Accord to the PLO's 1974 phased plan and a call made in a South African mosque for Muslims everywhere to "come and fight a jihad over Jerusalem."

In the secretly taped speech, Arafat went on to denounce Jewish control over the Holy City: "They say it is their capital. No, it is not their capital, it is our capital." Rabin termed the statement a violation of Arafat's promise to halt all verbal threats against Israel, prompting the Palestinian leader to reply that he was merely speaking of a "peaceful crusade" to retake Jerusalem.

It was not long before terrorist violence returned to the streets of Israel. Just two days after the Israel-Jordan peace accord was signed in an internationally televised ceremony, Gaza-based Islamic extremists blew up a city bus in the heart of Tel Aviv, killing twenty-one Israeli civilians and wounding more than forty others. The hideous attack— the worst since the 1978 coastal road massacre—came just two weeks after Muslim militants sprayed gunfire into a crowded Jerusalem café district, killing two (including an Arab patron) and wounding thirteen. The Tel Aviv assault came only one week after an Israeli soldier with dual American citizenship was kidnapped and murdered by HAMAS terrorists.

The horrendous splurge of barbaric attacks, which brought to almost one hundred the number of Israelis murdered since the Oslo Accord was signed, left stunned citizens with very little energy or desire to celebrate the peace accord with Jordan.

Rabin warned that the Israeli-Palestinian accord could not survive if Islamic terrorism was not halted. The statement came after several leading members of his Labor Party called for a reassessment of the withdrawal process. Meanwhile, the focus of terror attacks shifted to military personnel. Three soldiers were killed in a Gaza Strip ambush in November, which came one day after Arafat vowed in a fiery speech to "liberate Palestine in blood and fire!" The terrorism gloom was only briefly lifted in December when the Palestinian leader joined Rabin and Peres in receiving the Nobel Peace Prize in Norway.

Despair deepened in early 1995 when Muslim terrorists murdered twenty-one young Israeli soldiers at a bus stop north of Tel Aviv. The double suicide attack wounded sixty-two others, several of them severely.

As a result of the rash of deadly assaults, growing numbers of Israelis questioned the wisdom and veracity of Rabin's peace pact with the Palestinians. They decried the fact that the deal was obviously bringing with it a river overflowing with Jewish blood. President Ezer Weizmann called on Rabin to halt all negotiations with Arafat until the terrorism binge subsided. The call was a severe blow to the Labor government since the respected elder statesman and party member had been a strong advocate of the Oslo Accord.

Fearing that the second-stage pullback would not take place, Arafat finally began to seriously crack down on Palestinian Islamic groups, jailing suspected terrorist plotters. After several months of relative calm, negotiations resumed and a target withdrawal date of July 1 was agreed upon.

However, it was not long before Arafat freed most terrorist suspects from his Palestinian jails. Islamic militants struck again in April, leaving six soldiers dead in a Gaza Strip ambush. Peace talks were suspended in May after Rabin announced the expropriation of Arab-owned land in Jerusalem to build a major road and two new neighborhoods, one Palestinian and one Israeli. Despite the fact that such building was not outlawed under the accord, regional Arab leaders met and condemned the move, which was also blasted at the United Nations.

Negotiations resumed in June after Rabin rescinded his expropriation order, and a final second-stage withdrawal pact—dubbed "Oslo Two"—was signed in Washington on September 24. It called for Israeli troops to evacuate eight Arab towns in stages, ending with a partial pullout from Hebron by March 1996. Palestinian elections to choose a president and an eighty-two-member legislative council would be held in January. Three other redeployments would occur by the middle of 1997, leaving most of the disputed territories in Palestinian hands when scheduled final status negotiations got under way.

## THREE PRIME MINISTERS

Military withdrawals from parts of the perilous Gaza Strip and from the ancient town of Jericho had been widely supported by the Israeli public. Not so the scheduled pullbacks from Arab towns and villages close to the country's main cities. Although Rabin had already handed over tangible assets to the Palestinians, his people had not received the promised tranquility that they yearned for. In fact, many said they never felt more insecure. Among those who expressed reservations over the planned second-stage withdrawals was Armed Forces Chief of Staff Ehud Barak, a highly decorated military officer who would later enter the political arena.

Objections on security grounds were compounded by the fact that two of the Palestinian towns to be handed over to Arafat bordered sacred Jewish shrines: Joseph's Tomb near Nablus and Rachel's Tomb on the northern outskirts of Bethlehem. On top of this, Hebron contained Judaism's second holiest site on earth—the venerated graves of Abraham and Sarah, Isaac and Rebecca, and Jacob and Leah. Orthodox religious groups in particular protested against the promised army evacuations, saying they would threaten Jewish access to the holy sites.

Rabin's popularity ratings sank still further in opinion polls, which also predicted that Netanyahu would easily beat him in the upcoming 1996 elections. Several prominent politicians and rabbis blasted the premier for agreeing to abandon territory in Israel's biblical heartland. The phrase "Rabin is a traitor" arose from audiences at Likud Party rallies, although Netanyahu publicly rebuked such personal attacks against his opponent. Posters went up all around the country calling for the Labor Party leader—in an Arab headdress, or, in some cases, in a Nazi uniform—to be "punished" for the "crime" of ceding part of the Promised Land to the likes of Yasser Arafat.

Several Orthodox Jews gathered outside Rabin's official Jerusalem residence to recite an ancient curse of death against the Israeli leader. A mere one month later, he was a relic of history.

Yitzhak Rabin's November 4 assassination fell upon Israel like a blazing meteor from the black evening sky. Many believed it portended the death of the controversial peace process. The bullet that pierced the prime minister's chest also passed through and bloodied the written words to the "Song of Peace," which he had folded up and placed in his suit pocket only minutes before. With longtime rival Shimon Peres at his side, the esteemed war hero had awkwardly sung the song at a rally in Tel Aviv. The two Nobel Peace Prize recipients had achieved a tentative peace with Arafat's Fatah movement, but not with Muslim radicals or their regional backers, nor with a large segment of their own Jewish people who feared that the Oslo Accord spelled the ultimate demise of the tiny state.

To the shock and horror of the nation, it was one of Israel's sons—and an Orthodox Jew at that—who murdered Rabin. That news only further tore the traumatized country in two, even as world leaders made their way up to Jerusalem for the somber state funeral. Left-wing politicians and the slain leader's widow angrily blamed Netanyahu and his right-wing cronies for the assassination. The Likud leader refused to accept any blame, noting that he had frequently denounced verbal threats against his opponent. Several Orthodox rabbis did acknowledge that their condemnations of Rabin's policies may have been interpreted by some of their followers as a call to violence, although all maintained that they never dreamed an observant Jew would actually violate the biblical injunction against murder.

Sitting once again in the prime minister's chair, Peres vowed to proceed with the Oslo Two withdrawals. However, within one week of assuming office on November 22, Islamic militants made clear that they planned to make life difficult for the new leader, as they had for his assassinated predecessor. Lebanese Hizbullah forces pounded the northern Galilee region with more than thirty rockets, injuring eight Israelis. Peres warned the Assad regime that Syria would be held accountable for the aggressive actions of its surrogate ally. Yet soon afterward the Israeli leader renewed peace negotiations with Damascus, indicating that he was prepared to completely withdraw from the Golan Heights if certain conditions were met.

Israeli army forces evacuated seven Palestinian towns by Christmas, including Bethlehem. I was in the City of David reporting for CBS Radio News when Yasser Arafat helicoptered into town on the eve of the Christian holiday. In a defiant speech in which he called Jesus "the first Palestinian revolutionary," the PLO chief promised thousands of cheering

Arabs in Manger Square that they would soon march with him into nearby "sacred Al-Quds [Jerusalem], the capital of Palestine." One month later Arafat was overwhelmingly elected president of the expanding Palestinian entity. The contest was a foregone conclusion since no serious candidate dared to run against him.

Soon after Arafat secured his victory, Prime Minister Peres announced that Israeli elections would be moved up to May 29. In the wake of widespread revulsion over the heinous assassination of his longtime colleague, the new-old Labor leader was riding high in opinion polls. He wanted to capitalize on the predicted 10 to 20 percent "sympathy vote" that the polls showed he would receive from normally centrist and right-wing voters.

Islamic militants had other ideas. Backed by Iran, they set out to wreck the Israeli premier's lead by launching another wave of suicide terrorist strikes. The first attack came on the morning of February 25. A Palestinian from a refugee camp near Hebron boarded a Jerusalem bus dressed as an Israeli soldier. Among the twenty-two people blasted to bits by the bomber were two sixteen-year-old boys, along with an American Jewish student and his fiancée. Less than one hour later another jihad warrior blew himself up at a bus stop near the coastal town of Ashkelon, killing a female soldier and wounding many others. Hundreds of joyous Palestinians took to the streets in several towns under Arafat's control to celebrate the twin attacks. One week later Islamic militants struck again in Jerusalem. This time they murdered eighteen bus passengers riding down the city's main street, Jaffa Road.

The two Jerusalem massacres left dazed Israelis in a state of near hysteria, with many people fearing to venture out to public places. Realizing that his predicted election victory was endangered by the bloody blitz, Peres declared on March 3 that Israel was now "in a state of war against Islamic terrorism." As if to prove that the proclamation did not faze them, Palestinian militants struck again the very next day. This time they decided to hit the Labor Party's electoral heartland, the urban metropolis of Tel Aviv. A suicide "martyr" blew himself up outside a crowded mall in the center of the bustling city, filled with Israelis dressed in festive Purim costumes. Fourteen more Jews went to their untimely graves, including seven teenagers.

The total number of Israeli terrorist fatalities since the original Oslo Accord was arrived at now stood at 213, most of them civilians. This compared to less than one hundred victims in the corresponding thirty months before the agreement was signed in 1993.

"If this is peace, we don't want it!" declared a burgeoning number of Israelis as the election campaign swung into gear. Watching his ratings plummet in the polls, Peres suspended all peace talks with the Palestinians and postponed the scheduled March redeployment from Hebron. He also halted negotiations with Syria, pointing to hard evidence that the Assad regime, along with its ally, Iran, was backing Islamic terror attacks. Damascus showed its displeasure with the suspension by giving a green light to renewed Hizbullah rocket attacks upon northern Israel.

After dozens of Katuyshas landed in the Galilee panhandle, producing yet more Jewish victims of the Muslim fundamentalist holy war against Israel, Peres ordered a major military operation in southern Lebanon. In a repeat of Rabin's 1993 campaign, the April "mini-war" caused tens of thousands of Lebanese civilians to flee north. However, others took refuge in several south Lebanon U.N. outposts, which Israel charged were being used as cover for nearby Hizbullah rocket firings. More than one hundred were killed when Israeli artillery shells struck one of the bases. The incident enhanced world condemnation of the military operation and unleashed harsh Arab rebukes against Peres, even though he insisted that army gunners had been aiming at nearby rocket-launching positions.

The military operation did succeed in stopping Hizbullah rockets from crashing down upon northern Galilee. But it did not earn Peres many additional votes from his shell-shocked Jewish compatriots. Indeed, many Arab voters decided to sit out the election because of the Lebanon operation, depriving the Israeli premier of many traditional Labor votes. When television exit poll results were released on the evening of May 29, Shimon Peres was declared the winner. But when he got out of bed the next morning, the actual vote count showed that Binyamin Netanyahu had squeaked into office by less than 1 percent of the total vote. Among Israel's Jewish voters, the Likud leader was the clear favorite, capturing almost 60 percent of the ballots.

The new Israeli prime minister—the third man to hold the post in just seven months—sewed together a patchwork coalition of seven political parties. He needed to do so since his Likud Party, like Labor, had received far less seats than in previous elections. Among Netanyahu's coalition partners was a new immigrant party headed by former Soviet dissident Anatoly Natan Sharansky, which captured a surprising seven Knesset seats. Another partner was the new Third Way Party headed by former Labor Knesset member Avigdor Kahalani, who strongly opposed Labor's leftward tilt. Many secular Likud supporters expressed concern that just over one-third of the new government's seats were filled by three orthodox religious parties, which secured Netanyahu's commitment to back new legislation restricting the growing power of rival reform and conservative streams of Judaism.

## ARAFAT'S TUNNEL VISION

International leaders clearly wanted to see Shimon Peres retain the job that he inherited when his Labor party comrade was gunned down in Tel Aviv. This was especially true of most Arab leaders, who met in an emergency Arab League session in June to warn that they would "reconsider steps taken in the context of peace" if the new Likud premier did not continue with the U.N.-sanctioned "land for peace" withdrawal process.

Netanyahu, popularly known by his nickname, Bibi, denounced the Cairo summit resolution as an unnecessary threat, adding that "peace was and is Israel's strategic objective." He pointed out that while he had emphasized security and Palestinian reciprocity in his successful election bid, he had also promised to adhere to the Oslo Accords. Indeed, the Likud platform stated that all ratified peace commitments made by the Rabin government would be honored. But it also made clear that further land withdrawals would depend on Arafat's full compliance with his commitments, especially the crucial one to eradicate all Palestinian violence against Israelis, and threats of the same.

Although Netanyahu had many times castigated the Labor government's dealings with the PLO leader, he reluctantly met with Yasser Arafat in early September. Pointing to the Likud platform, he defended the move before several angry party colleagues by saying that Israel had no choice but to carry out the ratified Oslo Accords, however dangerous and flawed.

Barely two weeks after the two leaders met, unprecedented violence exploded in eastern Jerusalem and in Arafat's autonomous zones. The trigger for the outburst was, of all things, the official opening of a tourist exit door onto the Old City's Via Dolorosa. The door is located at the end of an ancient Jewish water tunnel that runs outside the northwestern retaining wall of the Temple Mount. With characteristic hyperbole, Arafat called the move "a great crime against our sacred shrines" and spurred on his people to take to the streets.

Netanyahu, who had ordered the exit opened after being advised by security officials that it would probably not inspire major unrest, denounced the Palestinian leader's statement as clear incitement to violence. He said Arafat knew that the tunnel was a mere tourist attraction that had been in operation under the previous Labor governments. He noted that the new exit, which was actually constructed under Rabin's watch, was nowhere near Muslim shrines on the Temple Mount and was only meant to alleviate congestion in the narrow tourist tunnel.

As is so often the case in the myopic Middle East, the details did not matter to the thousands of livid Palestinians who dutifully took up Arafat's call to man the trenches. Using tactics similar to those used during the riot described in the opening pages of this book, stones were hurled down from the Temple Mount onto Jewish worshipers at the Western Wall below. The Palestinian leader then called a general strike, which turned bloody when some of his security forces opened fire on Israeli soldiers, killing four of them. The worst violence occurred in the Gaza Strip, in Ramallah, and on the Temple Mount. Calm was finally restored at the end of September, but only after fifteen Israelis and sixty-nine Palestinians had lost their lives.

The small uprising set off alarm bells in Washington. President Clinton virtually ordered both Netanyahu and Arafat to fly to the U.S. capital for urgent consultations. He also invited King Hussein, who was more than a little piqued that he had not been told in advance about the tunnel exit opening. The American leader urged his Israeli counterpart to immediately pull his forces out of Hebron, which was almost eight months overdue according to the Oslo Two Accord. The new premier replied that he fully intended to carry out the delayed withdrawal, bringing sharp rebukes from some of his right-wing coalition allies who charged that he was too easily cowed by U.S. government pressure.

In the midst of the Jerusalem melee, war jitters were mounting in the north. Syrian leader Hafez Assad moved thousands of soldiers from the Beirut area to attack positions near the Golan Heights. The provocative action came after Netanyahu warned in August that Damascus would be held accountable for any renewed Hizbullah shelling of northern Israel. With war drums being pounded almost daily by Syrian officials and state-controlled media, Israeli defense minister Yitzhak Mordechai said in October that any nonconventional missile attack upon Israel would result in the annihilation of Assad's despotic regime. That ominous statement by the former army general was met the very next day by a Syrian attempt to penetrate Israeli airspace over the Golan Heights, and by provocative mobile missile movements.

Attempts to implement the army withdrawal from most of Hebron nearly caused the collapse of Netanyahu's multiparty government. Several cabinet ministers, including Ariel Sharon and Benny Begin, son of the former premier, argued that abandoning hills above the Jewish enclave to Arafat's armed forces was a sure recipe for future disaster. They were also upset that the Palestinians had still not revised the PLO charter, even though Arafat had promised to do so when the original Oslo Accord was agreed to and at every critical juncture of the withdrawal process. Begin resigned when the Hebron redeployment took place in January 1997. The pullback left Palestinian forces in control of 80 percent of the holy town. Israeli soldiers retained authority around the disputed Tomb of the Patriarchs and in adjacent Jewish neighborhoods, with some five hundred residents.

It was not long before jihad activists attacked thinned-out Israeli soldiers along the border of the Jewish enclave. The violence, which quickly spread to Bethlehem and other Palestinian towns, followed the Netanyahu government's mid-March announcement that construction would begin on a new Israeli housing project in the southeast corner of Jerusalem.

Ground breaking took place within sight of Bethlehem on a forested hill called Har Homa (Hebrew for the "Mount of the Protective Wall"). The new neighborhood, planned soon after the 1967 war, would complete a protective ring of Jewish housing around central Jerusalem.

Although the hill was more than 70 percent Israeli-owned, Arafat and company, along with most other Arab leaders, decried the construction project as a virtual declaration of war. As was the case when Yitzhak Rabin announced in 1995 that he would build in north Jerusalem, the Palestinian leader denounced the "illegal settlement building on occupied Arab land" as a violation of the Oslo Accords and demanded United Nations economic sanctions against the Jewish state. He then suspended sporadic peace talks with the Israeli government and had his information ministry issue a position paper claiming there was no historic or archeological evidence that Jewish temples were ever situated on the Old City's Temple Mount!

The moves were followed by another suicide terror attack in Tel Aviv, which left three female café patrons dead and dozens more wounded. Charging that Arafat had given the go-ahead for the Islamic attack, Prime Minister Netanyahu said he would not halt the Har Homa project under any circumstances. He added that no further land withdrawals would take place until such terror attacks were a thing of the past.

With the blood-soaked "land for peace" process teetering on the brink of collapse, both Israelis and Palestinians paused to consider some pressing internal matters. Social and political disputes between Orthodox and nonpracticing Jews, which predated the founding of the state in 1948, began to dominate the news. This was partly because the three religious political parties in Netanyahu's coalition had captured more Knesset seats in 1996 than ever before, giving them substantial weight in his government. Analysts said the unprecedented Orthodox electoral success— continuing a trend first noted in the early 1980s—was largely a reflection of the comparatively high birthrate among religious Jews, meaning Orthodox political power and influence would undoubtedly grow still more in the coming years.

Government-sponsored legislation designed to outlaw non-Orthodox conversions to Judaism fanned the smoldering religious-secular flames.

American Reform and Conservative Jewish leaders joined their local colleagues in denouncing the proposed law, warning that its passage would alienate non-Orthodox Jews around the world. The divisive issue was an almost identical rehash of another so-called "Who is a Jew?" debate that raged in the 1980s. Tensions also boiled up when Orthodox groups renewed their long-standing demand that a major road running through a religious neighborhood in north Jerusalem be closed on the Sabbath.

Seeing the demand as a sign of escalating religious attempts to trample on secular rights, various groups and politicians strongly resisted the move. As in earlier cultural clashes, calls were made for all healthy Orthodox males to be required to serve in the army (many receive almost automatic religious deferments).

Netanyahu's rule was threatened in early 1997 when Israeli police recommended that he be charged with fraud and breach of trust over a questionable political deal that he allegedly sanctioned. Although the Israeli attorney general later said there was not enough evidence to prosecute the prime minister, his personal credibility and political standing were seriously eroded. The affair was followed by an acrimonious cabinet revolt over various issues, which threatened to bring down his government and further weaken his authority. Several Likud Party leaders, including former Prime Minister Shamir, criticized Netanyahu's leadership style, saying he was too much of a one-man show.

Yasser Arafat's rule was also being questioned both at home and abroad, although the issues went beyond his personal integrity to the basic nature of his Palestinian Authority government. Critics said his formation of at least eight internal security services seemed to mirror one of the worst features of several surrounding Arab police states. While acknowledging Arafat's protests that it was not easy to establish self-rule in the face of Islamic opposition and Israeli intransigence, Palestinian journalists protested frequent censorship of their reports. Some stated publicly that they had actually faced less repression under Israeli military rule.

Palestinian human rights activists charged that dozens of Arabs had been tortured in Palestinian jails. They said fourteen prisoners died under suspicious circumstances during Arafat's first three years of autonomy rule. They also noted that a 1997 official decree that all Palestinians selling land to Jews would face the death penalty set off a wave of kidnappings and murders, allegedly by the hands of Arafat's security forces. The Palestinian Authority auditor stated that almost 40 percent of the autonomy government's budget was either squandered or misused by Palestinian officials, with some money going into personal bank accounts (Israeli officials later reported that Arafat himself had amassed a fortune of well over 1 billion U.S. dollars). The auditor's report was greeted by dismay in Washington and other donor capitals. Several important American politicians warned that further economic aid would be withheld if corruption and human rights violations did not cease. Prominent journalist Daoud Kuttab was jailed for a week on Arafat's orders after broadcasting a Palestinian council discussion of government corruption, even though his television station was licensed to transmit council sessions.

The internal Palestinian and Israeli scandals only added to the sense of gloom and pending doom that descended on the Middle East as negotiations on the explosive final status issues were set to get under way.

On the Palestinian side, the economy had not improved, as promised by Arafat when the original Oslo Accord was reached in 1993. In fact, living standards and salaries had actually declined for many people because of official financial mismanagement and the frequent border closures after terror attacks, which prevented many workers from getting to their jobs in Israel. Personal freedoms were seemingly no greater than under Israeli rule, although regular curfews no longer stifled life in towns and refugee camps. Islamic militants continued to threaten order in Palestinian society, as they did inside Israel's pre-1967 borders. The chances of setting up a sovereign Palestinian state with Jerusalem as its capital dimmed with Netanyahu's election. So, despite the widespread optimism when Rabin shook Arafat's hand on the White House lawn, the Oslo peace process seemed a mixed blessing at best.

In Israel, the faltering peace accord was not bringing the sense of well-being and security that many euphoric Israelis anticipated when the original agreement with the Palestinians was signed. Suicide terror attacks—which resumed in mid-1997 with two assaults in Jerusalem, leaving another twenty Israelis dead and scores seriously wounded—became a regular feature of life only after the accord was signed. Although many political, diplomatic, and economic benefits were apparent, the increasing trust and cooperation with Arafat and associates that were supposed to precede the difficult final status negotiations had not materialized. Deeply traumatized by the unprecedented terrorist blitz and the assassination of one of the "Fathers of Oslo," the Israeli public was more anxiety ridden and deeply divided than ever. All realized that a final dissolution of the crumbling peace accord could lead to a new regional war featuring chemical missile attacks on civilian centers.

# CHAPTER 11

# HOLY WAR OF TERROR

I vividly recall the first time I interviewed "Bibi" Netanyahu. It was October 1988, and his Likud party had just been declared the winner of that year's national elections under the leadership of Yitzhak Shamir. With a CBS Radio microphone in hand, I slowly edged my way up to the tall, American-educated politician through a crowd of enthusiastic well-wishers at Likud party headquarters in Tel Aviv.

Making his political debut, the eloquent Netanyahu was already known for his dramatic defense of the Jewish state as Israel's U.N. ambassador earlier in the decade, and from his frequent international television appearances since the outbreak of the Palestinian uprising more than one year before. As deputy foreign minister in Shamir's coalition, he would go on to be the Israeli government's main spokesperson to the world during the dark days before and during the Gulf War, which clearly irked his non-English-speaking boss, Foreign Minister David Levy.

However, the longer Netanyahu stayed in office as prime minister, the more people said he should go back to being an articulate government spokesman and leave the top job to someone else. His conservative coalition began to fall apart the moment he caved in to intense pressure from the Clinton White House and agreed to hand over most of Hebron to Yasser Arafat. Wobbly as it was, Netanyahu somehow managed to hold his patchwork government together for nearly two more years after Israeli troops evacuated their positions in the western part of the biblical town in early 1997. The Israeli leader also partially succeeded in convincing his aging Palestinian counterpart that a return to the level of terrorist violence experienced just before the Israeli election in 1996, and during the October tourist tunnel riots later that year, would spell the end of the Oslo peace process.

Following the twin 1997 terror attacks in Jerusalem, Israeli government pressure seemed to help Arafat keep a fairly tight reign on Islamic militants seeking to destroy the withdrawal accords. Still, occasional attacks did take place, with a rabbi stabbed to death in Hebron in mid-August 1998, followed by a HAMAS bomb blast one week later outside the Great Synagogue in Tel Aviv that wounded twenty-one Israelis. An angry Netanyahu said he would undertake no further land handovers until Arafat "fights terror everywhere in word and deed, whether in Hebron or Tel Aviv."

President Clinton kept pressing the photogenic prime minister throughout 1998 to implement additional land withdrawals. The Israeli leader and his cabinet agreed to do so if Arafat kept his peace process commitments, reiterated in the Hebron withdrawal accord. These included slashing his estimated 40,000-man paramilitary police and security forces to Oslo's 24,000 level, closing down illegal weapons factories, and halting incitement to violence on Palestinian radio and television. Arafat strongly resisted the Israeli pressure, charging it was meant to deflect attention from Netanyahu's alleged plot to retake land already handed over to Palestinian control.

Amid the frozen Oslo process and occasional terror attacks, Israelis celebrated the golden jubilee of their state in 1998—created fifty years earlier out of the ashes of the holocaust. The festivities, which angered many Palestinians, attracted a record number of foreign tourists to the Promised Land, most of them Christians and Jews who came to join in the widespread public observances. The visitors showed up despite renewed war jitters with Iraq in the spring. This caused the American and Canadian governments to issue travel warnings to Israel. Palestinians reacted to the escalating Middle East tensions by holding marches featuring the burning of U.S. and Israeli flags and calls for Saddam to bomb Tel Aviv. As a precautionary measure, gas mask distributions were increased throughout the land.

Soon after the late August terror attack in Tel Aviv, the government announced that 279 Israelis had been murdered by Arab terrorists in the five years since the preliminary Oslo accord was signed on the White House lawn in September 1993. Officials noted that this was three times the number slain by terrorists in the entire 15 years before the "land for peace" agreement was reached! The astonishing death toll only added to mushrooming right-wing calls for Netanyahu to abandon the blood-soaked Oslo process, with many arguing that Arafat's solemn promise to end all Palestinian violence had in reality been just a cover for stepped-up holy war.

Worldwide calls upon Arafat to clean up his corrupt government continued during Netanyahu's time in office, especially as evidence grew that many senior Palestinian officials—including the PLO chief—were pocketing international donor aid and building elaborate villas. Human rights groups questioned many Palestinian Authority practices, especially the 1997 deaths by torture of seven Palestinian prisoners being held in Arafat's jails, and the 1998 public execution of two brothers who served in his police force. The latter were shot dead by an official firing squad in Gaza City. Accused of killing two fellow policemen in a shootout the week before the brothers were tried by what many human rights groups termed a kangaroo court just before their executions—the first ones formally carried out by Arafat's administration. Despite the international protests, more Palestinian Authority executions followed.

## WYE ACCORD SPELLS NETANYAHU'S DEMISE

Despite the frequently heard Palestinian and Arab world contention that the nationalistic Israeli leader was not planning to implement any more army withdrawals, Netanyahu surprised his left-wing critics and shocked many of his coalition allies by agreeing to finish the pullback process begun by Yitzhak Rabin in 1994. As with the Hebron redeployment, it was intense arm twisting from Bill Clinton that clinched the deal—dubbed the Wye Accord since it was hammered out with Netanyahu and Arafat at a retreat center situated along Maryland's rustic Wye River. The agreement, reached in October 1998, came after increasing warnings from regional Arab leaders and others that the Palestinian street was about to explode if the moribund Oslo withdrawal process was not quickly revived. The Wye Accord consisted of three main sections. The first part detailed "further redeployments" that Israel would carry out to complete the withdrawals spelled out in earlier peace deals. The phased army pullbacks would be stretched out over a twelve-week period ending in January 1999. However, Netanyahu made clear that the actual timing of the redeployments would depend on Arafat's compliance with his end of the bargain.

In return for the additional land handovers, Arafat agreed in Wye's second section to confiscate illegal weapons in his autonomy zones and to keep captured Palestinian militants locked up instead of releasing them soon after arrest (the so-called "revolving door" practice frequently criticized by Israeli and American officials). He promised once again to reduce the number of armed men serving in his bloated security forces. Arafat also pledged to get his PLO executive committee to formally ratify his early 1998 letter to Clinton declaring that the PLO founding charter, with its many calls for Israel's destruction, had been effectively nullified by the Oslo Accords. The final section of the Wye pact dealt with the establishment of international committees to monitor the withdrawal process, and various economic issues related to the land-transfer process.

One of Netanyahu's main coalition partners, the nine-member National Religious Party, vowed to topple his government if he carried out the Wye withdrawals. Along with other cabinet ministers, party leaders broadly hinted that Clinton had forced the accord upon a reluctant Netanyahu and Arafat on the eve of U.S. congressional elections. They charged that the shamed president was trying to deflect voter attention away from the growing Monica Lewinski sex scandal and the pending impeachment process.

Several of Netanyahu's own Likud party colleagues also condemned the pact, with tourism minister and future president Moshe Katsav terming it "full of holes." This came in response to Netanyahu's contention that the Wye agreement "plugged many of the holes in the Swiss cheese that was Oslo." Benny Begin, son of the late Likud premier, blasted the deal as "a horror, idiocy and an agreement of defeat."

Palestinian militant groups expressed their fierce opposition to the "latest Arafat sellout" by launching fresh attacks to thwart any Wye implementation. Just six days after the accord was initialed in Washington, a HAMAS terrorist attempted to crash a car bomb into an Israeli school bus carrying thirty-four students in the Gaza Strip. The attack was thwarted when a quick-acting Russian immigrant soldier steered his army jeep into the path of the oncoming car—losing his life in the subsequent massive explosion. Israeli leaders demanded that Arafat publicly condemn the attack and crack down on the Islamic terrorist group.

Instead, the Palestinian leader merely termed the barely averted mass slaughter of children as "harmful to Palestinian national interests" and placed HAMAS leader Sheik Achmed Yassin under house arrest. The weak responses only strengthened opposition to the Wye pact inside Netanyahu's rebellious coalition.

The death knell to the prime minister's tottering government was sounded in early December. It came just days after he carried out the first Wye withdrawal from land surrounding the town of Jenin, released more than two hundred Arab prisoners from Israeli jails, and allowed the opening of a Palestinian international airport in the Gaza Strip. Netanyahu was astonished when widespread Palestinian violence erupted soon after the pullout, which left Arafat in control of an additional 9 percent of Israel's biblical heartland.

Dubbed the "prisoner intifada" by the Arab press, the revolt began when Palestinian security prisoners, unhappy that they were not among those released by Netanyahu, began rioting. The violence spread like the plague to all of Arafat's cities and towns, and then engulfed the eastern half of Jerusalem. Israeli troops responded with tear gas and rubber bullets, killing some rioters and wounding many others in the process.

Netanyahu's cabinet reacted strongly to the escalating unrest, which they said was egged on by Arafat and his comrades—as I confirmed by monitoring Palestinian television and radio. The government suspended the Wye Accord. The move angered President Clinton, who was about to be impeached by Congress over the humiliating sex scandal. But the U.S. leader barely had time to react before escalating Iraqi anti-aircraft fire on American and British jets prompted a four-day bombing campaign against Saddam Hussein. The air force action gave the Iraqi dictator the perfect excuse to send United Nations weapons inspectors packing, setting the stage for future confrontations with the United States and Israel.

Neither Middle East nor domestic tensions could stop the lame-duck White House occupant from attending a PLO National Council meeting in the Gaza Strip in late December, where he upset many Israelis by hailing Arafat and his colleagues for "standing tall for what you think is right for your future." The gathering voted to revoke clauses in the PLO founding charter calling for Israel's destruction, without specifically listing them as Netanyahu had demanded.

Increasingly upset that the charismatic Israeli leader had "brazenly gambled with the nation's security just to rescue Bill Clinton," as one of his cabinet colleagues put it, most of Netanyahu's six coalition partners revolted against him. Along with a majority of his own Likud Party legislators and the entire opposition, they supported an overwhelming Knesset vote to hold early national elections during the first half of 1999.

The crumbling Oslo peace process suffered another major blow in early 1999 when one of its strongest regional supporters, King Hussein of Jordan, died in February after ruling his desert country for more than forty-six years. Although the world's longest reigning monarch had often denied rumors that he was suffering from cancer, the reports proved to be true. Among his last acts in power was summoning Arafat and Netanyahu to his hospital room at the Mayo Clinic in Minnesota to plead with them to sign the Wye Accord. Indeed, both men said their subsequent decisions to do so, against their better judgments, were partly to honor the dying king.

Israeli officials were stunned when Hussein announced on his deathbed that his brother, world-renowned statesman Crown Prince Hassan, would not succeed him as everyone expected. Instead, the king chose his oldest son Abdullah, a relatively unknown and untested man in his mid-thirties. Fears were expressed in Israel and abroad that the young king, married to a Palestinian woman, would not be able to hold his fragile country together in the same manner that his father had done, let alone keep Hussein's 1994 peace treaty with Israel afloat.

Despite the collapse of the Wye withdrawal pact, the veteran Palestinian leader—who had presided over the PLO for more than thirty years—strongly hinted that he would declare the establishment of a sovereign Palestinian state in May 1999. Needing to win back as much right-wing support as he could before early national elections were held in mid-May, Netanyahu responded that the Oslo "land for peace" process would be dead and buried if the Palestinian leader carried out the threatened unilateral act.

## LIGHTNING TO THE RESCUE!

The 1999 Israeli elections were the first to feature a direct vote for prime minister. Until then, the electoral system only allowed voters to choose a political party to represent them in the Knesset, not an individual leader. Fierce horse-trading to select a premier usually followed. Israel's debut direct election prompted no less than five politicians to declare their candidacy for the top job: Netanyahu, Benny Begin, and Yitzhak Mordechai (who both quit the Likud Party to make their runs), plus new Labor Party leader Ehud Barak. The fifth candidate, Knesset member Azmi Bishara, was most notable for the fact he was an Arab citizen of Israel. Polls showed Netanyahu running neck and neck with his Labor Party rival, with the other candidates far behind. In the end, the three lagging politicians pulled out of the race, leaving a traditional two-man showdown in their wake.

Ehud Barak—whose last name means "lightning" in Hebrew—promised to revive the frozen peace process if elected premier. The former army general, who was the only Labor Party Knesset member to oppose the Rabin government's 1995 Oslo Two agreement, said he would yank Israeli forces out of Lebanon within one year of winning office. This was an extremely popular declaration, given that continuing Hizbullah attacks inside Israel's security zone were leaving more than thirty soldiers dead on average each year.

More boldly, Barak vowed to secure a peace pact with Syria during the first year of his administration, along with a final status accord with the Palestinians. Emphasizing his own security background and comparing himself to his assassinated political mentor, Barak promised to bring any final peace deal to a national referendum. He also vowed that there would be no return to the 1967 borders, no Palestinian army in Arafat's zones of control, and no redivision of Jerusalem. The short but stocky Labor leader said he would not abandon most Israeli settlements under a final peace accord, apart from isolated ones previously slated for handover by Yitzhak Rabin.

Predicting that Barak would fail to fulfill his campaign pledges, especially the one to keep all of Jerusalem united under Israeli rule, Netanyahu maintained that only he could "secure an enduring peace" with Arafat and company. However, his previous record, plus Barak's popular promise to "quickly exit the Lebanese quagmire," resulted in the Labor leader's landslide victory on May 17. The political novice took 56 percent of the vote. However, Barak's party shrank from thirty-four Knesset seats to just twenty-six.

Analysts said many traditional Labor voters either chose the new Center Party headed by Yitzhak Mordechai or the Shinui ("Change") Party, which captured six seats each. Most Arab voters selected Barak in the end, but not his party. A post-election breakdown showed that a substantial majority of Jewish Israelis chose Netanyahu over Barak, meaning the Arab vote had tipped the balance in the Labor leader's favor—a fact Barak would not forget when he later talked peace with Yasser Arafat.

Netanyahu's Likud Party was in even worse shape than Labor. It shrank from thirty-two Knesset seats to just nineteen. Many usual Likud supporters defected to Netanyahu's religious ally, the Orthodox Shas Party, which nearly doubled its Knesset representation to seventeen seats. The powerful Shas showing meant that Barak would be forced to include the hawkish religious party in his broad coalition government, and in his peace process formulations.

Ehud Barak moved like an electric bolt to keep his campaign promises. By August, he was busy bartering a revised Wye deal with the Palestinian leadership. With the besieged Clinton administration leaning hard on the aging PLO chairman, a deal was signed in Egypt on September 4. The accord stated that a final status framework accord would be hammered out by February 2000. It also featured a complete Israeli army withdrawal from an additional 11 percent of Judea and Samaria by then, along with the handing over of full administrative control to Arafat in an additional 10 percent of the disputed land. This would leave the Palestinian Authority in charge of more than 42 percent of Israel's biblical heartland when final status negotiations got under way, along with most of the Gaza Strip.

More importantly, almost all Palestinians would be under Arafat's direct rule. Thousands of Israeli residents of Judea and Samaria and their supporters demonstrated against the Wye Two Accord, as they had when Netanyahu signed the original agreement nearly one year before.

As he did when the Gaza-Jericho withdrawal agreement was signed in 1994, the Palestinian leader threw a last-minute spanner in the works just before the revised accord was due to be signed in Egypt. He demanded the immediate release of four hundred Arab prisoners from Israeli jails, including terrorists convicted of murdering Israelis. Barak refused to release anyone with "blood on their hands," prompting a two-day postponement of the signing ceremony while visiting U.S. secretary of state Madeleine Albright desperately bridged the gap. In the end, Arafat agreed to a slightly smaller release, but warned he would demand that all two thousand-plus Palestinian prisoners be set free as part of a final status accord, whatever their crimes.

Arab jihad warriors wasted no time demonstrating that Barak's peace process goals were just as naïve and unworkable as his political mentor's had been. Within eighteen hours of the Wye Two signing, twin car bombs were detonated in the northern port city of Haifa and Tiberius. The bombs apparently blew up prematurely while the vehicles were heading to their destinations in the center of both towns, killing only the three terrorists inside the cars. An elderly Jewish woman walking on the sidewalk near the Tiberius blast was seriously wounded. Israeli officials were later angered to learn that the dead Muslim terrorists were all Arab citizens of the Jewish-led state. Just one week before, another Muslim Israeli was arrested and charged with stabbing and bludgeoning to death an Orthodox Jewish couple who had been out walking in a Jezreel Valley forest.

## SYRIA SCUTTLES PEACE DEAL

With the Wye Two Accord under his belt, Ehud Barak set his sights on Lebanon and Syria. Intending to keep his campaign commitment to pull

Israeli forces out of southern Lebanon by the summer of 2000, he persuaded Bill Clinton to host meetings at the Wye River plantation between
himself and Syrian leaders. However, Syrian dictator Hafez Assad, who
was extremely ill, declined to attend, sending his bellicose foreign minister instead.

The Syrian official, Farouk Shara, blasted Israel in his opening speech
after refusing to shake Barak's hand. He repeated Syria's demand that the
entire Golan Heights be quickly handed over to full Syrian control, including the strategic eastern peak of Mount Hermon (the area is the
source of almost half of Israel's renewable supply of potable water). More
than this, he insisted that Barak guarantee that such a withdrawal would
be undertaken even before formal peace negotiations got under way. Shara
added insult to injury by refusing to promise that Assad would sign a full
treaty in return.

Despite a prolonged drought that parched Israel and most of the
Middle East in the late 1990s, Barak stunned many of his countrymen by
agreeing to a complete Golan withdrawal. However, he mollified some of
his critics by emphasizing that he would hold out for a phased pullback,
accompanied by a reciprocal Syrian military retreat from the Golan border, and various other security measures.

The shrewd Syrian strongman balked at Barak's relatively modest conditions (after all, it was Syria that attacked Israel from the strategic heights
in 1967 and again in 1973). He ordered his negotiators to present a coun-
terproposal that was a definite nonstarter. It stated that Syria would only
do a deal with Barak if he agreed to surrender the northeast shore of the
depleted Sea of Galilee—which includes the vital headwaters of the
Jordan River—along with the entire Golan plateau and Mount Hermon.
This astonished the two democratically elected leaders since Syria had
never legally controlled the seashore nor the riverbanks, but only captured
the areas in skirmishes with Israel before 1967.

Assad displayed his contempt for Clinton and Barak's desire to secure
a peace accord in an even more concrete and destructive way. In light of
the newly elected Israeli leader's pledge to pull his soldiers out of southern
Lebanon by July whether a peace pact was reached with Syria or not, the
widely feared despot unleashed his proxy Hizbullah holy warriors to

attack the detested Zionist enemy. Dozens of Russian-made rockets were lobbed at Israeli military positions in southern Lebanon and civilian targets inside Israel. Officials said more than 120 attacks were launched in the first six weeks of 2000 alone, more than in all of 1999, driving many Israeli border residents from their homes. Hizbullah assaults continued into the spring.

Meanwhile, the government-controlled media in Damascus lobbed fresh verbal assaults upon Israel, with the official *Tishrin* newspaper claiming that "Israeli crimes against the Arabs are uglier than the ones committed by the Nazis of old." Another editorial claimed that Israel "propagates the myth of the Holocaust" in order to "secure money from the West."

With fighting escalating in southern Lebanon, Barak suspended the peace talks with the Syrian regime in late January. However, Bill Clinton—seemingly desperate for some positive headlines to replace those heralding his raunchy Oval Office escapades—refused to give up, asking Assad to meet him in Geneva in late March. The confident American leader seemed certain he could use his personal charm and negotiating skills to produce a breakthrough. Instead, the ailing Syrian dictator, who would die a few months later and be replaced by his son Bashar, repeated his insistence that a peace deal must include an Israeli abandonment of the northeast shore of the Sea of Galilee.

Clinton was crestfallen, realizing that Israel would never give in to such an absurd demand, which would give Syria international legal rights to the decreasing water in Israel's main above-ground reservoir.

Acknowledging that the so-called "Syrian track" was leading nowhere, Prime Minister Barak turned his attention back to the Palestinians. Struggling negotiations had hit a brick wall when Arafat stormed out of a summit meeting with the Israeli premier in early January. The PLO chief was upset by Israeli maps that detailed the land Barak was offering in order to complete the Wye Two withdrawals. In particular, Barak wanted to hold on to Arab suburbs around Jerusalem, at least until the Palestinian demand to redivide the Holy City was dealt with during pending final status talks. Arafat's public pique caused the cancellation of a scheduled three-way summit between himself, Barak, and Clinton that was supposed to complete a final status framework agreement by mid-February. Before he walked out on Barak, Arafat had agreed to a mid-September deadline for achieving an overall peace accord.

As a result of sustained U.S. prodding, Israeli-Palestinian negotiations resumed in early March. The final Wye withdrawal took place later that month. Arafat was now in total control of more than one-fifth of the territory that Israel captured from Jordan in the Six Day War, with full Palestinian Authority administrative rule extending to an additional 21 percent of the disputed area. The army redeployment was followed by another round of final status talks between Barak and Arafat in Washington. The Israeli leader pledged to reach a framework accord by mid-May and an overall peace pact by the seventh anniversary of the original Oslo signing on September 13.

With the Israeli-Palestinian peace train apparently back on track, Arafat's security forces cooperated with their Israeli counterparts to confiscate a large cache of weapons found hidden in a HAMAS-run kindergarten in the Gaza Strip. This came after Israeli agents uncovered a terrorist cell inside an Arab Galilee town that was plotting with Gaza-based Islamic militants to blow up Jewish apartment buildings in Tel Aviv. The renewed security cooperation was welcomed in world capitals, as it was inside Barak's cabinet. Yet that did not stop fierce bickering between left-wing Meretz Party government ministers and their right-wing Shas Party antagonists. Barak worked hard to halt the internal bloodletting, realizing that his shaky coalition would fall apart if either one of the two parties, with twenty-seven Knesset seats between them, leaped from his tottering government ship.

As chilly Israeli-Palestinian relations warmed up, Pope John Paul came on a personal pilgrimage to the Holy Land. Delighted to be hosting the head of the world's largest church, Israeli leaders spared no expense to make the March visit a success. The costly effort paid off handsomely since the special pilgrimage brought with it a flood of mostly Roman Catholic tourists, boosting both the Israeli and Palestinian economies. However, politics was not entirely left out of the pontiff's spiritual tour. Just before his arrival, Arafat angered Israeli officials by signing a pact in Rome with John Paul that "guaranteed" that the Palestinian Authority would "protect the status of Roman Catholic churches and religious shrines" in Jerusalem once it gained full control over the walled Old City.

## LEBANON RETREAT

A massive Hizbullah rocket blitz exploded in northern Israel in early May, destroying several buildings and cars in the town of Kiryat Shmona. The attack prompted Ehud Barak to speed up his unilateral army withdrawal from the south Lebanon security zone. He argued that a one-sided pull-out was not overly risky since the United Nations had vowed to help se-cure Israel's border after his troops evacuated the area. If Muslim militia attacks continued and Israel needed to respond across the border, the world would understand and offer support, he maintained. Likud leaders scoffed at Barak's intended reliance on an international body that spent much of its time bashing Israel. They also pointed out that U.N. "peace-keeping forces" serving in the area for more than two decades had a mixed record at best in preventing Arab attacks upon Israeli targets.

Senior military leaders also expressed strong opposition to the pend-ing pullout. Armed forces chief Shaul Mofaz told Barak that the army could not guarantee the security of northern Israel once Israeli troops were withdrawn. He predicted that Hizbullah, and not U.N. forces or the Lebanese army, would end up ruling the abandoned security zone. Sadly, the warning proved to be right on target. Mofaz added that portions of Syria's expanding missile arsenal might be moved to the evacuated area, along with Iranian rockets.

Although the army pullback was not due to be completed before July, Barak decided to carry it out virtually overnight in late May. He reasoned that every additional day his soldiers were in the war-torn Land of the Cedars was another day they might be killed or wounded there. However, his sudden order to speed up and complete the withdrawal in just a mat-ter of days shocked the South Lebanese Army, Israel's local and loyal ally in the protracted war against Hizbullah. The mainly Maronite Lebanese militia had sacrificed hundreds of men in the military struggle against the Iranian- and Syrian-backed group, partly to protect southern Lebanon's Maronite Catholic community, but also to defend neighboring Israel.

Now, many feared a massacre once Israeli troops withdrew, especially among the hundreds of current or former South Lebanese Army soldiers. Their fears were compounded when Lebanese president Emile Lahoud announced on May 11 that there would be "no amnesty for those who collaborated with the enemy."

South Lebanese Army commander Antoine Lahad had been assured by his Jewish cohorts that the IDF pullout would not be completed for several more weeks. However, he and his men awoke on May 24 to find that the Israelis had evacuated their remaining positions overnight. With triumphant Hizbullah forces rapidly advancing into the crumbling Security Zone, more than six thousand South Lebanese Army-connected Lebanese citizens fled across the Israeli border for shelter. Most were forced to leave behind their possessions.

Bitter over the hasty Israeli retreat, Lahad said that Barak "destroyed in twenty-four hours relations which took twenty-four years to build." He added that his forces had "worked hand in hand with Israel, but suddenly Israel pulled back its hand and shook us off." Capping his critique, the South Lebanese Army commander said Barak's speedy exit had "given Hizbullah a victory it never dreamed of."

Many Middle East analysts surmised that the swift Israeli evacuation was precisely designed to cause the collapse of the South Lebanese Army. United Nations officials had made clear to Barak that they would not certify Israel's withdrawal, nor guarantee peace along the border, if the "rogue militia" remained in place. Analysts said Barak did not have the heart to disarm the mainly Maronite militia, as the U.N. demanded, and also feared that some angry South Lebanese Army soldiers might turn their guns on their long time allies if he ordered Israeli troops to do so. He concluded that a surprise pullback would do the job for him by forcing the soldiers to throw down their weapons and run for their lives.

Although most Israelis were pleased that their army had finally quit Lebanon after a long and dreary eighteen-year stay, Barak's overnight retreat—and the subsequent flood of desperate South Lebanese Army refugees fleeing with just the shirts on their backs—drew harsh criticism from many politicians. "We are sorry, ashamed, and ask forgiveness for the way you were treated," said Likud Knesset member Tzippi Livni while visiting shaken Lebanese families near Tiberius.

Among those who escaped from south Lebanon was a long time friend of mine who ran a dental clinic in the town of Marjayoun. Beverley Timgren, a Christian dental hygienist from Toronto who came to work at the clinic in 1984 and ended up running it, had to abandon most of her donated equipment, along with her car and other personal items. I was deeply saddened when she filled me in on some of the unpublished details of the South Lebanese Army flight, especially since I was acquainted with a few of the new refugees from my days at the Voice of Hope.

On top of that, I agreed with General Lahad, whom I had interviewed several times, that Ehud Barak's abandonment of Israel's only regional Arab ally was shameful. I was also concerned that the hasty pullout would significantly fan holy war flames by encouraging further attacks from Hizbullah jihad warriors, and even more importantly, from their militant Palestinian cousins.

## OMENS OF HOLY WAR

Basking in the glow of the "Zionist enemy's crushing defeat," Hizbullah leader Sheik Hassan Nasrallah declared before thousands of cheering Muslims in Beirut that "the sacred jihad will continue until Israel disappears!" More ominously, Iran's visiting foreign minister, Kamal Kharrazi, said Israel's swift withdrawal "shows us that resistance based on principals can impose difficult conditions on the occupier to force him to retreat in fear from the lands he occupies." Two days later, Nasrallah proclaimed to another huge crowd in southern Lebanon that Israel was "weaker than a spider's web!" He went on to crow that Lebanese "jihad martyrs" had demonstrated that determined Muslim warriors "can impose our demands on the Zionist aggressors."

Viewing the boastful comments on Hizbullah's popular television station, the Palestinian masses were watching and listening very carefully. Indeed, the holy war embers had already been stirred some ten days before the sudden Israeli pullout when fierce gun battles broke out between Palestinian and Israeli security forces. The armed exchanges—the worst since the 1996 tunnel riots—began when Palestinian policemen and Fatah activists opened fire with live ammunition on Israeli troops. Unarmed Palestinians quickly joined the mid-May fray, hurling rocks and firebombs at outnumbered Israeli soldiers. The violence, which engulfed all Palestinian Authority cities and towns and left four Palestinians dead and scores of Arabs and Israelis wounded, died down only after Israel threatened to send attack helicopters to blow up Palestinian police headquarters near Arafat's main office in Ramallah, where the heaviest clashes took place.

Israeli army leaders and many politicians blamed the Palestinian Authority for the unprovoked outburst of violence. As evidence, they pointed to a front-page notice that appeared in Arafat's official newspaper, *Al Hayat Al Jadida,* on the very morning that armed Palestinian attacks began. The notice was issued to mark *Al Nakba,* an annual event that commemorates "the catastrophe" of Israel's rebirth on May 15, 1948. It stated that "the fury of the masses must erupt like a volcano in the face of the Israelis, and the land must explode under their feet."

Analysts saw the published notice as an unabashed call by the Palestinian leadership for a return to the sustained uprising violence that led in 1993 to the faltering Oslo peace pact—a call that totally violated the accord. Leaving no doubt about where Arafat stood on the violent clashes, the PLO executive committee issued an official statement as the rioting calmed down. It hailed "the Palestinian martyrs" who had "given their lives in the great and popular awakening that swept all areas of our nation and refugee camps."

The "popular" rioting was an awakening of another kind for Ehud Barak and his pro-Oslo political comrades—an extremely rude one. They had generally dismissed the 1996 tunnel riots as an "understandable" result of Palestinian frustration over "intransigent Netanyahu government policies." Now, the Palestinian leadership was lauding, if not actually ordering, murderous attacks against Israelis while dovish Labor Party and Meretz politicians were running the political show.

The mid-May violence came just days after Palestinian leaders warned that a new uprising would be launched if they did not gain full sovereignty over all of eastern Jerusalem in a final status peace accord. As he had done several times before, Arafat declared that if Barak continued to ignore his Jerusalem handover ultimatum and a new *intifada* was started, it would end with Israeli Jews "drinking the water of the Dead Sea." In other words, the Israeli people would end up dead if they did not surrender the most hallowed portion of Judaism's most holy city to an autocratic Muslim-led regime.

Arafat's annihilation threat had come on the heels of yet another breakdown in the final status negotiations on May 5. The crisis began when Barak revealed that he wanted to retain control of around 20 percent of the disputed territories, including 144 Jewish settlements. Several of his coalition partners, especially the Shas Party and Natan Sharansky's Russian immigrant party, threatened to topple his government if the communities did not remain in Israeli hands. Palestinian negotiators flatly rejected the proposal, insisting it would leave isolated islands of Arab enclaves surrounded by Jewish settlements. Barak retorted that the Jewish communities he wished to retain sat on less than 5 percent of the land in question, leaving Arafat with a viable, if not entirely contiguous, state.

Ironically, the mid-May Palestinian assault was launched on the very day that Barak's cabinet reluctantly voted to withdraw from several Arab suburbs east of Jerusalem's Old City, transferring the villages to full Palestinian control as Arafat had demanded. The controversial decision—designed to get negotiations rolling again—left the southeast portion of the historic Mount of Olives in Palestinian Authority hands. This prompted the National Religious Party to warn that it would leave Barak's six-party coalition if any further concessions were offered over Jerusalem.

## CAMP DAVID DISASTER

The embattled premier concluded that Yasser Arafat himself was behind the intense rioting that blazed like a forest fire in May. This seemed to be confirmed in June when Arafat delivered several incendiary speeches sharply denouncing Barak and Israel. In one of them, he shouted out that "Palestine is ours, ours, ours!" to rapturous cheers from his Arab audience. He also stated that a new uprising was looming if Barak did not meet all of his negotiating demands. Nevertheless, Barak resisted right-wing demands that he halt tempestuous final status negotiations with the Palestinian Authority and freeze the Oslo "land for peace" process. Instead, the ex-general concluded that he must offer even *more* concessions to the veteran PLO chairman in order to secure a permanent peace deal.

That is exactly what Barak ended up doing at a drawn-out summit meeting with Arafat and Bill Clinton the second half of July. Longing for a breakthrough to rival the Egyptian-Israeli peace accord of 1978, the shamed American leader invited the two Middle East antagonists to negotiate at the Camp David presidential retreat in Maryland. He would play the role of Jimmy Carter, prodding the Arabs and Jews along where necessary with an assortment of carrots and sticks.

But a repeat performance was not to be. For one thing, three coalition parties resigned from Barak's unstable government even before he left for the United States, convinced he was planning to "give away the store." Barak had earlier resisted their demands that he form a broad national unity government to deal with the crucial final status negotiations, angering all three parties. The defections meant that any peace deal Barak might initial would be very unlikely to pass muster in the Knesset. Arafat was similarly warned by various Palestinian groups, including some connected to his own Fatah movement, that he would be met with massive resistance if he came away with anything less than everything.

Amid the growing signs that the trilateral summit would fail, many people, including Israeli foreign minister David Levy, called upon both leaders to stay away from Camp David. They warned that a seemingly unavoidable negative outcome would dash all hopes for peace and open the path for a return to full-scale holy war. But Barak and Clinton seemed determined to persevere, come hell or high water.

The writing on the wall was clear, and the acrimonious three-way summit ended in failure after nearly two weeks of round-the-clock negotiations. Instead of the smiles and handshakes that capped the original Camp David parley some two decades before, Arafat and Barak came away scowling, each accusing the other of having caused the climactic peace talks to fail. Left with yet more egg on his face, President Clinton put most of the blame for the failed meeting on the Palestinian leader, saying that Barak had "moved forward more from his initial position than Chairman Arafat, particularly surrounding the question of Jerusalem."

In the end, Arafat was apparently no more willing to bend than Hafez Assad had been. The two Arab leaders—bitter enemies for many years—were apparently cut from the same stubborn cloth. Both preferred to keep their suffering people locked in misery (and in Arafat's case, to once again hurl his children to premature graves), than to make serious concessions for peace. They refused to "lose face" by signing a compromise peace accord with Israel. So Clinton's high-stakes Camp David dice roll failed, and the seeds of a new violent uprising were planted firmly in the water-starved Middle Eastern soil.

Barak's unprecedented concessions were the final straw for several of his former coalition partners, who said they would now support early national elections in early 2001. David Levy then resigned from the cabinet, sealing the minority government's fate. On the other hand, Arafat returned home to a boisterous hero's welcome, seemingly riding higher in his political saddle than ever before.

Exactly what Barak offered at Camp David became the subject of some dispute itself, with Palestinian negotiators presenting a different version than either the Israeli or American leaders. But it seems clear that the novice premier was willing to hand over at least most of the walled Old City and surrounding Arab neighborhoods to full Palestinian Authority control, including the hallowed Temple Mount (this in response to a Clinton suggestion that Israel retain "sovereignty" inside the ancient walled structure, while the Palestinians got the top of it). Israel would only hold on to the southern portion of the Old City running from Jaffa Gate south and east to the sacred plateau. Almost all of the Christian and Armenian quarters would have been transferred to Palestinian Authority control, along with the entire Muslim Quarter.

Outside of Jerusalem, three populous settlement blocks were slated to remain under Israeli control, located south and east of Jerusalem and northeast of Tel Aviv. Dozens of isolated Jewish communities would have passed to Arafat's control, along with most of the strategic Jordan Valley. All fourteen Israeli settlements in the Gaza Strip would be no more. Barak suggested a land exchange in return for the estimated 5 to 8 percent of the former West Bank he wanted to hold on to, transferring Israeli territory to Palestinian Authority sovereignty near the Gaza Strip.

U.S. and Israeli officials said Arafat was tempted to accept Barak's offer, but decided after consultations with his top aides that Palestinian Islamic militants and their regional backers like Iran and Syria would strongly object if he let any portion of the "occupied territories" remain in the detested Zionist grip.

One other crucial issue proved to be a deal-buster as well: Arafat's refusal to make any real concessions on his oft-stated demand that all Palestinian refugees and their offspring have "a right to return to their homes" inside of Israel proper. Nearly every Israeli political party agrees that any significant Palestinian influx would end up destroying the world's only Jewish-ruled country. Arafat reportedly rebuffed Clinton's offer to mobilize international financial aid to help resettle such refugees inside the projected Palestinian state.

Yasser Arafat toured the globe in the wake of the failed Camp David summit, attempting to drum up support for a unilateral Palestinian statehood declaration on September 13. After visiting seventeen countries in three weeks, including Iran, which expressed full support for his hard-line stand on Jerusalem, he was forced to admit that very few world leaders were enthusiastic about his plans, including most Arab leaders. Meanwhile, American and European diplomats worked hard to get the two sides back to the negotiating table. Mid-level talks did take place in August and September, but they bore no real fruit, with Arafat still insisting on full control over Jerusalem's Old City. His continuing public belligerence did not help, with the Palestinian leader telling an Islamic summit meeting in Morocco in late August that "there will be no peace or stability in the Middle East if Jerusalem does not return to its legitimate owners."

Apparently worried that sporadic negotiations might somehow miraculously succeed in breaking the log jam, Palestinian terror groups warned that they would renew their deadly attacks if Arafat made any actual concessions, as he was being urged to do by Jordan's King Abdullah, Bill Clinton, and other leaders. At the same time, Israeli officials announced that they had uncovered a terrorist network working for Al Qaeda leader Osama Bin Laden. Palestinian security officials, who helped apprehend the suspects, said the network was planning a major attack inside Israel in order to fan billowing jihad flames over the emotional issue of Jerusalem.

## NEW PALESTINIAN UPRISING

On Monday night, September 25, Ehud Barak invited Yasser Arafat to his private home north of Tel Aviv for the first face-to-face meeting since the Camp David debacle two months before. The reportedly cordial gathering was interrupted by a telephone call from President Clinton, urging the two men to put aside their differences and reach a peace accord before he left office in January 2001. But by the end of the week, Palestinians and Israelis were once again caught up in another vicious chapter in the decades-old holy war for the Promised Land. Not surprisingly, the spark of war was the hotly contested Temple Mount.

Indications that serious trouble was brewing began to multiply soon after Likud Party leader Ariel Sharon announced that he would head an Israeli delegation on a visit to Judaism's most holy site on Thursday, September 28—one day before the start of the Jewish new year. The night before the visit, Palestinian terrorists emulated Hizbullah methods by setting off a powerful roadside bomb next to an Israeli army patrol in the Gaza Strip, killing one soldier and wounding another. Signaling that it was a well-planned operation involving a substantial group of attackers, camouflaged gunmen then opened fire from several directions on other soldiers who rushed to the scene. Israeli leaders immediately suspected that Palestinian Authority agents carried out the assaults.

Urged on by the Arab media and Palestinian Authority and Islamic leaders, hundreds of Muslims gathered on the Temple Mount the morning of Sharon's visit. They had come to rally against the supposed "desecration" of the disputed site. Palestinian schools were closed so students could attend the "spontaneous demonstrations." The protesters ignored the fact that Israeli officials often visited the sacred plateau after it was captured from Jordan in 1967, especially around Jewish religious holidays.

As the large Israeli delegation arrived, the Palestinians began hurling stones, bottles, and even chairs at Israeli security forces. Thirty policemen and soldiers were wounded during the barrage, including Jerusalem police chief Yair Yitzhaki. Israeli forces fought back with tear gas, and then with rubber bullets, wounding scores of people. The violence quickly spread to Arab neighborhoods throughout the eastern half of Jerusalem, and later to other locations. The uprising fuse had been lit.

Thousands of Palestinians woke up primed for jihad action on Friday, the Muslim day of rest. Most had spent Thursday evening listening to various Palestinian Authority leaders on television and radio, all of them harshly denouncing the Sharon visit and calling upon Muslims to "protect" their sacred sites from alleged Zionist plots to destroy them. Arafat led the incitement chorus, terming the pre-holiday visit "extremely dangerous to regional peace." Further demonstrating that he intended to milk the visit to the hilt, and giving a preview of the position he would take in the new uprising, he then called upon all Arab and Islamic nations to "mobilize your forces to protect our sacred shrines." In fact, the call for outsiders to come to his rescue was identical to the one he made when a tourist tunnel was opened at the base of the Temple Mount in 1996. But this time, he had a far more visceral issue at his disposal—a visit by the widely feared and detested Ariel Sharon.

Friday morning began with an unusual terror attack near the town of Kalkilya. Israeli and Palestinian security forces jointly patrolling the town stopped for a tea break. Without warning, one of the Arab policemen shouted out "Allah is great!" and then opened fire at his Jewish colleagues, killing one border policeman and wounding another. The unprovoked attack prompted Israeli military leaders to step up their alert for expected rioting following Friday Muslim services throughout Arafat's zones of control.

But the main action was again on the tense Temple Mount. Fired-up holy warriors piled out of Al Aksa midday prayers—featuring an impassioned call by Palestinian Authority—appointed grand mufti Ikreman Sabri to resist supposed Israeli plans to drive Muslims from the sacred site—and lobbed projectiles on Jewish worshipers at the Western Wall below. Israeli security forces again intervened. As casualties mounted on both sides, rioting spread to most other parts of the Palestinian-ruled territories. When the violence persisted into the next week, the Palestinian media labeled it the "Al Aksa intifada."

The international press largely echoed Arafat and his Palestinian Authority colleagues in maintaining that the violent new uprising was a spontaneous eruption that stemmed from Palestinian frustration over the stalled peace process. Certainly most people on both sides of the conflict, were upset over the slow pace of negotiations, and especially over the impasse that emerged from the Camp David gamble. However, a careful examination of the speeches and actions of Arafat and other Palestinian Authority leaders during the months leading up to the explosion of violence strongly suggests that the Palestinian street was being pumped and primed for renewed holy war. Sadly, the pushing was not just coming from militant Islamic groups this time, but from the very people who had signed a peace accord with Israeli leaders seven years before.

Watching Palestinian Authority television almost every day in the weeks before the rioting began, I surmised that the Arab masses, and especially young people, were being readied for battle. Regular programming was almost entirely suspended in early September, replaced by graphic footage of the original uprising and the 1996 tunnel riots. Images of brutish-looking Israeli soldiers firing on mostly young Palestinians fighters filled the screen, while Arabic singers hailed the slain warriors as *shahids* (martyrs) willing to give their lives for the "sacred cause of liberating Palestine" from detested Jewish control. The message was abundantly clear—you too will be hailed by your people, not to mention by Allah himself, if you join the holy struggle.

Palestinian officials fueled the new round of violence after it got going. This was later confirmed by several of them, including senior Fatah politician Marwan Barghouti, who headed two Arafat-linked militias until Israeli forces arrested him in 2002. On the first anniversary of the war of attrition in September 2001, he told the *Al Hayat* Arabic newspaper that he and other Palestinian leaders had been looking for just the right spark to set off a violent revolt in the weeks before Sharon ascended the Temple Mount. Barghouti quickly realized that the visit was the perfect match to light the holy war flame.

"After Sharon left, I remained for two hours to discuss the manner of response and how it was possible to react in all the cities and not just in Jerusalem," he told the newspaper, adding "we then contacted all the Palestinian factions." A joint uprising "steering committee" was quickly formed to manage the day-to-day "struggle" from Gaza City.

Thousands of Arab citizens of Israel joined their rioting Palestinian cousins as the violence spread. Clashes left thirteen of them dead and hundreds more wounded, mostly at the hands of outnumbered Israeli police forces. The damage to already strained relations between Israeli Arabs and Jews was just as severe, with many predicting that trust between the two communities would never be fully restored. Arab political leaders charged that security forces overreacted to the widespread rioting. Barak ordered an official investigation while decrying the propensity of Arab Knesset members to attack the government instead of trying to prevent further bloodshed.

Claiming with good reason that they were the real inspiration for the new uprising, Hizbullah militiamen joined in the battle by kidnapping three Israeli soldiers along the border with Lebanon in early October. Barak ordered air force pilots to bomb bases belonging to the Shiite group. Fulfilling his earlier warning to Syria that it would be held responsible if Hizbullah attacks resumed, the Israeli leader also commanded his warplanes to strike several Syrian positions east of Beirut. With Arafat screaming ever more loudly for regional Arab help, this raised the specter of a wider Middle East war.

Tensions were ratcheted up still further when Arab terrorists linked to Osama Bin Laden attacked an American naval ship in Yemen on October 13. Making things even worse, Saddam Hussein also began pounding his fists on the regional war drums, declaring he would form a special "volunteer jihad army" to "liberate Al-Quds from Zionist control" (he later claimed he had recruited 7 million soldiers). His threats gained weight when a senior emissary from Iran went to Baghdad in mid-October to bury the hatchet, declaring it was time for the former enemies to link arms and pursue the holy war together against Israel. This was followed by a thaw in frozen Iraqi relations with Syria.

Many Palestinians seemed convinced that the notorious "Butcher of Baghdad" was ready to rescue them at any moment. Upon learning that two Israeli army reserve soldiers had been lynched by a seething Palestinian mob in Ramallah as the new uprising entered its third week, thousands of Gaza City Arabs threw clothes into their cars and fled south. They were attempting to escape an expected Iraqi missile barrage on nearby Tel Aviv, which never materialized. Barak reacted to the lynching by declaring that "I no longer consider Arafat a partner for peace." He then ordered the aerial bombing of Palestinian Authority police headquarters near Arafat's Ramallah office—to send a warning message to the Palestinian leader that additional lynchings and the like would not be tolerated. He also urged opposition political parties to join him in forming an emergency unity government.

Arafat replied by attending a special Arab League summit meeting in Cairo, where he called for full backing for his ongoing revolt. Arab leaders pledged such support, with several scaling back official contacts with Israel.

## SEVERING TIES AND LIVES

As thousands of tourists made hasty exits from the Lord's land, hundreds of reporters flocked to it. Some were accompanying Bill Clinton and other world leaders who rushed to the region in futile attempts to halt the spiraling violence. I joined my media colleagues covering the latest phase in the ancient Isaac-Ishmael conflict, reporting part-time for CBS Radio and for other broadcast and print outlets. However, I soon found myself on the outs with the big American network due to an e-mail report that I sent out to around eighty friends the second week of the revived conflict. I had begun writing frequent updates in response to dozens of inquiries from around the world asking for my views on the escalating violence. Unfortunately, I mentioned in one of them that I was writing my message during a short break from reporting for CBS.

About one month later, that particular e-mail prompted a complaint to the CBS brass in New York from Palestinian legislator and media personality Hanan Ashrawi, who somehow got hold of it. I was told she objected to the biblical references I made in it, especially to my statement that I felt the violence could ultimately lead to a prophesied Middle East war over Jerusalem. This also bothered some CBS executives, who were obviously not used to their reporters expressing personal religious convictions. In fact, I was told my views were "an embarrassment" to the network.

I replied that I found it a bit incredible that the folks behind Howard Stern were blushing because of *my* religious convictions, which I pointed out are shared by millions of Americans—most of them no doubt living outside of New York City.

Ashrawi maintained that I had slandered Yasser Arafat by stating that he was doing precious little to halt the violence (a comment also made by Bill Clinton, who did not lose his job over it). In fact, Arafat was asked just one day before how long the new uprising might go on. He bluntly stated that his people "will never stop at all." Ashrawi was apparently also upset over my eyewitness testimony that I had seen armed Palestinian gunman firing weapons from amid crowds of ostensibly unarmed demonstrators—a fact later confirmed by many other journalists. She demanded that the network stop carrying my reports, which they immediately did even though my boss in New York admitted that radio department heads had absolutely no problems with my on-air journalism work.

So my CBS career, which began on the most violent day of the first uprising in April 1988, came to an abrupt end at the beginning of the second revolt more than twelve years later. Despite this, I stayed in the land and covered the escalating conflict for other media outlets. Meanwhile, my unplanned e-mail update list grew into thousands of subscribers.

The violent Palestinian revolt quickly escalated into a terrorist war of attrition. With street demonstrations dying down in late October, the Palestinians took their war directly into Israeli cities. Since it was the "Al Aksa uprising," the natural first target was Jerusalem. Skilled Palestinian snipers opened fire on Jewish homes in the southern Gilo neighborhood. From then on, the area became the regular target of attack from the nearby Bethlehem suburb of Beit Jala. Many nights I was shaken from my slumber by the jarring sounds of Israeli tanks and helicopter gunships firing in response to Palestinian sniper attacks upon Gilo, situated just one mile southwest of my apartment. On more than one occasion, I thought for a few seconds that I was back on the border with Lebanon.

A car bomb was detonated amid the modern office buildings of western Jerusalem on November 2, killing two Israeli civilians. One just happened to be the daughter of a prominent political leader, and the other a young lawyer who was a friend of a close friend of mine. I was sitting with him watching the evening news when we learned that his attorney friend had been blasted to bits earlier that day. The single man, who had given my friend free assistance in starting a business, was killed while walking back to his office after eating lunch in a nearby restaurant.

The powerful autumn blast would turn out to be just the first of a series of deadly terror assaults in the Israeli capital. The atrocities would take dozens of civilian lives in the following months on city buses, in a crowded pizzeria and several cafes, at Hebrew University, etc. The terror attacks soon spread to Tel Aviv, Haifa, Netanya, and most other Israeli cities and towns. Palestinian terrorists would slaughter more than six hundred Israelis by the time the war of attrition entered its third year in late September 2002, along with several tourists and foreign workers from the United States, China, France, the Philippines, and elsewhere. Over one hundred were Jewish soldiers and policemen killed while on active duty.

The Palestinian death toll was more than two times higher, although around two hundred of the slain were killed by fellow Arabs. Israeli officials pointed out that the vast majority of Arab casualties consisted of active male combatants, with relatively few women or children among them, compared to the growing Jewish fatality list. Four out of five Israeli victims were civilians, and 30 percent were women—compared to less than 3 percent on the Arab side. Another 30 percent of slaughtered Jews were teenagers or children. Entire Jewish families had been suddenly wiped out or children made orphans in the hideous Palestinian assaults, increasingly carried out by suicide bombers, many of them directly connected to Arafat's Fatah movement, as the attrition war raged on.

Attempting to quell the escalating terrorist war and win reelection in February 2001, Ehud Barak tried one last time to reach a peaceful settlement with his Palestinian nemesis. Still attempting to grab the golden ring, retiring U.S. President Clinton urged each side to accept his new "Outline of Principles," which put forth possible solutions to the peace process impasse. Barak and Arafat discussed the plan at a summit meeting in the Sinai Peninsula just after Christmas. Afterwards Arafat flew to Washington to get some "clarifications" from Clinton, and pledged to halt the violent uprising. But Arab League foreign ministers bucked up the PLO chief's hard-line Camp David stand by declaring in early January that the Palestinian refugee "right of return" to inside Israel's pre-1967 borders—one of the main sticking points in the Sinai talks—was "sacred."

The renewed talks went nowhere, even though Barak actually added more sugar to his saccharine Camp David offer. Clinton and Barak were soon out of office, with only Yasser Arafat, the veteran survivor, left holding any political reins. But even the autocratic Arafat had to deal with growing upheaval in his camp as the Palestinian uprising wore on, with many questioning what benefits the ongoing violence was bringing them in the face of soaring unemployment and growing poverty.

## ARIEL SHARON TAKES CHARGE

With the Oslo "land for peace" process in tatters and the Palestinian holy war raging on, Israeli voters went to the polls in early 2001. However, they did not have the opportunity to choose a new legislature as usual but only to vote for the position of prime minister. Although former Premier Binyamin Netanyahu desperately wanted to run again, he refused to do so unless Knesset elections were held as well. But the ruling Labor Party and its left-wing allies refused to dissolve the Knesset, suspecting that polls predicting Labor would get trounced were dead on the mark. That left the door open for longtime politician and war horse Ariel Sharon to come marching onto the stage, which he did in a landslide electoral triumph on February 6.

The new-old Israeli leader, who had run on a platform promising security first and then peace, set about forming a broad national unity coalition with the Labor Party and others. While he did so, Palestinian terrorists continued to snuff out Israeli civilian lives. A prominent Jewish doctor was among the growing list of victims, along with a baby girl shot dead in her stroller by a Palestinian sniper in Hebron.

The attacks outraged the public. Still, the ex-general surprised many Israelis, and certainly the international community, by his relatively moderate response. Defending himself against growing right-wing criticism, Sharon noted that his coalition accord with the large Labor Party gave his two top ministers nearly equal decision-making status to his own. Many hawkish politicians decried this arrangement, given that his foreign minister was none other than Oslo architect Shimon Peres. They were somewhat happier with Defense Minister Binyamin Ben Eliezer, a Baghdad-born tough former general like Sharon.

After twenty-one people, mostly teenage girls, were slaughtered at a Tel Aviv disco in June, Sharon was ready to pull out all the military stops, but was prevented from doing so by his two junior cabinet colleagues. A terror attack in August on a crowded pizzeria in Jerusalem nearly lit the fuse as well, but American and Labor Party pressure held Sharon back once again.

Things began to change after Middle East Muslim suicide terrorists blew up the World Trade Center and part of the Pentagon in September. With the American people and government seemingly more sympathetic to Israel's struggle against terror than ever before, Sharon's military response to the continuing stream of deadly atrocities was stepped up. This was especially true after Palestinian gunmen assassinated his close friend and colleague, Tourism Minister Rehavam Ze'evi, in a Jerusalem hotel on October 16.

When the Bush White House sent a special envoy to the region in late November to try to end the continuing bloodshed, a new wave of Palestinian terror attacks followed. Sharon then declared that Arafat was no longer free to move outside of his Ramallah office headquarters. The Bush administration quietly supported the move, indicating that it was also becoming fed up with Arafat's apparent unwillingness or inability to curb such vicious attacks. American anger was further amplified when Israeli naval vessels intercepted a ship in January 2002 carrying more than fifty tons of illegal Iranian-supplied weaponry, paid for by a senior Palestinian Authority official. The stage was set for even stronger Israeli military action ahead.

The trigger for a massive armed forces response was the outrageous massacre of twenty-nine Jewish civilians attending a Passover Seder meal at a Netanya hotel in late March. This prompted the exasperated Sharon government to launch Operation Defensive Shield, the largest military campaign since the Lebanon war two decades before. Islamic strongholds in Jenin and other Palestinian Authority towns came under sustained army assault, along with Arafat's own Ramallah headquarters. Israeli forces entered the Palestinian leader's surrounded compound and seized documents that they said confirmed his direct role in sanctioning terror attacks carried out by the Fatah-linked Tanzim militia and by the Al Aksa Martyr's Brigades terrorist group. Although Palestinian officials claimed that the documents were forgeries, American officials said they were convinced otherwise.

The month-long military campaign featured fierce fighting in several towns, especially in the Jenin refugee camp, where many homicide bombers hailed from. Another hot spot was Bethlehem's ancient Nativity Church, taken over by Palestinian gunmen who fled there as Israeli troops reentered the historic town. Still holed up in Ramallah, Arafat claimed that Israeli soldiers had massacred some five hundred Palestinians in Jenin, and he demanded a formal U.N. investigation. Israeli leaders resisted the call, insisting that some sixty Palestinians had died in the intense April fighting, most of them active combatants. The U.N. and human rights groups later confirmed the lower toll, although they also charged Israeli soldiers with using excessive force in the campaign to find and destroy terrorist hideouts.

Israel's antiterror campaign resulted in a sharp drop in Palestinian assaults, but not the desired complete halt. That would only come with an overall political solution, said many observers. Others countered that the political route had already been tried, with terrible results. Ariel Sharon, who authorized the building of a security fence to keep Palestinians out of Israel's pre-1967 borders, said he was willing to head to the negotiating table, but only if Palestinian terror attacks ceased.

Meanwhile, President George W. Bush joined the Israeli government in labeling Arafat a major obstacle to lasting peace. He also called for political reforms in the Palestinian Authority and new elections. Other senior U.S. officials went even further, saying a return to the Oslo formula would be suicidal for tiny Israel. This came as Bush indicated he was ready to launch a military campaign to oust Saddam, whose financial gifts were propping up the families of Palestinian terrorist "martyrs."

Facing mounting internal criticism for choosing violence over negotiations after the collapse of the Camp David summit, Arafat appointed several reformist cabinet ministers and announced that Palestinian elections would be held in early 2003. But he also said he would be a candidate for Palestinian Authority leader once again, whether Bush or Sharon liked it or not. Arafat cancelled the elections in December, claiming they could not be held while Israeli troops were occupying his land. Sharon had sent his forces back in to most Palestinian towns following a new wave of terrorist atrocities in the fall. Meanwhile Al Qaeda terrorists took responsibility for a deadly assault on Israeli tourists in Kenya and vowed to launch many more attacks on Israeli targets.

With the combustible Middle East seemingly poised on the edge of another horrific explosion, Israelis wearily dusted off their gas masks once again in early 2003 as officials warned that any U.S. strike on Iraq would probably be met, or even preceded by, repeat missile attacks from Saddam. With nothing to lose, everyone realized that the infamous dictator might just use chemical, biological, or possibly even nuclear weapons this time around. But many Israelis also hoped that Saddam's ousting—and Arafat's, as well—could turn out to be the starting point for a less radical Middle East in the years ahead.

k ✡ †

# THAT ELUSIVE PEACE

D espite intensive efforts by many world leaders and organizations to resolve the Arab-Israeli conflict, the long and bitter dispute continues to boil. While peace treaties have been signed between Israel and two of her immediate neighbors, Egypt and Jordan, and with Yasser Arafat's PLO, all Middle East nations are still arming for war. World opinion seems to have concluded that Israel is largely to blame for the absence of tranquility in the region. Polls show that support for the Jewish state declined in all Western nations as a result of the first Palestinian uprising, although there was at least a temporary upsurge of sympathy during the 1991 Gulf War and after peace accords were signed with the Palestinians and Jordan.

The hideous suicide terrorist campaign that followed the collapse of the Oslo peace process also produced some support for Israel, especially among Americans after the Al Qaeda attacks in New York and Washington. Still, most people in the world seemed indifferent at best toward the tiny Jewish state, if not openly hostile.

According to several surveys taken in the U.S. and elsewhere, Christian evangelicals continue to overwhelmingly support Israel's right to exist. But the traditional feeling of warmth and sympathy for the Jewish state has declined from heights reached just after the Six Day War. The rise in recent years of restoration, or reconstructionist, theology, which generally reflects the "replacement" view that the church has completely taken over Israel's role in God's plan for humanity, has added significantly to the growing evangelical move away from Israel. Polls show that mainline Protestant and Roman Catholic support, never as strong as evangelical backing, has eroded as well. Critical voices can also be heard increasingly in the worldwide Jewish community, always Israel's staunchest supporters.

The tiny Jewish state, so popular in the West and with much of the church in the 1950s and 1960s, is seemingly becoming a pariah, an embarrassment, even to her most tenacious Christian and Jewish admirers. Have events in the Middle East over the past few decades finally proved that Christian backers of Israel are way out of line, as many restorationists and others maintain, or do her supporters still have a leg to stand on?

My answer to that question should be obvious by now. Jacob's children have a right to live in the mostly Muslim Middle East, I believe, on moral, legal, and biblical grounds. Yet supporters of this contention must be the first to acknowledge that Israeli Jews are human beings, prone to the same sins and selfishness as the rest of humanity—including Christians. Far too much has been expected from Israel by her supporters, and even by many detractors. She has too often in the past been placed on a pedestal and judged by unrealistically high standards.

But now, in my opinion, the nation of Israel is being driven into the ground by an overly critical world—a world still stinking from the smoke of Jewish bodies burning in the ovens of "Christian" Europe.

It seems to me that many Christians and Jews, especially Americans, have held an overly sentimental view of Israel and have, therefore, been overly disappointed when Israelis have not lived up to expectations. While it is true that some Israeli Jews have hoped that Israel would be a "light to the Gentiles," most have never had any other ambition but to survive in an extremely hostile world. Israel's behaving at times like a typical Middle Eastern nation should surprise no one. Israel is, after all, a nation in the Middle East—one whose right to exist is constantly called into question. Still, Israeli self-criticism, self-restraint, and human rights standards remain far ahead of other regional states, such as Syria, Lebanon, Iraq, and Libya.[41]

## THE ANCESTRAL FAITHS

Israel's friends cannot and should not ignore the fact that there were Arabs living in the Holy Land before large-scale Jewish immigration began in the 1880s, and that most Palestinians, especially those who fled or were expelled from their homes during the war of 1947–49 and again in 1967, are still suffering today. This is certainly the case for the estimated 1.3 million Palestinians still living in nearly sixty refugee camps around the region. The "Palestinian problem" will not go away by simply denying that it exists, or by ignoring it.

Yet friend and foe alike should also be prepared to concede that there may *not* be a satisfactory human solution to the intense Arab-Israeli conflict. This is the conclusion I came to after a decade of studying the conflict, not in some classroom, but in the places where it is played out every day. I've discovered, as have others before me, that the dispute is *religious* at its core. With millions of Muslims and not a few Jews, it boils down to a question of "whose God is God?"—Allah from the Koran, or Elohim, the God of Israel revealed in the Bible.

This fact is not often emphasized in discussions or books about the dispute, probably because most people who write or speak about it, including many Israeli Jews and Palestinian activists, do not themselves have significant religious beliefs. They therefore tend to underestimate the strong religious struggle at the center of the Arab-Israeli conflict and thus often overestimate the potential for a negotiated solution.

Such authors and speakers make the mistake of seeing many of the leading Jewish and Arab actors as basically *secular* people. While this may be true on the surface, the fact is that Jewish-Israeli society and thinking is heavily influenced by Judaism, as Arab society is overwhelmingly by Islam. Ariel Sharon, like other Israeli leaders before him, may not have a deep personal faith, as may also be true of Bashar Assad, King Abdullah of Jordan, or Yasser Arafat. But all are heavily influenced by the religious concepts held dear by many, if not most, of their citizens.

While Israeli Jews are definitely less religious overall than their Arab cousins, Judaism still plays a significant role in people's everyday lives. Israelis are married and buried by Orthodox rabbis. Most major holidays, such as Passover, Rosh Hashanah (the Jewish New Year), Yom Kippur, and the Feasts of Weeks (Pentecost) and Tabernacles, are straight out of the Bible. Many of Israel's most popular folk songs, sung enthusiastically by even the most atheistic Jews, come from biblical passages. It is no coincidence that most major state ceremonies, including military inductions and Memorial Day ceremonies, are held at the hallowed Western Wall. Having lived in Israel for more than two decades, I can attest that Judaism's influence here is far greater than most casual observers might imagine.

Islam plays an enormous role in the lives of Muslim Arabs, whether they are deeply observant or not. Islamic holy days are national holidays. Allusions to the Koran pepper everyday speech. The call to prayer from tall mosque minarets is a familiar sound to all Arabs, from cradle to grave.

Islam is not only the religion of most Arabs; it is their shared cultural heritage. The dominant Middle Eastern religion has also been the most important factor in the Arab world's rejection of the Jewish state of Israel. Several Arab leaders have reportedly told their Western counterparts that their efforts to make, or sustain, peace with Israel have been greatly constricted by the religious beliefs and prejudices of their Muslim citizens. On the other hand, basically secular Arab leaders like Saddam Hussein have often found Islam quite useful in promoting their own political goals and in undermining their opponents.

It is not only modern analysts who underestimate the religious dimension of the Arab-Israeli dispute. Many of the earliest Jewish immigrants, familiar with the latest medical and agricultural methods, naively believed that local Arabs would welcome their move to "Palestine," or at least not resist it. The largely secular and socialistic northern European and Russian immigrants simply did not have an adequate understanding of Islam, although they were more familiar with replacement theology in Christianity.

At the same time, many Zionist leaders, preoccupied with the Jewish need for a homeland in the face of vicious anti-Semitic pogroms, downplayed or ignored the fact that hundreds of thousands of Arabs, most of them devout Muslims, were already living in the Holy Land.

While the role of the Jew in God's economy is still debated by Christians, the Koran leaves no room for doubt that Allah is finished with them as a sovereign people. As I have already mentioned, it was inconceivable to Muslims that the eternally subjugated dhimmi Jews would once again have control over Jerusalem. If Islam were required to wage jihad against the Christian crusaders until they were pushed out of Jerusalem, then certainly war would be doubly waged against any Jewish attempt to regain or retain sovereignty over "Al-Quds." This was, and remains, the root cause of the decades-old violent Arab resistance to a Jewish state near the center of the Muslim world.

Had Islam not mandated such resistance, and had replacement theology not been so dominant in the ancient established churches of the region, the Arabs would have undoubtedly been more sympathetic toward early Jewish immigrants fleeing violent pogroms. Still, no one could have expected them to welcome the arrival of hundreds of thousands of foreign Jews, even though all realized that Judaism sprang up in the Holy Land. After centuries of rule from Istanbul, nobody was too excited at the prospect of being a minority citizen of a Jewish state. And yet, some empathy for incoming Jews would have at least been a possibility if preconceived religious prejudices had not been so strong.

Many historians have written that Arab hostility against the proposed Jewish national home was greatly enhanced by British and Jewish insensitivity and arrogance toward the Arabs of Palestine. There is little doubt that European Christians and Jews saw their way of life as superior to that of local Arabs.

Still, we must remember that Arabs first expressed strong opposition to the proposed Jewish state *before* Britain had issued the Balfour Declaration or had any role in the Holy Land, and before many Jews had moved there. It was the *idea* of a sovereign Jewish state, more than Jewish or British actions, that produced loathing in many regional Arabs. Actual encounters with British officials, soldiers, and immigrating Jews only moderately enhanced the strong antagonism toward Christians and Jews that was already deeply inbred in most Muslims.

Palestinians and other Arabs argue that the League of Nations had no right to vote a special status for the area known in the West as Palestine when affirming the San Remo mandates for creating sovereign states in the Middle East. I strongly disagree. The land was sacred to Muslims and

Christians precisely because it was first holy to Jews. Islamic Arab warriors occupied the Holy Land by force, ending Christian control of such ancient historic sites as the Temple Mount and Abraham's Tomb. Centuries earlier, the Jews had largely been pushed out—against their will—by the Romans.

The League of Nations rightly recognized that the Holy Land is a unique place, still sacred to millions of Jews and Christians as well as to Muslims. Members of the two older religions—especially the wandering, persecuted Jews—legitimately expected the League of Nations to treat Palestine differently. Had most Muslims been able to emulate the moderate Iraqi King Faisal and concede that the Holy Land demanded special treatment (as did Lebanon), the Jewish-Arab strife of the twentieth century might have been averted.

While the new immigrants didn't speak often of their people's ancestral religion, the well-established and overwhelmingly observant Jewish communities of Jerusalem, Hebron, and elsewhere had lived and worshiped in the Holy Land for centuries. Local Arabs certainly knew that religious Jews still regarded Jerusalem as the centerpiece of Judaism, even if the faithful had been scattered to the most remote parts of the earth. Many must have realized that Zionism was not a new Jewish movement, but only a new expression of a very old Jewish yearning—to return to the hills and valleys of the Promised Land, *Eretz Yisrael.*

## EVERLASTING LAND COVENANT

The religious struggle over the Lord's land centers on who has the God-given right to possess it. Polls show that an overwhelming majority of Israeli Jews, even most who don't regularly attend synagogue, believe in the existence of the God of Israel. Many of them are convinced that the Bible teaches that God gave them title to the land forever. Muslims and most Christians who subscribe to replacement theology strongly disagree. As we saw in the Muslim fundamentalist HAMAS charter, the Holy Land is seen by observant Muslims as part of the Islamic heritage forever bequeathed to Islam by Allah. The Roman Catholic and Eastern Orthodox churches have traditionally viewed the land as a Christian heritage, as demonstrated during the Crusades.

What does the Bible say? In Genesis 17 God promised to give Abraham and his descendants the land of Canaan for "an everlasting possession" (v. 8). He did so after telling Abraham that he would be "a father of many nations" (vv. 4–5). Then God clarified that his covenant promises would be passed on through the descendants of Isaac (v. 19), although he reassured Abraham that Ishmael's descendants would also become a great nation (v. 20).

On his deathbed, Isaac's son Jacob told his son Joseph that God had appeared to him at Luz in the land of Canaan, saying, "I am going to make you fruitful and will increase your numbers. I will make you a community of peoples, and I will give this land as an everlasting possession to your descendants after you" (Gen. 48:4). God's eternal land covenant to Israel is recalled in Psalm 105:

> He has remembered His covenant forever,
> The word which He commanded to a thousand generations,
> The covenant which He made with Abraham,
> And His oath to Isaac.
> Then He confirmed it to Jacob for a statute,
> To Israel as an everlasting covenant,
> Saying, "To you I will give the land of Canaan
> As the portion of your inheritance" (vv. 8–11 NASB).

To those who believe in God and his Word, these foundational promises seem to reveal clearly the Most High's intention to give "the land of Canaan" to the tribes of Israel forever. Of course, the Scriptures are full of warnings of what will happen to the Jewish people if they disobey God's commands, including being thrown out of the Promised Land. Twice the Jews have been scattered from the land as a result of sin. Yet throughout the Hebrew Bible, or Old Testament, God promised to regather the descendants of Jacob to their ancient ancestral homeland in the "last days," just before he fully establishes his kingdom on earth.

Many regathering promises were fulfilled in the return from the seventy-year Babylonian exile. But others, such as the one recorded in

Isaiah 61:4, speak of the Jews returning and rebuilding their nation after having "been devastated for generations," in other words, after a very long exile. Still other Scripture passages speak of Jewish people returning from the four corners of the earth. This did not occur in the Babylonian return but is clearly happening in our day.

Yet even if the Jewish people have been given a permanent divine title to the Holy Land, there is no biblical reason why Arabs and others cannot also live in it. Various peoples resided in Israel and Judea along with the Jews in ancient times. Modern Jewish Zionist leaders assumed in the beginning, undoubtedly naively, that most Arab residents would not be too unhappy to become citizens of the emerging Jewish state. It was thought that some might want to move to neighboring lands in order to live in an Arab-controlled state, but most would be content to stay where they were.

Among Christians and Jews who do believe that God forever promised the land to the Jews, some argue that the current ingathering is not the one spoken of in the Bible. The end-time prophecies, they say, indicate that the Jews will come back to the land only after the Messiah either comes or returns. It seems to me that this argument is irrelevant to the question of whether or not the Jews have a God-given right to live in the Holy Land. If the land was promised to Jacob's descendants as an "everlasting possession," then it still rightfully belongs to them, even when they are scattered from it.

Apart from this, as a Christian I find it hard to believe that the re-creation of a sovereign Jewish state in 1948—which was accomplished against incredible odds—is just an accident of history or a "Western imperialist plot," of no meaning to God or humanity. Either the sovereign Lord who determines the boundaries of nations (Acts 17:26) has allowed the establishment of Israel in our time, or he is not sovereign after all.

Can Christians, Jews, or even Muslims—reading of God's promises to and love for Jacob's descendants—see the creation of a Jewish state after almost two thousand years of exile that culminated in the Holocaust as simply a historical accident? Is there no prophetic significance to the fact that the Jewish people, scattered as foretold all over the earth, once again have sovereignty over Jerusalem, their beloved ancient Holy City?

No one, not even the Arabs, can deny that the long-desolate, sparsely populated land of Israel, which the Romans renamed "Palaestina" to erase all Jewish association, has been transformed into a major agricultural center with beautiful forests and cities over the past century. Visitors coming from Egypt and Jordan often comment on the lushness of the land compared to those neighboring countries. Is it just an accident—a mere coincidence—that the Jews have even made portions of the desert bloom, as the Bible foretold they would?

## JEWS, ARABS, AND JERUSALEM

To call the Jewish migration to the Lord's land "the greatest crime of the twentieth century," as the Arabs have generally done, ignores the history of humanity over the past one hundred years. Mass migrations have taken place all over the globe. Large-scale refugee flights have also occurred in many places, especially in Asia and Africa. For example, the 1980s Afghan refugee exodus of several million Muslims was considerably larger than the Palestinian flight, yet little was heard about it. The Palestinian flight was not even in the twentieth century's top ten in terms of overall size.

National boundaries in Europe, Africa, and much of Asia were either created or redrawn many times during the 1900s, usually as a result of war.

The Arabs, like other peoples, were promised an independent state or states by the victorious European powers who helped liberate them from Ottoman control during World War I. They now have not one but seventeen states stretching from the west coast of Africa to Iran.[42]

After centuries of oppression and persecution in Muslim and Christian regions, the Jews were also promised a national home in the Middle East, a proposition essentially agreed to by Arab-Muslim leader Faisal Hussein and endorsed by the League of Nations and later by the United Nations. While many Jews did not see the need for such a state in the early 1900s, almost all did so after the fires of the Holocaust were finally put out.

Jews immigrating to their ancient ancestral homeland did not "steal Arab land" as is so often charged, but legally bought what they could, as

Arieh Avneri fully documents in his book *Claim of Dispossession*. It is true that much Arab-owned property was seized by Israeli authorities in 1948 and 1949. Many abandoned villages, usually partially destroyed, were either completely razed or rebuilt for Jewish settlement. Palestinians understandably reacted with much anger and bitterness when they learned, in many cases, that their homes either no longer existed or were being occupied by Jews.

But the Israeli land seizures must be placed in their historical context. This is usually not done by Palestinians and their advocates. It was the Arabs who initiated a self-declared total war of destruction against the fledgling Jewish state after turning down the U.N. partition plan and refusing, as is generally still true today, to recognize that the Jews might have a legitimate right, and certainly a need, for a sovereign state in their beloved Holy Land. If the Arabs had agreed to a land partition, there would have been no war, no refugees, and no land seizures. Socialist and Western-orientated Jewish leaders like David Ben Gurion—keenly aware that world support was vital for the new state—were not about to initiate military action to drive Palestinians from their homes and farms.

It was in the midst of the 1948 and 1967 wars, waged by a number of Arab countries against the vastly outnumbered Jews, that Palestinian land was seized. Unpleasant as it may be, land is often taken by victors in war, especially if the other side initiated the conflict and threatens to do so again in the future. The United States did not expand by land purchases alone, nor has any other nation in recorded history.

It is also important to remember that Jewish properties and other assets were seized all over Europe before and during World War II and from parts of the Arab world as Jews fled to the newly established state of Israel. Plundered Jewish wealth in Arab lands has never been compensated for, although West Germany paid war reparations to most holocaust survivors. Other countries like Switzerland and Sweden are only beginning to admit that they benefited economically from stolen Jewish assets.

The more than one hundred thousand Jews who fled Baghdad in the early 1950s were allowed to carry only one small suitcase with them and could take out of the country no more than the equivalent of 140 American dollars. The Iraqi government seized all of the remaining Jewish assets, which were substantial. The Jews of Europe and parts of the Arab world lost their property and valuables because of unprovoked attacks upon them, or they were forced to give them up in order to buy safe passage from hostile Arab lands. In contrast, Palestinian refugees lost their assets in the course of wars initiated by their own leaders and surrounding Arab states.

Yet even if one accepts the Jewish people's biblical right, or at least practical need, to return to the Promised Land, the pictures and stories of suffering Palestinians grip the heart and mind. I have witnessed Palestinian agony firsthand. Many are my neighbors, my business contacts, my friends. I have visited their war-ravaged camps in Lebanon and watched them battle Israeli soldiers patrolling crowded camps in the West Bank and Gaza Strip. I have interviewed local Palestinian leaders and regularly read translations of their East Jerusalem–based newspapers. The Palestinians are not just statistics or "terrorists," but flesh-and-blood people who have legitimate needs and desires like anyone else. Many of them have poured out their problems and feelings to me, and I have listened with an open heart. A person would have to be extremely callous not to realize that these people are really hurting.

The Palestinian Arabs are victims—but not primarily of the Israelis. They are, in my opinion, mainly the victims of an often-violent religion based on a corruption of the Bible. While I have great love and respect for the Muslims as people made in the image of God, I grieve for them as prisoners of a religious system, based on the Koran and Hadith, that exalts warfare and almost mandates hatred, or at least scorn, of the Jews. Of course, many Muslims—Palestinian and otherwise—are basically fine people who shun violence. But this is in spite of what their holy book and oral tradition teaches, not because of it. Many Palestinian Christians also disdain the Jewish people and Judaism, based on selected biblical passages and church tradition. But at least they have no scriptural basis—unlike Muslims—to wage war against Jews.

It was Haj Amin Husseini's use of Islamic motifs that cemented Palestinian Arab opposition to the emerging Jewish state in the 1920s and 1930s. And Islamic teachings, above all else, inspired the entire Arab world to wage or support wars of annihilation against the Jewish state in

1948, 1967, and 1973. Saddam also used them as the basis for his Scud missile attacks in 1991. Although many PLO founders were Marxists or atheists, deeply rooted religious prejudices against the Jews were clearly reflected in the PLO's founding charter, as they were in the 1988 HAMAS charter.

If Islam's supreme prophet Muhammad personally killed Jews, as most Palestinian Muslims believe, then what were they to do to the Jewish "infidels" who were building a nation in the midst of the Arab-Muslim world, and who subsequently captured some of their holy sites during the 1967 war? Such actions seemed to contradict Islam's Allah-ordained role as conqueror and ruler of the entire Middle East, and eventually of the entire world.

Many Muslims have a hard enough time accepting that Christian shrines are allowed to exist in the Holy Land, since Christians follow the "abominable" practice of worshiping Jesus. How then can they ever accept the fact that the doubly rejected Jews now control the Old City of Jerusalem, where Muhammad is said to have ascended into heaven from the Temple Mount? This reality seems to call into question the validity and truthfulness of Islam itself.

The Temple Mount is not Judaism's third most holy site, as it is Islam's (actually several other locations share "third place" with the Jerusalem site). I have often observed Muslims saying midday prayers near my home south of the Old City. I note that they always face *away* from the Temple Mount, which I can clearly see behind them. The Muslims are praying toward Islam's most holy site, the Kaaba Shrine in Mecca, Saudi Arabia. But religious Jews pray facing *toward* the Temple Mount, which is far and away Judaism's most holy site.

Many people think that the Western Wall is Judaism's most sacred site, but it is the Mount itself that is holy to praying Jews. They gather at the Wall to pray that God will soon reveal the chosen Messiah and allow the construction of the third Jewish temple on the sacred Mount. Then, they believe, the prophecies recorded in the Books of Isaiah and Micah will be fulfilled, that "in the last days, the mountain of the house of the LORD's temple will be established as chief among the mountains," with all nations and peoples streaming up to it (Isa. 2:2–3; Mic. 4:1–2). Until such a time, observant Jews are forbidden to walk around on the Mount lest they accidentally tread over, and thus desecrate, the site of the ancient Holy of Holies.

Just as no Arab leader could ever agree to recognize permanent Jewish control over the Mount's holy mosques, so no Israeli leader could ever voluntarily concede Jewish sovereignty over the spot that has been at the center of Jewish hearts for three thousand years. (Although Ehud Barak came close to doing this at Camp David in 2000, the Knesset would probably not have sanctioned such a controversial concession). If Yitzhak Rabin was assassinated for agreeing to withdraw from Hebron and other sites less holy than Jerusalem, what would happen to an Israeli leader who willingly abandoned the sacred Temple Mount? While a majority of Israeli Jews might agree to an arrangement under which Islam is guaranteed permanent control over the Mount itself, many Orthodox Jews and Israeli nationalists would strongly resist such a move, probably violently.

Indeed, the struggle for control of the Temple Mount and the rest of the Old City is the central point of contention in the Arab-Israeli conflict—a fact often obscured in the day-to-day media coverage of the latest happenings in the conflict. Islam—the world's fastest-growing religion with well over 1 billion followers—will never willingly accept permanent Jewish sovereignty over any portion of "sacred Al-Quds," and especially over the Temple Mount and adjacent Muslim areas of the Old City. Just as clearly, Israeli Jews will never willingly abandon control over most of the Old City, and especially over the Western Wall and Temple Mount.

Of course, many Israeli Jews couldn't care less about holding on to the Temple Mount for religious reasons. Either they view Judaism in a more universal sense—no longer needing a "sacred spot"—or they are not religious at all. But even for many such people, the Mount seems to be a powerful and important, although frequently subconscious, symbol of their national and personal identity. This is undoubtedly the main reason why opinion polls show that an Israeli pullout from the eastern half of Jerusalem, and especially from the entire Old City, is considered unthinkable.

During my many years in Israel, I have yet to come across a peace proposal that contains a workable solution to the intensely emotional holy war being waged by both Muslims and Jews over the ancient Old City of Jerusalem. The Muslim world, still bristling with deep humiliation over the loss of the area in 1967, wants a total end to Israeli sovereignty—period. This view is shared by moderate, pro-Western countries like Egypt and Morocco and by more radical states like Syria, Libya, Iraq, and Iran with the latter states demanding that Jewish control be eliminated not only over all of Jerusalem but over all of Israel.

Orthodox Jews, remembering that they were completely barred from even approaching the gates of the walled Old City from 1948 until 1967, believe that continued access to the Western Wall will be assured only if their government retains absolute control of the area. Many are prepared to fight, if they must, to retain such control.

Another major obstacle to a peaceful solution of the Arab-Israeli conflict is deep Israeli suspicion that nobody really cares whether or not Israel survives as a distinct nation, let alone has access to Jerusalem's Old City. In fact, Israeli friends tell me they suspect that many non-Jews would be quite happy if a violent "final solution" led to their demise as a nation.

## STRATEGIC HILLS

While a majority of Israelis do not really care about holding on to religious sites outside of Jerusalem, they do see at least portions of Judea and Samaria as strategically vital to Israel's defense. A number of military analysts maintain that Israel does not need such a territorial buffer zone any more, since any future full-scale war will most likely be fought largely by missiles and jets, leaving ground forces basically irrelevant. Iraqi missile attacks against Israel during the Gulf War seemed to confirm this view.

However, many other analysts argue that Iraq's 1991 use of medium-range missiles against the heavily populated coastal plain—ballistics that could have carried chemical or biological warheads, or even nuclear warheads if the Israelis had not bombed Iraq's nuclear reactor in 1981—illustrates why it is more essential than ever for Israel to keep control of at least part of the strategic Samarian and Judean hills. If many Israeli soldiers and civilians were killed or injured in a full-scale Arab missile attack, then a follow-up ground invasion could be fatal, even if Israel responded by firing nuclear missiles at long-range Arab targets.[43]

With Arab and Iranian missile technology advancing, a surprise strike against Israeli air force bases could substantially cripple Israel's most important segment of military power, thus weakening the ability of relatively small ground forces to withstand attacking armies. Following a missile strike, Israel's full-time and reserve army would need every inch of territory up to the Jordan River in order to halt a ground invasion.

Israelis keenly remember how easily Hitler discarded his prewar "peace" commitments as soon as it suited him. Even left-wing activists, who are generally not religious, tell me they realize that Israel has taken great military risks in agreeing to hand over portions of the hilly regions to Palestinian control. In light of Jewish history, the breakdown of the Oslo peace process, and constant threats of attack from Arab leaders like Saddam Hussein, one can hardly blame many Israelis for opposing potentially suicidal concessions.

But shouldn't it be easy for Israel to achieve full and lasting peace with the Palestinians and Syria since she was able to do so with Egypt in 1978 and Jordan in 1994? It was relatively simple to resolve the differences with Jordan and Egypt. No substantial land was demanded back by King Hussein, who renounced Amman's claim to its annexed West Bank in 1988. Although Egypt used the Sinai Peninsula as a staging ground for two attacks against Israel, the desert area was not considered absolutely vital for Israeli security. The substantial financial aid that the United States pledged to give both countries in order to shore up the peace, and, in Israel's case, to partially compensate for the loss of Israeli-developed Sinai oil wells, was an obvious incentive.

But the main reason why the Camp David Peace Accords were signed was that the two sides agreed not to deal with the thorny religious-based issue of east Jerusalem, nor of the other captured territories near Israel's heartland. Anwar Sadat knew he could not seriously address those concerns and still get back the Sinai.

It is quite obvious that the alternative to a peaceful resolution of the Arab-Israeli struggle is continuing violence and warfare. Nearly everyone, including most Israelis, recognizes that the Palestinians will not rest until their stateless status is resolved. It doesn't matter that Palestinian statelessness may be largely due to their leaders' having "never missed an opportunity to miss an opportunity," as former Israeli foreign minister Abba Eban put it. Although it is undoubtedly true, it is now irrelevant to argue that the Palestinians would have long ago been citizens of their own state if they hadn't rejected the British and United Nations partition plans or subsequent Israeli peace proposals. The frequently heard Arab contention that the West solved its own "Jewish problem" by creating Israel also does very little to bring the dispute to a peaceful resolution.

All those involved should recognize that religiously based conflicts are especially difficult to resolve. The late Iranian leader Ayatollah Khomeini taught that Satan created "that cancerous tumor" Israel, with Allah's approval, as a judgment on backslidden Muslim nations. When Muslims, especially decadent Western-inspired leaders, repent of their wicked ways, then Allah will destroy the "infidel" state. To say the least, this view—shared by many Palestinians—greatly impedes efforts to establish a lasting peace between the Muslim world and Israel.

If the powerful Arab-Israeli struggle were basically an ideological one, such as between communism and capitalism, a peaceful resolution could probably be achieved with relative ease. In 1989 the world witnessed the fall of discredited communist governments in Eastern Europe and then watched in amazement as communism unraveled in its "mecca," Moscow.

Although *like* a religion in many respects, communism is ultimately open to change because it is acknowledged to be a belief system based solely on the teachings of human beings. However, Islam and Judaism are long-established *religions,* and therefore not subject to sudden abandonment by most observant followers. The average Muslim is fully convinced that Allah revealed Islam, the final religious truth, to Muhammad through the Angel Jibril. Religious Jews are just as convinced that the God of Israel established their nation and religion through his covenants with their forefathers.

Western leaders trying to forge a new world order following the end of the East-West cold war must remember that Abraham, Moses, and Muhammad are revered as prophets of God by millions of people, not simply as philosophers or politicians whose teachings and ideas can be easily put aside.

## THE LORD'S TINY LAND

Even if the overall Arab-Israeli conflict were not basically religious in nature, the Israeli-Palestinian dispute would still be extremely difficult to resolve. The reason is simple—two peoples are struggling to control a very small piece of earth. It is hard for many Westerners to conceive just how tiny the land in question is. It is on average only 50 miles from Israel's western Mediterranean Sea border to the Jordan River. This extremely narrow land is much longer than it is wide—260 miles from the northern upper Galilee border with Lebanon to the southern port city of Eilat on the Red Sea. Israel minus the territories is only 7,993 square miles overall, just slightly larger than New Jersey or Wales.

If a Palestinian state were to be established in the entire area that Israel captured from Jordan in 1967 and in the Gaza Strip, as Palestinian leaders constantly demand, it would be only 2,123 square miles in its "West Bank" part and 139 square miles in the narrow Gaza Strip. The eastern portion would be on average just 83 miles long and 34 miles wide. The densely populated Gaza section would be even smaller: 24 miles long and less than 5 miles wide. The eastern part of the proposed state is dominated by the Judean and Samarian hills, which afford a commanding view of Israeli coastal areas. The section of the coastal plain adjacent to Israel's pre-1967 border, from the southern Tel Aviv suburbs north to the town of Hadera, is only about 12 miles wide on the average.

If the entire area that Israel captured from Jordan becomes a Palestinian state, the narrow coastal plain, home to nearly half of all Israelis, would be the only land bridge connecting northern Israel with the center and south, as it was before the Six Day War. This is a strategic nightmare for a small Jewish state situated as an island in an Islamic sea.

Israeli military analysts are naturally quite concerned over the potential for armed assaults from the proposed Palestinian state, especially from the hilly eastern section. Any pledge to keep such a state free of heavy weaponry could, of course, be broken (in fact, many illegal arms have poured into Arafat's autonomy zones since the 1993 Oslo Accord was signed, and others have been manufactured there).

Another worry is who would ultimately control such a state. There are six major factions and several splinter groups inside the PLO. Although Fatah is the largest, the Popular Front and the Democratic Front groups—which strongly opposed the Oslo peace accord and have launched armed attacks during the Al Aksa war of attrition—have many followers. The other three major PLO factions are also often at odds with Fatah. How Fatah will restrain its PLO rivals in an "independent Palestinian state" is anybody's guess.

Apart from internal PLO disputes, there is the huge problem of the two Palestinian Islamic fundamentalist movements that strongly oppose all peace moves toward Israel. Supported by many Muslims around the world, the two groups have pledged to wage holy war until the "infidel state" is destroyed. Each at times launched violent attacks against Fatah supporters during the pre-Oslo Palestinian uprising and later staged massive demonstrations against Arafat's autonomy rule. It was their suicide attacks that led to Shimon Peres's electoral defeat in 1996. They again set the pace by launching a majority of the major terrorist assaults in the Al Aksa war of attrition, leading to a sharp upswing in their popularity according to Palestinian opinion polls. Their demands, based on religious beliefs, are nonnegotiable.

How will Fatah insure that these popular movements abide by a permanent peace settlement with Israel? And how can Israel be certain that a final Israel-Palestinian peace treaty will not be just another step toward the fulfillment of the PLO's 1974 "phased program" to destroy Israel in stages, as Arafat himself indicated the shattered Oslo accords were? Will international sponsors of the Oslo peace process, especially the United States, always be close at hand to guarantee that the tiny Jewish state, surrounded by Muslim countries, is not eventually swallowed up by a "secular democratic Palestinian state" or by a Muslim fundamentalist-ruled state?

Another major obstacle in the way of an overall Arab-Israeli peace settlement is the small portion of land known in the West as the Golan Heights. Had British Mandate officials not ceded the volcanic plateau to the French in 1923, the strategic area would probably have been part of the state of Israel from 1948. But instead, the Golan Heights was in Syrian hands until the 1967 Six Day War, and Damascus wants it back. Even if Syrian strongman Bashar Assad were to be replaced by a more moderate leader, Syria could hardly give up its claim to the green plateau overlooking the Israeli Hula Valley and the Sea of Galilee.

It is certainly true that Israel is much more likely to vacate the Golan Heights than to pull out of east Jerusalem. Still, the more than twelve thousand Israelis living in thirty-three settlements there would strongly—possibly even violently—protest such a turnover, as would many other Israelis, especially those who live in the valley below the Golan Heights. Far too many people remember the constant shelling and machine gun attacks that the Syrians launched from the area before the 1967 Israeli capture. In a final peace settlement with Syria, Israel would probably insist that it hold on to the sloping hills and ridge just above the valley. While demanding all of the area back and the dismantling of every Israeli settlement, Syria might agree to the stationing of an international peacekeeping force on the Golan Heights just above the ridge.

For any overall Arab-Israeli peace accord to be fully effective, Arab leaders from Morocco in western Africa to Oman on the Persian Gulf must support it, along with non-Arab Muslim states like Iran and Pakistan. Such a development seems remote, at best, as illustrated by supreme Iranian leader Ayatollah Khameini. He has vowed several times that Iran, the main backer of the Hizbullah militia in south Lebanon, will not rest until Israel is destroyed. Certainly Israel cannot fully rest until all of her declared enemies prove that they are ready to cease hostilities. It will not be true peace for Israel if, for example, Fatah subdues its Palestinian rivals and establishes a fully independent state in the territories, while Iran, Syria, Sudan, Libya, and Iraq continue to support Palestinian and Lebanese groups working for the destruction of "the Zionist entity." Lebanon would cease to be a base of anti-Israeli activities only if the Christian-Muslim divide is fully overcome—a seemingly unlikely prospect.

Divided Arabs and Jews must also deal with a growing regional water crisis. The precious commodity is in short supply in all Middle Eastern countries, with the few water sources under increasing pressure. Israel,

Syria, and Jordan all vie for the waters that eventually flow into the Sea of Galilee and the Dead Sea. Growing populations are already taxing these and other water sources to the limit. Water would also be a major problem in the proposed minuscule Palestine state, with Arab wells siphoning off water that flows into Israel's vital aquifers underneath the coastal plain. Analysts say the Middle East water shortage itself may well lead to future regional wars.

## MIDDLE EASTERN POWDER KEG

The vast wealth that poured into many Arab countries following the 1973 Yom Kippur War enabled Israel's enemies to purchase untold billions of dollars' worth of the latest Western and Soviet weaponry. Such large-scale arms purchases were made by countries whose land and population bases are vastly superior to Israel's. The ending of the Cold War in 1991 led to stepped-up purchases of "bargain" weapons, such as Soviet T-72 tanks, that were dumped in Eastern Europe and republics of the former Soviet Union.

This forced Israel to increase her defense spending in the 1990s, despite the regional peace process. It shot up even further after the Palestinians went back on the warpath in September 2000. Some 20 percent of Israel's annual budget is now devoted to military spending, which amounted to more than 10 percent of the country's gross national product of more than $90 billion in 2001.

On the ground, Israel's armed forces are overwhelmingly outnumbered by its Arab and Iranian enemies. Syria alone has a well-trained standing army of around 400,000 soldiers, compared to Israel's estimated 170,000. Israel can muster another 750,000 reserve fighters from its civilian population, but the Arabs and Iranians can do much better than that. Jordan and Saudi Arabia have relatively small but highly trained regular forces, with the Saudis frequently purchasing large quantities of the latest Western and Chinese weaponry. Despite heavy losses in the Gulf War, Iraq emerged with most of its elite fighting units intact and set out to rebuild its large regular army. With a population of nearly 60 million, Iran can produce many soldiers for the holy war against Israel. In any future full-scale Arab-Israeli conflict, Libya, Algeria, Yemen, Sudan, and other Arab states could potentially contribute soldiers and equipment to the battle.

Israel's worst nightmare is that Muslim fundamentalists in Egypt—whose substantial military forces have been well trained and equipped by the United States—might one day seize power, renounce the peace treaty with Israel, and support an Arab-Iranian assault on the small Jewish state. Even if this does not occur, Israeli military analysts fear that Egypt might be inclined to tacitly support its Arab friends in any new war with Israel, forcing some Israeli brigades to remain stationed along the Sinai border. They note that massive Egyptian war games staged in September 1996 were ominously code-named "Operation Badr," the very name used for the 1973 Yom Kippur surprise attack. The ten-day maneuvers simulated a deep offensive against Israel, including a major amphibious landing on the Sinai coast and nighttime crossing of the Suez Canal.

Of even greater concern to Israel is the rapidly escalating missile proliferation in the region. With generous Saudi financial help, Syria went on a military spending spree after the Gulf War, especially focusing on surface-to-surface missiles. Apparently heartened by Saddam's success at striking Israel's urban centers with his modified Scuds, the Syrians have built up a stockpile of more than one thousand such missiles, say Israeli and international military analysts. Damascus is now able to hit most Israeli civilian and military targets with conventional or nonconventional warheads supplied by Russia or North Korea.

Among the deadly chemical poisons that the Syrians are busy producing is VX nerve gas. Experts say the toxin—first developed by the U.S. in the 1960s but subsequently made even more potent by the Soviets—is more deadly than other chemical agents because it penetrates the skin and remains active in the target area for several days, rendering ineffective the sealed rooms used during the Gulf War.

Iran and Libya are busy producing or acquiring advanced missiles that can strike Israeli targets, and both countries are known to be manufacturing chemical weapons. Iran is working hard to produce nuclear weapons. In fact, a London-based newspaper and *U.S. News and World Report* magazine reported in early 1992 that the Islamic regime in Tehran had actually purchased three nuclear bombs from the former Soviet Muslim republic of Kazakhstan. Although Iraq's vast chemical, biological, and nuclear weapons programs were curtailed by the Gulf War and U.N. actions following the war, Israeli leaders were concerned by U.N. reports in the mid-1990s that Iraq was secretly pursuing its nonconventional weapons programs while hiding missiles and other weapons from U.N. inspectors. Their worries multiplied after Saddam kicked out U.N. inspectors altogether in 1998.

The number of tanks and combat jets that Syria, Jordan, Iraq, the Gulf states, and Iran possess are well over three times that of Israel's. Syria and Iran stepped up purchases of bargain Soviet-built warplanes after the Gulf War, focusing on advanced SU-24 long-range bombers and MIG-29 jets. To the west, Libya has around five hundred warplanes. Algeria, Morocco, Tunisia, and Yemen also have military resources that could be offered to frontline states in a full-scale war against Israel.

Israeli military analysts believe that some of these countries, especially Egypt and Morocco, are not likely to actively support any future military campaign against the Jewish state. Still, they admit that the Al Aksa revolt sharply increased public hostility against Israel in both countries. Other Arab states and Iran seem intent on pursuing the jihad struggle, despite growing international attempts to bring a final resolution of the Arab-Muslim–Israeli conflict.

World history has shown that even states that sign peace treaties with their enemies can later break them. Iran, which will never make peace with Israel as long as Shiite Muslim fundamentalist clerics rule the country, is trying to widen the conflict by bringing other non-Arab Islamic countries into the holy war against the Jewish "infidels." The radical state stepped up recruitment efforts following the collapse of the Oslo peace process in 2000.

Many argue that Israel's nuclear weapons give the Jewish state a huge advantage over all of its declared or potential enemies, whatever their power. While it is now virtually undisputed that Israel does possess such weapons, this fact alone cannot compensate for Israel's extremely small population, land, and economic base in comparison to those of its enemies. Iraq alone is about twenty times the size of Israel. Saudi Arabia is one hundred times larger. Tripoli, the capital of Libya—which is a mere eighty-five times the size of Israel—is well over a thousand miles west of Tel Aviv. Iran, some nine hundred miles east of the Jewish state, has a population base ten times greater than Israel's. Therefore, even if Israel responded to a devastating conventional, chemical, and/or biological attack with all of her nuclear warheads—which is highly unlikely—most of the vast Arab world and Iran would remain untouched.

Tiny Israel, just slightly larger than Kuwait, could suffer overwhelming damage and loss of life in a full-scale military attack, especially if nonconventional weapons were fired at the narrow coastal plain, where 80 percent of Israel's Jewish population resides. But the vast Arab world and Iran, nearly five hundred times the size of Israel, with a population approaching 300 million people and massive underground oil deposits, could certainly recover in time from an Israeli nuclear response. If one adds to all this the likelihood that one or more of Israel's enemies will succeed in acquiring or producing nuclear weapons, the position of the small Jewish state seems extremely precarious.

## AMERICAN AID TO ISRAEL

With the end of the unprecedented economic boom of the 1990s, American financial aid to Israel—about 3 billion dollars a year since 1985, to Egypt's 2 billion or so—has come under increasing scrutiny. Critics note that aid to Israel and Egypt amounts to more than one-third of the annual foreign aid budget of the United States. The statement is often heard that America supplies the equivalent of ten thousand dollars for every Israeli citizen, as if U.S. government checks are being handed out in the streets of Tel Aviv and Jerusalem!

Israeli analysts note that most of the foreign aid immediately returns to the United States to pay off bank loans, helping somewhat to shore up America's loan-stretched banking system. About 1.2 billion dollars is military aid that must be spent by law in the U.S.—helping to keep people working at American defense establishments that are struggling to survive in the post-Soviet era. So, in the end, most of the dollars sent to Israel end up right back in American pockets.

Israeli financial experts say that Israel would not need to receive so much U.S. aid, borrow so much from American and European banks, or invest so heavily in military procurement if the United States, Britain, and other world powers were not selling vast quantities of advanced weaponry to Israel's Arab enemies. Trying to keep up militarily with her neighbors, Israel has the highest per capita defense budget in the world. They also note that Israel, unlike Egypt, has provided highly valued military and intelligence information to the West over the past few decades. Military analysts say such information has been worth tens of billions of dollars to NATO and the United States.

Israel also acts as a land-based "aircraft carrier" for American jets operating in the region, while the highly trained Israeli air force helps to patrol the strategic eastern Mediterranean Sea. Haifa serves as a friendly and secure port for Western ships in the region. All of these acts of assistance are important assets in this volatile part of the world. In one display of the deep military relationship between the U.S. and Israel, giant American Galaxy planes transported twelve Israeli-made portable bridges to Saudi Arabia on the eve of the Gulf War. Israel also reportedly supplied launchers for American Tomahawk cruise missiles.

Although the United States cemented alliances with Saudi Arabia and Egypt during the war, both countries still have many Muslim citizens and clerics who are hostile toward the West, as demonstrated by some anti-American reactions to the 2001 Al Qaeda terror attacks in New York and Washington. Israel remains the only true Western-style democracy in the oil-rich Middle East whose ties with America and Western Europe are based on shared political and religious values. Even with the demise of the mighty Soviet Union, Israel remains an important ally. As Western armies and defense budgets shrink, Israel's military power will continue to act as an important deterrent against anti-Western Middle Eastern countries such as Syria, Libya, Iraq, and Iran.

## ISRAEL MEETS THE PRESS

During the Palestinian uprising of the late 1980s, many Israeli friends blamed me and my media colleagues for what they saw as growing

Western perceptions of them as hate-filled, intransigent people, gleefully oppressing Palestinians. Unfair press coverage contributed heavily to a rise in worldwide anti-Semitic vandalism and other attacks in the past decade, they said. Israelis were portrayed as willfully depriving human rights to an oppressed minority, they complained, as if the Palestinians—part of the larger Arab world—were imported black slaves whom the Israelis consider racially inferior, and therefore have a right to dominate.

Although the comparison was often made, the situation was quite different from that in South Africa, they argued, where white minority leaders with no historical claim to the land deliberately set out to suppress the black majority based on racist beliefs. The Palestinians have not suffered because they are Palestinians, my Israeli friends argue. Israeli "oppression" is in reality mostly suppression of unwarranted Palestinian violence directed from the 1920s onward against Jews settling in their ancient homeland.

It seems to me that these arguments have much merit. Israel, like any country, does have its racists and religious bigots, such as the late Rabbi Meir Kahane (shot dead by an Arab in late 1990 while delivering a speech in New York) and his followers. Yet I have found most Israelis to be anything but racists. The Israeli supreme court banned Kahane from running for Parliament in 1988 precisely because Israel is not a state that condones racial hatred. The Jewish people have suffered greatly from bigotry and racism down through the centuries, leaving most of them keen supporters of the concepts of tolerance and equality. Yet many Israeli Jews, especially those who have lost loved ones in the various wars and terror attacks, do harbor hatred for their Arab cousins. However, I believe this is not primarily because of religious or racial reasons, but because the Arabs in general have repeatedly attacked the Jews both verbally and physically in the past one hundred years.

There is no denying that Arab citizens of Israel suffer discrimination in jobs, government funding, and so on. But again the reason, I believe, is Israeli suspicions of the Arabs based on past wars and continuing Palestinian terror attacks, and not because of ingrained racism. It is also true that Israeli businessmen usually pay Palestinian laborers less than Jewish workers and would rather employ fellow Jews if they had a choice.

But it seems to me that the apparent double pay scale is not the result of inherent racism, but simply because the market, saturated with Arab job seekers, allows it. Israeli businessmen's preference for Jewish workers is easily explained by the growing numbers of Palestinian killings of Israeli employers and coworkers in recent years.

In racial terms Arabs and Jews are indeed cousins, as is obvious to anyone living in Israel. Israeli society is heavily influenced by the larger Arabic Middle Eastern culture, which is natural enough since more than 1 million Israeli citizens are Arabs and many Israeli Jews were born in Arab countries. Unlike blacks and whites, Jews and Arabs are of the same racial stock and have many shared cultural, religious, and social values that go back many centuries. This is why David Ben Gurion thought in the 1930s that there was a chance that the emerging Jewish state could join a regional federation with neighboring Arab states.

The most popular Israeli foods and music reflect a strong Arab influence. The Hebrew and Arabic languages have many common words, since both originated in the same region. The Arab-Israeli dispute is a tribal religious conflict between relatives, not a racial struggle between two totally foreign and unrelated cultures.

Yet even if we journalists were scrupulously even-handed toward both the Palestinians and Israelis, there is no way that television pictures of armed soldiers shooting stone-throwing teenagers, or of young people being arrested and sent to crowded detention centers, could make Israel look like anything but a major human rights violator, no matter who is ultimately to blame for the situation. The Palestinians know this and have used such knowledge to their advantage.

Palestinian stringers working for Western news agencies during the early months of the original uprising would sometimes call to recommend that a camera crew be sent to a location in order to film a Palestinian demonstration. Such "friendly advice" helped assure that a constant stream of violent confrontations between Israeli soldiers and Palestinians made it on to television screens around the world. The ethics of acting on such tips bothered me, as it did some of my colleagues, yet everyone knew that action shots were what the editors back home wanted (in my case "action sounds," since I mainly work in radio).

Naturally enough, the Israeli army also tries at times to direct our efforts to gather the news, usually by limiting access to trouble spots. More than one reporter has been kicked, shoved, or arrested, and film has been confiscated. However, the Palestinian Authority has been guilty of this as well. And such restrictions and actions by Israeli officials or soldiers have been the exception rather than the rule.

In comparison to the almost total news blackout that Britain imposed during the 1982 Falklands War, or the severe restrictions enforced during the American invasion of Grenada in 1983 and during the Gulf War, Israel's record seems pretty good, considering that the Palestinians are backed morally and financially by Arab states that threaten to destroy her. Neither Britain nor the United States faced military threats to their homelands or national existence from Argentina, Grenada, or Iraq.

Was press coverage of the uprising biased against Israel, as my Israeli friends generally believe? Overall, I would say that the reporters I know strove, as I did, to present a balanced and accurate picture. Yet we journalists are fallible human beings. We have our own opinions. So do our editors overseas. Many of my colleagues tend to favor the Palestinian position over Israel's. A few are downright hostile toward the Jews. Other reporters display more subtle evidence of traditional Western anti-Semitic attitudes, usually without even realizing it.

I believe one of our faults is that we often judge Israel—located in the heart of the autocratic Middle East and on the western edge of Asia, a continent not exactly known for its great democracies—by the standards of a Western democracy at peace. I am frankly amazed that the perennially despised Israeli Jews, facing not only stones and firebombs but continuing threats of widespread death and destruction from heavily armed neighbors, have maintained their democratic principles over the years as well as they have.

Israeli and foreign human rights groups have been especially critical of Israeli army shootings that allegedly occurred in non-life-threatening situations. Other deaths resulting from illegal use of firearms or beatings have been roundly condemned. More than two dozen soldiers were court-martialed for such abuses during the first Palestinian uprising, and scores more during the fighting that began in September 2000.

Human rights groups often insist that soldiers are punished too lightly, thus failing to deter further violations. Israeli officials respond that such groups fail to take into account the warlike context in which the violence occurs, adding that many Israelis, some of them children and most of them civilians, have also been killed or wounded. PLO and HAMAS uprising leaflets often called on Jewish soldiers and civilians to be killed, they note. They say human rights groups usually failed to condemn the inter-Arab killings that escalated dramatically as the first uprising continued, leaving more than six hundred Palestinians dead by mid-1992.

Some eight hundred Palestinian deaths by Israeli soldiers in the first four years of the original uprising were relatively small numbers, even though tragic. Israeli leaders complained that the world media highlighted each and every death during the first few years of the uprising, while giving scant coverage to other violent world struggles. This criticism seems justified, although there are understandable political, historical, and religious reasons the press pays more attention to the Arab-Israeli dispute than to other conflicts.

Israeli officials said the international media hardly reported the deaths of more than two hundred thousand Sudanese civilians—many of them children—during the first year of the original uprising, 1988. Pro-Israel media analysis groups echoed this criticism, pointing out that American press reports featuring young Palestinian deaths were widespread during 1988.[44] Relatively few reports dealt with the Sudanese tragedy, they note, even though many times more were actually dying in the African nation. The groups did note, however, that the Palestinian casualties came mostly from army gunfire, while the Sudanese deaths mainly resulted from starvation caused by civil war.

It seems to me that in real-life Mideast, African, and Asian terms, Israel acted with relative restraint in the face of an ongoing, violent civilian uprising led by PLO and Islamic groups. This did not excuse Israeli abuses, but it should be noted. Israeli response was even more measured in the Al Aksa revolt that began in September 2000, given that many Palestinians were armed with rifles, mortars, and other deadly weapons. It is a fact that twice as many Palestinians were killed in the first two years of the post-Oslo conflict as in the entire first uprising, but then again ten times as many Israelis were killed by Palestinians—many of them literally blown to bits. While most of the Palestinian casualties were adult males, many of the murdered Israelis were women or children.

On July 14, 1989, in the midst of a civil war, Somali soldiers fired indiscriminately into crowds of unarmed Muslims in Mogadishu, killing around 450 people. Saudi forces killed more than 400 unarmed Muslim rioters, mostly Iranians, in Mecca in late July 1987. The U.S. State Department said Iraq used chemical weapons to kill up to 3,000 Kurdish civilians in 1988. Around 500 civilians, some of them children, were killed in just a few days as Algerian forces put down fundamentalist-led food riots in 1988. Some 600 civil war refugees huddled in a church were massacred by Liberian government soldiers on July 29, 1990.

Nobody knows how many unarmed civilians were killed when Chinese forces crushed the Tiananmen Square student protests in early June 1989; when Iraqi soldiers overran Kuwait in 1990; when Croats, Bosnian Muslims, Serbs, and Albanians engaged in the most savage fighting in Europe since World War II in the 1990s; when Russian forces put down an armed rebellion in Chechnya in 1994, and 1995; in the bloody civil war in Rwanda; or when American forces bombed Taliban and Al Qaeda positions in Afghanistan. Of course, most of these countries do not even claim to be real democracies. But others that do, such as Pakistan and India, have regularly employed live fire against unarmed civilian rioters.

Israeli critics charge that media coverage of the Arab-Israeli conflict often lacks historical context, especially in television and radio reports. Both Israelis and Palestinians complain that background context to individual clashes is also often nowhere to be found. Both charges are generally on target.

But in defense of my trade, I must point out that such omissions are mainly due to time constraints and not because most reporters are historically ignorant (although I do recall a newly arrived Associated Press reporter—one of hundreds of nonresident journalists who descended on Israel during the early days of the first uprising—asking me to check her "facts," which I quickly saw were anything but that). More than once I complained to CBS Radio editors in New York that my thirty-five to forty-second spots sometimes seemed to obscure, rather than clarify, certain stories. But what can a reporter do? There is simply very little room for background information on most commercial network newscasts.

Television reports tend to emphasize immediate, dramatic pictures over background context. Commercial networks naturally want the viewer to stay tuned, since more viewers means better ratings, which mean more money. But overemphasis on "action shots" tends to give a false impression. Having used modern computer video editing equipment, I know how easy it is to rearrange shots to highlight the exciting.

Most people don't stay home because three people were shot during a local bank robbery. Yet, if my friends in the United States are any indication, when three are killed during rioting in Hebron, viewers far away from the action tend to think the whole of Israel is on fire. I have pointed out to my friends that many more people are murdered each year in major American cities than in Israel or the disputed territories, yet people still flock to Los Angeles, New York, and Chicago. Still, it is quite understandable that overseas viewers, watching frequent media reports focusing on scattered violence, while seeing few if any reports on the overall peaceful situation in most of Israel, would be reluctant to travel here.

Israeli tourism officials say overdone television reports of violence keep many potential tourists—whose visits are essential to the economy of both Israel and the Palestinian autonomy areas—away from the Holy Land.

Another problem I see in the media's coverage of Israel is the use of certain descriptive terms that convey more emotion than information. I cringed, for instance, when I used the words "occupied territories" in my reports, even though the phrase may have been technically correct. I believe the argument made by many Israelis, that the term was legally a misnomer, had validity. But more than this, I was aware that to many listeners, especially older ones, the words "occupied territories" conjured up pictures of Nazi Germany and Japan deliberately and ruthlessly occupying various sovereign nations before and during World War II.

There is a vast difference between Germany's and Japan's occupations and Israel's control—resulting from a war forced upon her—of two small strips of disputed land not far from her central cities. It would have been far more accurate in historical terms to have called the formerly

Soviet-occupied Baltic States "occupied territories," yet media reports generally did not do so. Certainly Tibet, forcibly taken over by China, is under resented military occupation. Many other portions of land are controlled by one nation and disputed by another. Yet with heavy media usage, everyone in the world knew that "*the* occupied territories" were the ones controlled by the tiny state of Israel.

The same problem arises with the frequently used phrases "Arab East Jerusalem" and "occupied East Jerusalem." The latter is questionable since the entire city was supposed to temporarily pass from British to international U.N. control in 1948, but instead was quickly divided up between Israel and Jordan. It is certainly true that many residents of the disputed eastern half of Jerusalem are Arabs, and that Arab Muslims have constituted the majority community for most of the past fifteen centuries.

But it is also a historical fact that Jews have continuously lived in the Old City over the past three thousand years, except when forcibly expelled for brief periods of time. Thousands resided there until the Jordanians expelled them in 1948. Tens of thousands of Israeli Jews have moved back to the Old City's restored Jewish Quarter and to other parts of eastern Jerusalem during the past three decades. Indeed, more Jews than Arabs now live in areas captured from Jordan in 1967 and annexed to Jewish west Jerusalem. Given these facts, it would be far more accurate, if politically incorrect, to simply call the area "east Jerusalem," or at the most, "disputed east Jerusalem."

Are the major news organizations determined to bash Israel? Probably not, at least for the most part. But they are certainly not immune to the forces that exist in the real world, especially financial ones. Although it would be hard to prove, it at least seems plausible to suggest that some of the media's major commercial sponsors—the large oil companies that operate in the Arab countries; automobile manufacturers whose customers won't purchase cars if there is no gasoline to run them; and major banks full of petro-dollar deposits—have an interest in pleasing the Arabs more than the Jews. It doesn't seem far-fetched to assume that such business giants might have some influence in corporate media headquarters, as well as at the White House and in other world capitals.

The American president is certainly cognizant of the fact that the U.S. has been importing increasing amounts of oil from the Middle East in recent years. The region has around 70 percent of known world oil reserves. With Europe increasingly reliant on Middle Eastern oil supplies, as Japan always has been, it is not hard to imagine that Western governments and businesses will be increasingly receptive to Arab concerns in the coming years, despite the Islamic terror attacks in America. Indeed, the evidence in the months after the horrendous September 11 assaults in New York and Washington suggested that many governments were more prone to take into consideration Muslim interests and attitudes than they were before the Al-Qaida assaults were launched.

Would the quick Western military buildup in the Persian Gulf region in 1990 have occurred if Iraq had been a medium-sized African state that overran a small, poor neighbor? The rapid multinational response to Saddam Hussein's occupation of Kuwait was certainly undertaken with strategic Western oil interests in mind. There's a lot of black gold under those Arab desert sands, and everybody knows it.

# CONCLUSION

The Arab-Israeli struggle is unique among world conflicts. At its center is a city sacred to almost half the people on earth. After centuries of domination by Christians, then by Muslims, then by Christians during the Crusades, then once again by Muslims, Jerusalem is now under Jewish control, although Jews comprise only a tiny proportion of the world's population.

The two religions that dominated the Holy Land for many centuries are, for the most part, unhappy that the Jewish people once again control the land. But both realize that the ancient prophets they revere, plus most other great men and women of the Bible, including Jesus, were Jews. While Christians debate whether or not the Jewish people have a biblical right to sovereignty in the ancient Jewish homeland, Muslims overwhelmingly agree that it is not the will of Allah, as revealed in the Koran.

Immigrating Jews over the past hundred years encountered deepseated resistance and growing hostility from many Palestinian Arabs—Muslim and Christian. The Arabs' opposition was partly due to understandable fears of what a sovereign Jewish state might mean for their future. But it was even more so the result of preconceived prejudices based on religious beliefs.

The Jewish people suffered frequent persecution during their centuries of exile from the Promised Land, mostly from self-professed Christians, but also from Muslims. Such persecution did not wane, but actually increased, as the "enlightened" industrial revolution spread in Europe and

Russia. The overwhelming majority of Jewish immigrants who came to the Holy Land from the 1880s until 1948 were trying to escape powerful attempts to destroy them, first during the pogroms in Russia and Eastern Europe, and later during the Nazi reign over most of Europe and parts of northern Africa. Most Jewish immigrants since 1948 have fled oppression in Muslim-Arab countries and under communist regimes in Eastern Europe and the Soviet Union. The need for a Jewish homeland is quite evident to such immigrants and their offspring. Israel is indeed a refuge for the Jewish people, especially those suffering persecution or threats of annihilation.

Many Palestinian Arabs became refugees as the Jewish state came into existence. Others fled their homes during the 1967 Arab-Israeli war. With natural growth, some 1.5 million Palestinians living in Jordan, Syria, and Lebanon today are registered as refugees. Another 900,000 live in Judea, Samaria, and the Gaza Strip. Although wealthy Arab states and others could have supplied money to resettle them, the Palestinians "would remain refugees, to be utilized during the following years by the Arab states as a powerful political and propaganda pawn against Israel," as Benny Morris puts it.[45] The refugees are housed, fed, and receive medical attention through United Nations relief agencies (which receive more than one-third of their operating funds from the United States), along with private charitable organizations.

It was not inevitable that hundreds of thousands of Palestinian Arabs became refugees. Western-oriented Jewish Zionist leaders did not intend to displace them, believing the land was big enough to house both peoples, which it was. However, the Arabs, of whom most are Muslims, were basically duty-bound to reject the idea of Jewish sovereignty in the Holy Land. Many also assumed that immigrating Jews would take revenge for the centuries of oppression, and sometimes persecution, suffered by their Jewish coreligionists under Islam. Muslim religious leaders, especially the Jerusalem grand mufti, played upon those fears. Violent attacks were launched upon the Jews in the 1920s and 1930s, leading naturally to a hardening of Jewish attitudes toward Palestinian Arabs.

In the midst of a war launched by calls from the entire Arab world for the Jews to be thrown into the sea and on the heels of the Holocaust, most

Jews were not sad to see the Arabs flee when the main refugee flight occurred in 1948.

Finding a lasting peaceful solution to the Arab-Israeli conflict is next to impossible, as many world diplomats have discovered over the past five decades. Hatred of the Jews is still strong in much of the Arab world, as any casual reading of the Arab press will show. The idea of a sovereign Jewish state in the heart of the Muslim world is, and will always be, grating to many Muslims. Jewish sovereignty anywhere in the Middle East seems to contradict the teachings of the Koran, and thus calls into question the validity of Islam itself.

Jewish Israelis, while deeply desiring peace, are quite skeptical of Arab, and especially Palestinian, intentions. The various Arab-Israeli wars and years of PLO and Islamic terrorism have left deep scars. The collapse of the Oslo "land for peace" process added enormous weight to widespread Jewish skepticism of Yasser Arafat's claims that his people were ready to live in peace next door to Israel. Undoubtedly most Palestinian refugees, stateless and dwelling in substandard conditions, harbor deep hatred of Israeli Jews.

Although Western secular society obscures the fact, the Arab-Israeli dispute is largely a struggle over an ancient city that is holy to both peoples. The Jewish people have yearned for Jerusalem—Judaism's most sacred city—ever since their expulsion from the Holy Land. Most Muslims, whose ancestors fought hard to prevent Christian domination of Islam's shrines in the land, are not about to abandon the demand for complete sovereignty over east Jerusalem, where the Dome of the Rock and Al Aksa Mosque sit on the ancient Temple Mount. Anwar Sadat made this point even as he received back the Sinai Peninsula in 1978. Palestinian and other Middle Eastern Christians are generally more sympathetic toward the Jews, having also suffered under Islam. Yet most are still opposed to Jewish control over all Jerusalem.

Jewish attachment to Jerusalem's Old City has existed for three thousand years and continues to play a central role in the religious life of modern Israel. Israel annexed East Jerusalem in 1967, a move supported by the vast majority of Israeli Jews. Polls show very few Israelis would willingly surrender sovereignty even if they came to believe that the Arabs as a whole were truly ready to make peace.

To most Palestinian Muslims, and to not a few Orthodox Jews, the Arab-Israeli conflict boils down to this crucial question: Whose deity, Allah or the God of Israel, is the actual supreme sovereign of the universe? Related to this is another important question: Which holy book, the Koran or the Bible, contains the final and divine revelation of ultimate truth? Politicians and diplomats on both sides of the conflict can never ignore these enormous questions, which are of great importance to many of their people.

■ ■ ■

I realize I have painted a fairly dark picture. What can I do? I wish I could honestly say, as some of my colleagues and many world governments do, that lasting peace will come only if "Israeli intransigence" is modified, especially regarding a pullout from East Jerusalem. But I believe that the conflict runs much deeper than *any* political party, statesman, or government. Having extensively covered the conflict at its center, I believe my analysis is an accurate portrayal of the situation that exists in the heart of the muddled Middle East.

I know of many good and sincere people—Arabs, Jews, and others—who are working to bring about reconciliation and an end to violence. I am also acquainted with many hurting people on both sides of the conflict, and I wish I could write that lasting peace is just around the corner. But strong forces, based on ancient religious beliefs, are at work in the struggle. They are not about to disappear. Of course, it is always possible that a more powerful force will one day succeed in ending the Arab-Israeli dispute. I do not believe that the world powers alone have such strength, despite the tremendous economic influence they exert over the antagonists, especially Israel. Still, they will probably keep trying and may surprise me and many others by somehow forcing the two sides to lay aside their deep division, especially over Jerusalem. A devastating war could also lead to a de facto resolution of the Arab-Israeli conflict.

Many Christians, basing their beliefs on Daniel 11 and Paul's second letter to the Thessalonians, expect that a worldwide leader with supernatural powers—the "antichrist" strongman of the Books of Revelation and Daniel—will impose a peace settlement in the strife-torn region. This leader will allow the Jews to rebuild the temple in Jerusalem or construct it himself, and eventually sit inside the Holy of Holies and declare that he is God. In the end, he will prove to be no friend of the Jews, nor of true Christians, who will refuse to worship him or participate in his worldwide economic system.

Although a journalist and not a prophet, I am personally convinced that there are strong supernatural forces at work behind the Arab-Israeli dispute. I cannot help mentioning that I often perceive a certain glowing, otherworldly light behind the conflict—a light that shows up some very dark shadows. Why does the United Nations spend such a disproportionate amount of time on this struggle? Is it simply because the world body helped to create the Jewish state? Why does one of the smallest countries on earth have one of the largest permanent foreign press corps? Is it just that "Jews are news," or because wealthy oil states and three major religions play a role in the Arab-Israeli conflict? There is a fascination, an intensity to this struggle, that seems to go beyond normal explanations.

If it is true, as the Bible says, that the God of Israel has forever wedded his name to this tiny strip of disputed land, then *that* is what makes this conflict so unlike any other. If he indeed intends to establish his earthly reign in Jerusalem, and this design is opposed by his heavenly and earthly adversaries, then no other reason must be given for the fact that Jerusalem is "an immovable rock" (Zech. 12:3) in the way of a man-made peace process. If these things are true, then Arabs and Israelis are participants in a story whose ultimate implications are far greater than any human being can fully comprehend.

Israel is increasingly at the center of international criticism, protest, and condemnation. With serious threats all around and growing trials at home, it seems that Jacob's troubles can only increase as the world moves further into the twenty-first century. I think it is fair to speculate that the many biblical prophecies that speak of extremely dark days just before the kingdom of God is fully established on earth may be nearing the time of their fulfillment. Is an "antichrist" dictator about to appear who will enforce a "final solution" of the Middle Eastern conflict? Will a full-scale military attack leave Israel greatly weakened and open to foreign domination during the short time span known to many Christians as the Great

Tribulation, as Revelation 11:2 and Zechariah 14:2 seem to indicate? What of the long-anticipated and dreaded final battle of Armageddon, which the Book of Revelation says will involve armies numbering 200 million soldiers (Rev. 9:16)? Only God and time will fully reveal the answers to these questions.

Whatever lies in the future, it is quite clear that the complex Arab-Israeli conflict already reeks of hatred, death, and destruction. Yet I believe there is hope even today for the troubled Middle East. Every one of Abraham's children—Arab and Jew—has the same opportunity as I of receiving God's gift of eternal life, offered in his chosen Messiah, Jesus. Quite understandably, this does not seem like a valid road to peace to most Muslims and Jews, who have witnessed much hypocrisy and violence over the years from Gentile followers of Jesus—further stoking the holy war fires blazing in the world. But Israel's Messiah does have the power to bring reconciliation and peace to both individuals and societies. I believe that this is the only peace process that will ultimately succeed in forever turning Arab and Israeli swords into ploughshares . . . resulting in everlasting *shalom* for the Promised Land.

# APPENDIX: KEY MAPS

## The British Mandate, 1920

Map 1

# The British Mandate, 1922

Map 2

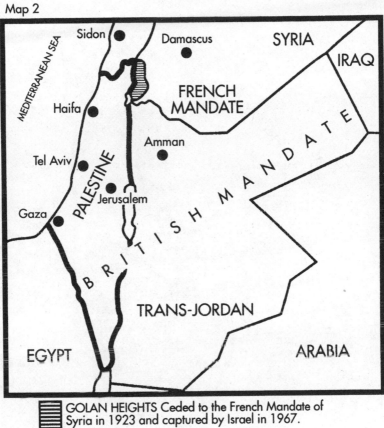

GOLAN HEIGHTS Ceded to the French Mandate of Syria in 1923 and captured by Israel in 1967.

# The U.N. Partition Plan, 1947

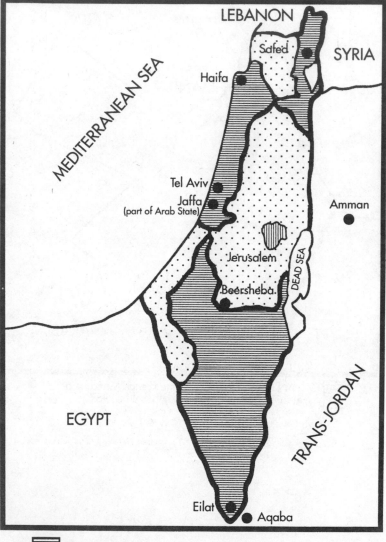

Map 3

LEBANON

SYRIA

Safed

MEDITERRANEAN SEA

Haifa

Tel Aviv

Jaffa
(part of Arab State)

Amman

Jerusalem

DEAD SEA

Beersheba

EGYPT

TRANS-JORDAN

Eilat

Aqaba

 Proposed Jewish State

 International Zone (Jerusalem and its suburbs)

Proposed Arab State (Includes Jaffa)

# The Armistice Demarcation Lines, 1949

Map 4

LEBANON

SYRIA

MEDITERRANEAN SEA

Haifa

Tel Aviv

Amman

Jerusalem

DEAD SEA

Gaza
Strip

ISRAEL

EGYPT
(SINAI PENINSULA)

JORDAN

Scale of miles

0    20    40    60

Eilat    Aqaba

**✱**Area annexed by Jordan in 1950 and renamed "West Bank"

# NOTES

1. This is a summary of events based on testimony and interviews of Arabs, Jews, and foreigners at the site. I believe this is as accurate an account as can be given, although both Palestinians and Israelis might dispute some of the points. All agree that it was a chaotic and fast-moving event, and so a complete reconstruction is not easy to make.

   Many Palestinians insist that no calls to jihad were made over the mosque loudspeakers, but many witnesses testified under oath that they heard such calls at the beginning of the riot. I believe their testimony is accurate, although I think calls to "slaughter the Jews" may have come from the rioters themselves and not over mosque loudspeakers, as some testified.

2. Edward H. Flannery, *The Anguish of the Jews: Twenty-three Centuries of Antisemitism* (New York: Paulist Press, 1985), 1.

3. Ibid., 40.

4. Ibid., 41.

5. Ibid., 50.

6. Ibid., 51.

7. H. L. Ellis, *The Lion Concise History of Christianity* (London: Lion Publishers, 1983).

8. In fact, proportionally fewer Jews than Gentiles died from the plague, undoubtedly because of strict Jewish dietary and hygienic laws garnered from the Bible, such as ritual hand-washing before each meal.

9. The Koran, translated from Arabic into English by N. J. Dawood, (London: Penguin Books Ltd., 1978), 317. All subsequent quotations from the Koran are from this translation. Also note that most

Arabic versions of the Koran are in chronological, not numerical, order.

10. Ibid.

11. Ibid.

12. G. H. Jansen, *Militant Islam* (New York: Harper & Row, 1979), 21.

13. Samuel Katz, *The Jewish Presence in Palestine* (Jerusalem: Israel Academic Committee on the Middle East, 1976).

14. The Koran.

15. James Parkes, *A History of Palestine from A.D. 135 to Modern Times* (London: Victor Gollancz Ltd., 1949), 214.

16. Mark Twain, *The Innocents Abroad* (London: 1881), quoted by Parkes, *History of Palestine.* 441–42.

17. Ibid., 349.

18. Arieh Avneri, *The Claim of Dispossession: Jewish Land Settlement and the Arabs* (Tel Aviv: Yad Tabenkin, Hebrew ed. 1980, English ed. 1982).

19. Walter Laqueur, *A History of Zionism* (New York: Holt, Rinehart & Winston, 1972), 239.

20. Ibid., 240.

21. Ibid., 239.

22. Ibid., 242.

23. The population of Palestine at the beginning of the first immigration wave is disputed. Most Arab sources say estimates of 400,000 are too small. Avneri, quoting Professor Roberto Bacci, who authored a book on the topic, says 523,000 people lived in the land in 1890— 431,800 Muslims; 57,400 Christians; and 42,900 Jews.

He thus calculates that 425,000 to 440,000 Arabs lived in Palestine in 1880. The numbers at the beginning are important since disputes also rage over how many Arabs immigrated into Palestine before 1948. British records show that the Arab population increased by 120 percent between 1922 and 1947, writes Avneri.

He and others believe this unusually large population increase must have been at least partially due to wide-scale Arab immigration—legal and illegal—into Palestine during the period (desert and mountain borders were largely open, notes Avneri). Therefore, at least a portion of the "Palestinians" who fled in 1948 were relatively recent immigrants from Egypt, Syria, Trans-Jordan, etc.

24. Laqueur, *A History of Zionism,* 529.

25. Ibid., 573.

26. Reports at the time spoke of more than two hundred killed; but a survivor from the village, Muhammad Sammour, told correspondent Eric Silver of the British *Guardian* newspaper in April 1983 that 116 residents had died. Sammour said he was one of the representatives of the five clans who lived in the village and who met in Jerusalem just after the slaughter to count the dead.

27. Laqueur, *A History of Zionism,* 585.

28. Benny Morris, *The Birth of the Palestinian Refugee Problem, 1947–1949* (Cambridge: Cambridge University Press, 1987, paperback ed. 1989).

29. Ibid. This latter conclusion is one of the things that has made Morris's book so controversial. Israeli critics say he has deliberately ignored evidence that local and regional Arab leaders did indeed order out prominent Palestinians, knowing this would lead by example to widescale flight. Such commands, mainly issued verbally, they say, were picked up by Israeli and British intelligence.

They say Morris, who was born the same year as the Jewish state, tends to exaggerate Israeli confidence and military strength, viewing the 1948 struggle through the eyes of one who has known Israel only as a military giant.

Morris notes that he lacked Arab documents on the period, but says he pieced together a fairly accurate picture of Arab activities from Israeli and British documents. Some question the validity of this approach. The fact that he relied on Hebrew and English translations of Arabic radio broadcasts and other Arabic material in Israeli and British archives has also been criticized. Despite uneasiness with the way Morris interprets some of the material he presents, and agreement with some of the criticism mentioned above, I believe his book is overall the best to date in detailing the refugee flight.

30. Ibid., 298.

31. Ibid., 294.

32. Quoted by historian Martin Gilbert in *The Arab/Israeli Conflict: Its History in Maps,* 2d ed. (London: Weidenfeld and Nicolson, 1976), 67.

33. Ibid., 103.

34. Thomas Friedman, *From Beirut to Jerusalem* (New York: Farrar, Straus and Giroux, 1989), 69.

35. Ibid., 70.

36. Ibid.

37. Ibid., 73.

38. Ibid., 58–59.

39. Eugene Rostow, U.S. Undersecretary of State for Political Affairs in the late 1960s, presented the legal arguments behind this position in the April 16, 1990, issue of *New Republic* magazine: "The Jewish right of settlement in the West Bank is conferred by the same provisions of the Mandate under which Jews settled in Haifa, Tel Aviv, and Jerusalem before the State of Israel was created." He notes that article 25 of the Mandate gave Great Britain and the League of Nations "discretion to 'postpone' or 'withhold' the Jewish people's right of settlement in the Trans-Jordanian province of Palestine," adding that the British did just that in 1922. "The Mandate does not, however, permit even a temporary suspension of the Jewish right of settlement in the parts of the Mandate *west* of the Jordan River." He adds that the 1949 armistice line—which in effect became Israel's pre-1967 borders—did not legally constitute Israel's permanent borders.

The Mandate provisions for settlement in *all* of Palestine west of the river did not end in 1948, writes Rostow, but continue to have legal force to this day. Therefore, Israel has a legal right to build settlements in those portions of Mandatory Palestine captured in 1967. Other legal arguments concerning the application of the Fourth Geneva Convention are also given in the article.

40. It has become popular among Middle Eastern Arabs in recent years, along with neo-Nazis and others, to maintain that East European and Russian Jews are not descendants of ancient Jews at all. Therefore, they have no right to live in the Holy Land. This case was made in a Saudi Arabian–sponsored ad printed in October 1988 in major

American newspapers: "In A.D. 740 a large kingdom of Europeans, located in modern-day Russia, converted to Judaism. This group had no biological connection with any of the original Jews." Therefore, "most" of the Jews in Israel are not biological Jews, but descendants of European converts, also known as "Askenazi" or "White Jews," who can "make no Biblical claim to the Arab lands in Palestine, including Jerusalem." This argument is based on the conversion to Judaism in the eighth century of leaders of the Khazaria Kingdom located in south central Asia. Subsequently many Khazars converted to Judaism and were dispersed when the Russians destroyed the kingdom in the eleventh century. However, history records that at least some Jews from the West moved to Khazaria to escape persecution.

More importantly, it is well documented that many west European Jews moved east to Poland, Lithuania, etc., during the Middle Ages after they were forced out of France, Germany, Austria, and other areas. (This is why Yiddish, a German-Hebrew mixture, was the main language of such east European Jews.) Certainly Khazar's Jewish converts, as converts elsewhere, mixed over the years with known physical descendants of Abraham, but it is historically absurd to maintain that "European White Jews" have no ancient Jewish ancestry. Such widely believed myths, propounded by a leading "moderate" Arab state, illustrate the deeply held Arab prejudices against Israel.

41. For instance, Israel's more than 1 million Arab citizens, unlike Arabs in some other Middle Eastern nations, have full voting rights and read non-government-controlled Arabic periodicals, subject to occasional Israeli censorship, but still freer than in all regional states except Egypt and Lebanon. Unlike in Syria, Iraq, and elsewhere, they cannot be held in prison without being formally charged with a crime. They have full religious freedom, unlike Muslims in Saudi Arabia, who are still officially subject to the death penalty if they convert.

Palestinians living in parts of the territories still under Israeli control do not enjoy all of these rights, and many have been imprisoned without trial and others apparently tortured. Yet overall, they have been treated with relative restraint in comparison to the way Syria, Iraq, Algeria, Saudi Arabia, and other countries have handled internal riots and rebellions in the past decade. (Read Thomas Friedman's excellent report on Syria's crushing of the fundamentalist rebellion in the city of Hama in *From Beirut to Jerusalem,* cited above.) Israel's comparatively good human rights record may not be apparent to many people because media reports tend to highlight criticism of Israel by such groups as Amnesty International, while only lightly reporting stronger but routine allegations of torture and other abuses in the Palestinian Authority zones of control and in Syria, Sudan, and other regional countries.

Media outlets rightly maintain that Israel's record is and should be of more concern to Americans and other Westerners because of strong Western political and economic support for Israel. Still, media focus on Israeli human rights abuses, paying less attention to the misdeeds of other regional states, may leave some Westerners with the false impression that Israel's overall record is the poorest in the region.

42. Twenty-one states were members of the Arab League following the 1990 merger of North and South Yemen. Several African member states are mostly non-Arab, but largely Muslim.

43. Israel and the U.S. have jointly produced an "antimissile missile" to intercept and destroy incoming missiles. Part of the SDI program, the so-called "arrow" missile is thought to be more effective in intercepting incoming missiles than the U.S. "Patriot" system. It was successfully test-fired for the first time in 1995.

44. Among the groups that monitor media coverage of Israel are: CAMERA (Committee for Accuracy in Middle East Reporting in America), P.O. Box 17322, Washington, D.C. 20041; and Americans for a Safe Israel, 114 E. 28th Street, New York, NY 10016; and Zionist Organization of America, 4 East 34th Street, New York, NY 10016.

45. Morris, *The Birth of the Palestinian Refugee Problem, 1947–1949,* 296.

# INDEX

# ABOUT THE AUTHOR

David Dolan has lived in Israel since 1980. He began broadcasting news from the Middle East in 1982, reporting for Moody Radio, CBN Radio and Television, and for the CBS Radio Network from early 1988 until late 2000. He has traveled the globe as an international public speaker since 1989.

While covering the Arab-Israeli conflict for more than two decades, Dolan has come to be recognized as an expert on this important topic. He is a frequent guest on many radio and television programs around the world.

Along with several books, Dolan has written many articles on the intense Middle Eastern struggle for various newspapers and magazines, including the *Jerusalem Post*. The first three editions of this book, originally published in 1991, sold more than 100,000 copies, together with thousands of copies in German and several other languages. Dolan's second book, an apocalyptic novel set in Israel titled *The End of Days,* has recently been updated. His third book, *Israel in Crisis: What Lies Ahead?* was published in 2001.

Dolan sends out regular E-mail updates on the Middle East. You may sign up for them via his Web site at www.ddolan.com.